HERE
and
THERE

HERE
and
THERE

Reading Pennsylvania's Working Landscapes

BILL CONLOGUE

THE PENNSYLVANIA STATE UNIVERSITY PRESS
UNIVERSITY PARK, PENNSYLVANIA

Chapter 2 was first published as "Merwin and Mining," in *Interdisciplinary Studies in Literature and Environment* 18.3 (Summer 2011): 594–614. Reprinted by permission of Oxford University Press. Part of chapter 5 first appeared as "Other Places," in *Black Earth and the Ivory Tower*, editedby Z. M. Jack (Columbia: University of South Carolina Press, 2005), 282–88. Reprinted by permission of University of South Carolina Press.

Library of Congress Cataloging-in-Publication Data

Conlogue, William, author.
Here and there : reading Pennsylvania's working landscapes / Bill Conlogue.
p.   cm
Summary: "A collection of essays exploring the social, economic, and environmental elements of the anthracite coal region of northeastern Pennsylvania"—Provided by publisher.
Includes bibliographical references and index.
ISBN 978-0-271-06080-4 (cloth : alk. paper)
1. Pennsylvania—Social conditions—History.
2. Anthracite coal mines and mining—Environmental aspects—Pennsylvania—History.
3. Anthracite coal mines and mining—Social aspects—Pennsylvania—History.
4. Pennsylvania—Economic conditions—History.
5. Land use—Pennsylvania—History.
6. Coal mines and mining in literature.
7. Conlogue, William.
I. Title.

F149.C765 2013
974.8—dc23
2013018986

The Pennsylvania State University Press is a member of the
Association of American University Presses.

It is the policy of The Pennsylvania State University Press to use acid-free paper. Publications on uncoated stock satisfy the minimum requirements of American National Standard for Information Sciences—Permanence of Paper for Printed Library Material, ANSI Z39.48–1992.

This book is printed on paper that contains 30% post-consumer waste.

Frontispiece:
Marvine colliery, 1922. Courtesy of the
Lackawanna Historical Society.

For Bridget, *who knows*

here and there *adv (14c)*

1 : in one place and another

2 : from time to time

. . . our season: Memorial Day, Fourth of July, Labor Day.

As far as we knew them, we followed the formal rules of softball, but in
a casual way, given our amateur status and the topography of the field,
which was a side hill cut by a stony driveway, two ditches, a barbed wire fence,
the house, and three barns. Each game surprised us with lessons
in chance, improvisation, and judgment.

Sure of snagging a grounder, you could get a rude awakening when the
ball popped up and smacked your chin. Catching a fly meant accounting for the
ball's trajectory and the height of its arc, but also the slope of the ground and
the location of holes, pipes, and posts. Aunts and uncles, cousins and kids
watched from the porch along third-base line, ribbing batters and pitchers,
laughing at infield errors, and applauding spectacular plays, which often enough
meant someone snaring a fly ball against the gas tanks in left field, stopping a
pinball up the driveway, or beelining a strike from barn to home.

All the littlest kids batted at least once, each hitting a home run, of course,
though it required repeated directions and dramatically dropped balls to
get them around the bases. For the rest of us, making it home meant
remembering that reaching second, uphill and from grass to gravel, required an
instinctive understanding of different types of ground; that balls knocked into
the pasture sometimes disappeared into wet spots, which required both teams to
double as a search team; and that behind home plate stood a stone wall.

So that the cows could be milked, the first innings ended just before five; some of
us tossed aside mitts and bats to pick up shovels and pails.
Others ate, drank, talked.

The rest of the game ended in twilight, the ball a moth . . .

Contents

Figures and Maps

Preface: Homework

Not far from where I now live, beyond the Scranton grid, along Boulevard Avenue, on the other side of Green Ridge Assisted Living and Mike's Scrap Yard, stands the Lackawanna Recycling Center, which occupies ground of the former Marvine colliery, on whose culm dump, once site of a fire that burned blue and red for years, sprawls a U.S. Armed Forces Reserve complex.

During the 1950s, my grandfather, a resident of West Side in Carbondale, worked as a conductor for the Delaware and Hudson Railroad, which hauled Marvine colliery coal. Although he had to start work in Wilkes-Barre, he refused to drive a car or to take a train, so every time he had to report to the rail yards, my widowed mother drove him, which meant managing two toddlers for the hour trip, one way, through a nest of narrow streets. Traveling a straight line to Oneonta, New York, and coming back the next day, the D & H train rumbled through Carbondale, passing a few blocks from their house. On the day of his return, he told my mother, she was to listen for the train's whistle at the Seventh Avenue crossing, pile everyone into the car, and time her arrival in Wilkes-Barre with the train's easing into the station. They practiced this commute while a mine fire burned beneath their home, threatening their displacement.

Over the Moosic Mountains, in Wayne County, we heated the farmhouse with anthracite, which came, like as not, from a Hudson Coal Company mine. A kid keeping the furnace alive, I nightly fed its fire with baskets of "rice," which I dumped over the lip of a fifty-five-gallon drum attached to the stoker. The ashes I piled against the cellar's fieldstone foundation, banking them for use on snow-filled mornings when the milk truck couldn't make the hill.

I write about land use. The first example above suggests the ironies of spatial and temporal orientation, the second nods to how our patterns—in this case, fuel and travel—wear on others, and the third acknowledges the interconnections—for good and ill—between very different lands. To write about land use is to write about how different types of work create these ironies, patterns, and inter-connections. Evidence of land-shaping work surfaces repeatedly in my home region's literature and history, in my own interactions with these lands, and in my native places' cultural and economic forms—the organization of farms and mines, for example.

I offer here my homework, a record both physical and textual. Whatever I do or read becomes, no matter how briefly, a part of my ordering of the world. Even when I read or labor alone, I'm in the company of another mind; I participate in conversations about the world that extend before and after me. With reading and lived experience so interdependent, I overlay in this book texts and contexts, near and far. I keep returning to the local, though, because good work dwells in the details, always.

Here and There refuses to back away from any kind of knowing, especially narrative. A lived experience, land use unfolds in place, over time. In revealing familiar tensions within this unfolding, I trespass freely across genres, chronologies, and disciplines. Anecdotes and footnotes may compete for your consideration in *Here and There*, but each asks only that you pay attention.

Acknowledgments

Many people and organizations helped me to complete this book: my debts exceed my capacity to repay them. Any errors in the book are mine.

Several people read and responded to early drafts. My Marywood colleagues Laurie McMillan and Mike Foley offered me detailed feedback that improved my arguments. I am grateful to Ian Marshall and Christine Cusick, who reviewed the manuscript for Penn State University Press; their responses sharpened the manuscript into a book. My coffee conversations with Virginia Kennedy, who read parts of the manuscript, renewed my faith in the project at key moments.

Mary Ann Moran-Savakinus, Director of the Lackawanna Historical Society, was always there with her tremendous knowledge of the history, people, and places of Lackawanna County. She often dropped what she was doing to help me find sources of information. Behind this book also stands the work and expertise of Gloria McCullough, research librarian at the Wayne County Historical Society, who guided me to important sources for Wayne County history; archivists Jim Sullivan, at Marywood, Sr. Anitra Nemotko, at the Scranton IHM Center, and Michael Knies, at the University of Scranton, who led me to key texts; and interlibrary loan specialist Becky Kohinsky, who aided me tremendously in accessing books and articles that I otherwise would not have been able to use. The staff at the Luzerne County Historical Society was very helpful to me in my research of the Jason Torrey Papers. All of these folks were very generous with their time and talents.

For all I learned in interviews with them, I am grateful to John Hambrose, Alliance Landfill; Dave Messersmith, Wayne County Extension Service; and Norma Reese, Forest Hill Cemetery. In our several conversations, Bernie McGurl, Director of the Lackawanna River Corridor Association, taught me much about many aspects of the Lackawanna Valley and the Lackawanna River. For their assistance, I thank art historian Darlene Miller-Lanning, University of Scranton; S. Robert Powell, Director of the Carbondale Historical Society; Paul

Reining, Forestry Specialist, Wayne County Conservation Office; John Kameen and Patricia Striefsky, publishers of the *Forest City News*; and Brian Fulton, librarian at the Scranton *Times-Tribune*.

Several experiences inspired me in my research and writing. The 2002 National Endowment for the Humanities Summer Institute "Regional Studies for Liberal Arts Learning: An Appalachian Exemplar" bolstered my confidence about the importance of writing about northeastern Pennsylvania. I thank NEH, Peter Crow, my institute colleagues, and Ferrum College for a great experience. A 2003 Pennsylvania Historical and Museum Commission summer grant to conduct research at the Anthracite Museum expanded my understanding of the richness of the region's history. During my subsequent trips to the museum, Chester Kulesa and John Fielding, who always made me feel welcome, went out of their way to give me access to the Anthracite's collections. Marywood University granted me a sabbatical that allowed me extended time to work on the book.

At Penn State University Press, I am in debt to acquisitions editor Kathryn Yahner and editorial assistant Charlee Redman, who made the submission and production process run smoothly, and to Nicholas Taylor, who copyedited the manuscript. I thank Erin Greb, of Erin Greb Cartography, for making the maps of Scranton and northeastern Pennsylvania.

I am grateful to *Interdisciplinary Studies in Literature and Environment* for permission to reprint "Merwin and Mining," which appears here as chapter 2, and to the University of South Carolina Press for permission to reprint my essay "Other Places," which is now part of chapter 5.

My extended family deserves credit for hearing about this project for several years. My greatest debt, however, is to my wife, Bridget, who made this book possible in more ways than she'll ever know.

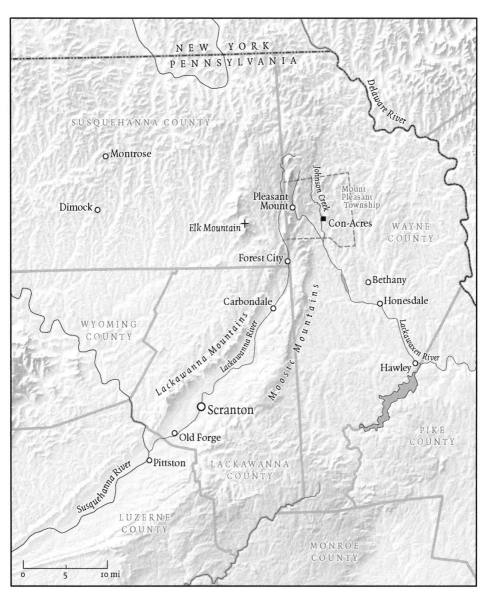

Map 1 Northeastern Pennsylvania. Map by Erin Greb Cartography.

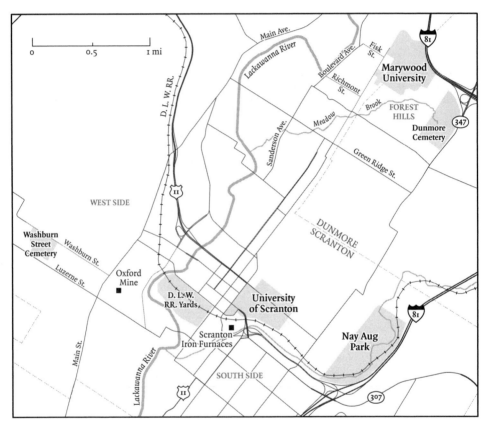

Map 2 Scranton. Map by Erin Greb Cartography.

Introduction: Orientation

Perception is inference.

—Atul Gawande, "The Itch"

In *Here and There* I challenge the assumption that literature and local places matter less and less in a world that economists describe as "flat," politicians insist has "globalized," and social scientists imagine as a "village." Through the prisms of literature and history, I explore tensions and conflicts within northeastern Pennsylvania, tensions and conflicts created by national and global demand for the region's resources: farmland, forest products, anthracite coal, and college-educated young people. Powerful ways of knowing, history and literature tell stories of people in time and place; they are not simply dates or fictions. The project pivots on the interplay between other places and my native ones: Scranton, where I now live and work, and the family dairy farm, where I grew up and to which I often return. Sharing the Moosic Mountains, each ground is a place of beginning, becoming, and homecoming. My experiences in this "rough terrain" may be unique to me, but I know they are common, ordinary, shared.[1]

The local and the global intersect most visibly in how people treat the land where they live. Because we must use land to survive, we need to think carefully about the ethics of land use. Responsible not only to themselves, but also to the community, landowners touch the lives of next-door neighbors, others living in a watershed, and those residing a world away. These responsibilities encompass, literally, everyone, everywhere, living and to come. It cannot be otherwise, because our lives are profoundly connected to and shaped by the world beyond our home ground. We inhabit, as they say at Marywood University, a "diverse and interdependent world."

The interplay among places that I invoke has become increasingly important to scholars of environmental literature and history. For example, in *Writing for an Endangered World* (2001), literary scholar Lawrence Buell offers a critical framework for understanding the sort of rural/urban interchange that I describe.[2] Buell juxtaposes depictions of "'green' and 'brown' landscapes" to argue that environmental writers and critics must attend to a single, complex environment that interweaves the found and the human-made. Adding to Buell's argument another layer of complexity, I study the altered landscapes of the mine-scarred Lackawanna Valley, home to what I describe as dark fields.

Somewhere between a green field and a brown field, a dark field has been industrially developed and polluted, but people live there, often unaware of the site's history and danger. The natural and the constructed may intersect most obviously in the green fields of a farm, but the dark fields of mined land testify to the thoughtless, forgotten abuse of the natural and the human-made. In traversing meadows and woods, culm banks and mineshafts, towns and cities, I uncover a past that remains all too present. This past is like dark matter in the universe: it's everywhere but nowhere visible.

Any discussion of literature, history, and the environment is insufficient if it does not address the human need for food and fuel. Anthracite coal mining, the foundation of nineteenth-century U.S. industrialization and urbanization, erased in no time the northern hardwood forest of a very local geography, planting in its place an unstable, boom-and-bust economy. Agriculture, the work that I knew growing up, turned the adjoining beech and hemlock forest into a patchwork of fields and woods that another forest may now be reclaiming. Although our family farm survives, barely, farmers as a group have statistically disappeared from the American landscape;[3] our shrinking farm, once a member of a thriving neighborhood, limps along as a remainder and a reminder of another time. With food and fuel basic to people's lives, environmental writers and historians need more than ever to re-envision rural and urban places as parts of a single tapestry, one that is rapidly fraying. Mending the damage starts with remembering what damage has been done.

Acutely aware of their proximity to this damage, several scholars of environmental history and literature have recently called for more attention to a "literature of everyday nature."[4] These writers place landscapes within their historical and cultural contexts, and they encourage examination of the working landscapes where most people live. For example, in reminding us that "wilderness" is a socially constructed concept, one that did not take on its current resonance as a place of escape until the late nineteenth century, William Cronon asserts that "most of our most serious environmental problems start right here, at home, and if we are to solve those problems, we need an environmental ethic that will tell us as much about *using* nature as about *not* using it." To show us how our attention to home can be diverted, Bart Welling analyzes ecopornography, a "type of contemporary visual discourse made up of highly idealized, anthropomorphized views of landscapes and nonhuman animals," a discourse that hides "damage inflicted on the *non*represented, nonphotogenic landscapes that are logged, mined, dammed, polluted, or otherwise exploited to provide the materials and energy required for producing and distributing images of more visually appealing places." Although Scott Hess wants us to imagine nature as the everyday world of the "unspectacular, developed, aesthetically ordinary environments where most of us live and work," he points out that everyday nature is "not just a location, but rather a kind of attention, or better yet, a way of defining our identities and values through local relationship rather than through imaginative escape."[5]

Here and There explores working landscapes. I understand work to include duty, craft, and creativity. As an expression of ideas, our work reveals how we answer moral questions that arise in our use of land. When one adds the present participle, the word places us in time: working means "used as a guide" and "capable of being used as the basis of further work."[6] I define the word "landscape" to refer not to land so much as to human perceptions of land; landscape is about point of view. Examining working landscapes, which are both places and depictions of places, demands then that I judge what I have been seeing and doing in the world.

Regions Within Regions

Regions are "culturally constructed" landscapes. The American West, for example, is much more a product of human imagination than it is a fact of nature.[7] As human constructs, language and literature necessarily shape our definitions of region. However, as modes of representation, each can, at best, only point to what it seeks to express. In the gap between thing and word stretches not only a world of error and deception, but also the possibility of powerful insight. In this gap, we imagine our lives and communities. Because such gaps pockmark my understanding of northeastern Pennsylvania, I can make sense of the region only by tracing its interdependent relationships with other people and places, across time.

Named for an industry that all but disappeared sixty years ago, the Anthracite Region, a series of distinct coalfields, has a rich ethnic and labor history, a long record of social and environmental upheaval, and a reputation as the first major example of U.S. deindustrialization. A collection of fragments defined by the geology of its coal, the Anthracite Region consists of four geographies—northern, eastern middle, western middle, and southern fields—and three commercial zones: Wyoming, Lehigh, and Schuylkill.[8] Found in patches within the folds of the Appalachian Mountains, from Schuylkill County north to Susquehanna County, each field is distinct from the others because of its type and quantity of anthracite, its settlement patterns, and its links with New York and Philadelphia. For example, the northern field, which includes the Lackawanna Valley, has the deepest deposits and its coal has the highest carbon content, but it was the costliest to mine and the last to develop.[9] While the southern field looks to Philadelphia, the northern field faces New York.

A region within a region, the northern anthracite field exerted a gravitational pull on places and people far beyond the mines. For example, the Pennsylvania Coal Company purchased props from farms in neighboring Wayne County to shore up its mines in Forest City, at the extreme northern tip of the northern field. Miners latticed their workspaces there with white and red oak, chestnut, beech, maple, birch, and locust—until, that is, they exhausted the local supply. After nearby forests all but disappeared, companies imported loblolly pine from the South and, later, Douglas fir from Oregon via the Panama Canal. Companies preferred wooden props, by the way, because they failed over time, thus warning of a working mine, rather than crumpling all of a sudden, as steel often did.[10] Beneath towns and cities up and down the Lackawanna Valley a mixed phantom forest still stands, a forest cut from faraway farms.

My mother heated our Wayne County farmhouse with anthracite until January 2004, when her old Van Wert stoker gave out and she switched to oil. Until then, she had long been in the minority, hanging on to the fuel she grew up knowing. Today, her heating oil is trucked from where she grocery-shops, Forest City, about ten miles away, just below the headwaters of the Lackawanna. In June 2008, my mother, a native of Carbondale, taught me a lesson about the power of place: "I've been here [on the farm] forty-five years, and I have no interest in Wayne County; only Lackawanna County. That's why I get the Scranton paper." To write about the farm I must write about mining, which is to write about U.S. industrialization, which is to write about the end of farming.

I grew up on a Wayne County dairy farm, lived in Scranton for a time as an undergraduate, and spent four years living as a graduate student near Washington, D.C. My experiences in these different places gave me different contexts for understanding the relationships between human work and the land. Farm life engrained in me an awareness of nature's rhythms and whims, my familiarity with Scranton taught me that some work can irreparably damage a place, and my time within the Beltway showed me that distant decision makers can thoughtlessly alter local lives and lands.

A renewed sense of home will be increasingly important to us all as more and more local cultures—family farm networks, urban neighborhoods, and native peoples—disappear into the global industrial economy's regimentation and homogenization. If we do not remember the remnants, our connections with one another will wither. If we do not keep varied communities and healthy places, how can we be decent to one another in a world that is ever more uncertain, claustrophobic, and hostile? And if we cannot be decent to one another as human beings, what hope is there that we can be decent to the rest of life?

At work, I'm a generalist, a professor who teaches in a small English department at a comprehensive Catholic university. I still wonder that I have a job doing what I enjoy: studying language and literature, explaining poems and plays, interpreting novels and films. Sometimes I think that the world around me values these activities less and less. Teaching undergraduates, writing essays, and thinking about where I am and the work that I do here and there are the main threads that make up my life; they're not separate parts of a "career." The literature and history I profess tell stories about what it means to be human; each explores the narrative of our connection, alienation, combativeness, and generosity. In asking questions about good and evil and right and wrong, they matter—and the humanities in general matter—because our lived experience demands that we each think carefully about our answers to this question: How am I at work in the world?

The best literature teaches us that other people are people. Inviting us to see with others' eyes, it increases our capacity for empathy and mercy, and reminds us that human lives are bound up with and dependent on a living earth that pre-dates us and will outlast us. Within this context, we realize that we are keepers of a shared gift that we hold for only a little while. In *Here and There*, I practice what Wendell Berry calls "practical reading," a phrase he uses to remind us that literature teaches us something about the world; it's not simply a display of verbal virtuosity.[11] Is it really possible to read *The Grapes of Wrath*, for example, and not think through the social and economic dilemmas its characters confront?

Practical reading empowers us to think critically and carefully about ourselves, our relationships with others, and our connections to the world beyond us. Reading fine writing gives us the courage to confront the paradox at the heart of a liberal arts education: to be free is to understand—never fully, never completely—one's dependence on others, living and dead, human and nonhuman.

Each chapter here begins at home, journeys elsewhere, and returns to northeastern Pennsylvania. A thoughtful coming and going is, I believe, the essence of knowing where one stands. For example, what has my teaching to do with what happens in the world around me? How do everyday issues within these places help me to understand what's at stake in larger debates about land use, the value of the humanities, and the role of the teacher/scholar? How does the story of my home ground contribute to the human story? If we don't look around us, I keep telling myself, we won't see what's beyond us.

At Home

In the Anthracite Museum hangs a map of the Lackawanna Valley, dated 1886. Depicting land from Scranton to Forest City, the map traces in red the valley's underground mines. Particularly striking is the sinuous circulatory system that overlays Scranton's street grid, which is almost invisible. Although many maps divide land into counties, states, and nations, this map marks company property; the usual political divisions compete with blocks of corporate control. The map reminds me that the region's geology holds hostage its geography, even its urban geography. The city of Scranton, like most cities and towns in the Anthracite Region, has its doppelganger in a city below, a dark Atlantis peopled by the ghosts of the men and mules who worked both into existence. Today's visible city rests on the crumbling pillars of the buried one, a fact expressed in every mine subsidence.

Bridget and I live within that tangle of red, in an old Scranton suburb, on a quiet street, in a shingle-style, balloon-frame house nestled between a home owned by a banker and one owned by a casket salesman. In the three houses across the street live a social studies teacher, a widow, and a retired couple, the man a former composing room worker at the *Scranton Times*. Educators, lawyers, and businessmen live up and down the block. Shaded by two silver maples, our house has a wide front porch, a white picket fence around the back yard, and uneven bluestone sidewalks. Like much of the valley, though, our home sits on hollowed ground.

Developers added Richmont Park to the more exclusive Green Ridge section in the early 1900s. Hoping to take advantage of the valley's increasing wealth, the cachet of Green Ridge, and middle-class people's desire to leave the industrial city center, investors Jordan, Hannah, and Jordan purchased the ground in 1893 from the Pennsylvania Coal Company. As a condition of sale, Pennsylvania Coal stipulated that subsequent land purchasers could not stop the company or its heirs from mining under the development. Homeowners here, Bridget and I included, own no mineral rights. Deeds also note that Pennsylvania Coal has already mined beneath Richmont Park, and that neither the company nor its heirs are to be held liable for later injuries or damages as a result of this prior work. This would include, I imagine, mine water flooding one's basement, one's house disappearing into a mine subsidence, or coal gas killing a family member. These things have happened.

The house has had eight owners in its hundred-plus year history. Carpenter William Erhardt and builder Ernest Latham purchased the lot in 1906; they constructed the house the following spring and summer, when the first people to occupy it, the Reinhardts, moved in. Designed to appeal to people of a certain income, the house included a finished attic room, a servant's quarters with fixtures that combined gas and electric lighting.

A mine foreman, John Reinhardt owned the house until 1913, when George Llewellyn, a superintendent for Prudential Insurance, bought the place. By 1915, Llewellyn had moved to Clay Avenue, but he kept the house until 1919, when he sold the property to George Vasey, who manufactured diamond tools.[12] Vasey soon sold the house and land to Fred Frederickson, who lost the property in 1935 due to delinquent taxes. The bank held the house in trust between 1935 and 1946, when George and Elizabeth Simms bought it. They, in turn, sold it in 1948 to the Harrises, Dorothy and her husband, Luther, who worked for Scranton Lace Company. They occupied the house for the longest time, forty-six years, the years of Scranton's steep economic decline. In 1994, the widowed Mrs. Harris sold the property to William Conway, whose grandfather happened to be Fred Frederickson. We purchased it from Conway in 2001, two months before 9/11. At the closing, he gave us a box of tools, which we accepted with appreciation—and apprehension.

Stonework

Going home began with understanding the rock at my feet.

The bone structure of this region accumulated slowly, horizon upon horizon. Despite epochs of ice and mountain building, ages of deposition and erosion, millennia of migration and extinction, this land has never stopped working. A thousand million years ago, time immemorial, a continent ripped apart and formed the sea Iapetus, approximately where the Atlantic is now, and lasted longer than today's ocean. In the Paleozoic era, Iapetus, named for the father of Atlas, closed as the split continent "came together in a crash no less brutal than slow," thrusting aloft, miles high, the Appalachians. Valleys appeared, and were buried, their rivers coursing in one direction, another, and then, maybe, not at all. During the Mesozoic era, the stitched-together continent tore apart again, widening to form today's Atlantic, which still grows. As this collision and declension unfolded, glaciers advanced and retreated, a dozen times, more or less, across northeastern Pennsylvania.[13]

The last glacier, the Wisconsin ice sheet, erased the work of ancestral glaciers, leaving in its wake Wayne County: more than two hundred feet of clay and silt, sand and gravel. As the head of the Second Geological Survey of Pennsylvania observed in 1881, the county is "an unbroken sheet of Drift, with the usual aspect of Till, with loose boulders, striae on exposed outcrops, drift dams, buried valleys, reversed drainage, and innumerable drift inclosed ponds and lakes." Beneath most of this drift stretches the county's bedrock, the Catskill continental group, mainly red and brown sandstone and shale; another, younger bedrock, Pottsville and Post-Pottsville formations, underlies a sliver of the county, along the west edge, in the Lackawanna Syncline, part of the Ridge and Valley Province.[14] Poor farmland, yes, but we could move the drift, which could also move us.

On a Sunday afternoon in the early seventies, not quite ten years old, Mike O'Neill and I unearthed Iapetus in the dirt behind his house in Pleasant Mount. On tableland two thousand feet up and a hundred miles from the Atlantic, an old sugar maple shading us, we sat in cool soil, surrounded by ragged grass that greened at a stream in the neighbor's yard. We had little else to do but dig. Making a hole for no good reason, we turned up a stone. At first it looked like any half loaf, the kind of rock we'd seen often enough. But then we turned it over. A constellation of shells studded the flat side; each sharply etched, fine grained. Seashells? Astonished, we met each other's eyes, realizing we had in our hands evidence of another time, an alien wonder. Only later, in school, did we find out that an ancient sea had covered the place, a warm and shallow sea that mountains and glaciers had replaced. Still later, the wonder drained, we learned about buried valleys, erratics, drift, debris.[15]

Devonian, Pennsylvanian, Carboniferous.

In April, we'd pick rock. Plowing and harrowing the Flat was never enough; to plant corn the ground had to be cleared. A kid, I was little help as my father and older brothers, sweating away two or three long afternoons, wore their hands raw tossing rock onto a stone boat, sheet metal with three-inch pipe welded to the sides, an upturned end serving as a prow. My father, a Lucky Strike in the corner of his mouth, guided the John Deere 3010 at a crawl, Bob and Jack behind, bent to the ground, hardly glancing with each throw. I kept ahead, loosening a stone here and there for one or the other, itching for shade and a sip of water. A half hour, the boat loaded, we'd climb aboard for the ride to the creek, the soil shearing off smooth behind us. Bankside, we'd toss the rock on a pile meant to keep floods from eating the field, but even after generations of stone picking and piling, the water found a way.

Swollen with snowmelt or storm rains, Johnson Creek ate at basher silt loam left from the Wisconsin ice sheet.[16] After sweeping around, or over, the rock pile, the waters often enough swept soil into the woods or carried it on to alluvial fans on farms far downstream. There, in other fields, other stone boats ferried across similar flats the same glacial drift, stone buried when ice retreated from the land in the last cold spell, during the Pleistocene Epoch, about twelve thousand years ago.

To pick stone was to choose. You didn't need to throw on every rock, just ones you judged capable of doing damage. Occasionally the plow would resurrect a stone large enough that it took two to handle, but more often than not we picked rock no bigger than a good book or a loaf of bread. Every once in a while, someone would discover an odd rock, black and crumbly, maybe, or one shaped like it had come fresh from a mason. As far as I know, we never came across a star, only pieces of mountains.

We stopped planting corn in the late seventies—too expensive—but I discovered picking rock again when in college I came across "A Star in a Stoneboat" (1923), a Robert Frost poem that offered me a new context for moving rock. In the poem, a laborer, clearing plowed ground of glacial drift, levers a meteorite into a stone boat. He doesn't realize, however, that he's come upon a "smooth coal," a onetime fire in the sky that's gone "stone-cold" (4, 10). Once an awe-inspiring sight, this star, come to earth, has died, but in dying has recharged the "very nature of the soil" (21). Now "burning to yield flowers instead of grain," the star has been resurrected as a poet's metaphor for art making (22). After the laborer removes the rock, a kind of waste where it is, he uses it to enclose space with a wall, a human-made artifact whose pattern across the land makes a place, the field. Although the laborer "noticed nothing in it to remark" (7), the speaker, a poet, marks the star so that he feels "Commanded" to "right the wrong" that the once-transcendent stone has been made marginal, ordinary (35, 36).

The heavens may fail, but wonder sings on in the mundane. The speaker cannot undo what's been done by placing the "star back in its course"; telescopes long ago made such stars into stones (30). And if the meteorite is left "lying where it fell," its former glory is known—and meaningful—to no one (30, 39). Reshaped for human use, the star still carries within it its "long Bird of Paradise's tail," and "promises the prize / Of the one world complete in any size" that the speaker is "like to compass, fool or wise" (16, 55–56, 57).

The promised "prize" is a reoriented, recharged relationship with this magnetic world. The meteorite, a smaller version of Mars or Earth, stars of "death and birth" and "death and sin," possesses "poles, and only needs a spin / To show its worldly nature" (46, 49, 50–51). Held in the speaker's "calloused palm" (i.e., the palm of the poet, the poem's other laborer), the stone will "chafe and shuffle . . . / And run off in strange tangents with [his] arm" (52–53). No longer oriented by the stars, the poet/laborer holds a lodestone made erratic by the tension between the sublime and the ordinary, between the mystery of the universe and the earth's magnetism. Following a new course in an old world, the poet looks not to "school and church" for answers but goes about "measuring stone walls, perch on perch" to find inspiration in the land, the "one thing palpable besides the soul / To penetrate the air in which we roll" (11–12, 43, 45). Despite his calluses, this singer is electric with feeling.

My homeland divides in two like no other place in Pennsylvania. The multifold map accompanying the 1881 geological survey of Susquehanna and Wayne counties sharply separates the geologies of the Lackawaxen and Lackawanna riversheds. The map's pale grays and browns, depicting the Appalachian Plateau, contrast with the bright red line of Mauch Chunk shale that rings the Lackawanna Valley's northern tip. Geologist I. C. White marvels at this, the map's "most striking feature . . . the very curious curling up of the end of the Carbondale coal basin, northward; and the continuation of the axis of its trough (or synclinal) in a nearly due north direction along the mid-county line." He describes the formation as a "remarkable violation of the general law of direction which governs the whole system of anticlinals and synclinals in Pennsylvania; virtually cutting off those of the Alleghany mountain region . . . on the west, from all connection with those of the Catskill mountain region of New York State." The result: "No one of the Susquehanna river folds can be identified with any of the Delaware river folds—the two systems of folds flattening out as they approach each other and being kept apart by the north and south fold which cuts transversely across and between them."[17] Maybe because they are so sharply separated in their suturing, crossing and recrossing these folds has been, for me, an education in metaphor.

For example, commuting to high school, and then college, I passed a rock that gradually grew symbolic of the watersheds' separation. I. C. White described the rock as a "massive grayish-white sandstone, with a few pebbles . . . still dipping northwestward . . . most probably the representation of the *Cherry Ridge conglomerate*."[18] Unlike any rock nearby, in color or size, this erratic rests in Griswold's Gap, on the crest of the Moosic Mountains, between Curtis Valley and Browndale, and marks, in my mind, the exact divide between the Lackawanna and Lackawaxen watersheds.

These watersheds, however, are not really separate systems; as neighbors, they interlink, and each opens to other watersheds, on end. A rain shower near Belmont falls to each river, to the Lackawaxen, which flows across the Appalachian Plateau to the Delaware, and to the Lackawanna, which drops off the same plateau at Stillwater to cut a course through the ridge and valley system of the Susquehanna rivershed. Even when I lived furthest from the farm, for four years in College Park, Maryland, near the Chesapeake, Mount Pleasant Township showers found the sea through the bay. So these waters have stayed with me.

Colliding continents folded and refolded the earth's crust here, rolling up layers of dead Devonian trees, plants, and marine life. As mountains rose, their weight compressed the dead, pressing from them almost all but carbon. The folded layers hardened, over millennia, into anthracite, or hard coal. In the trough of one fold rides our house, and beneath us stretch seams of carbon. A slight correction: one bed, the Clark, lay there until the 1930s, when it was hacked out and shipped off to disappear into heat and light. Only the shell of what was remains.

I visited the void in July 2010. The Lackawanna Coal Mine Tour, a Scranton tourist attraction, brought me under in a car that descended at a 25° pitch. The circle of light at the mine entrance receded, smaller and smaller, the deeper we went; as we rounded a bend, natural light winked out, leaving only lamps to show the way. With a jolt, the car stopped, and we clambered out beside a shack 250 feet below the surface, in the ten-by-fifteen Clark vein. Rail thin, a retired miner, the only one of us wearing a hard hat, collected us before a chart of the region's coal beds: Rock Bed, Big Bed, New County Bed, Clark Bed, Dunmore #1, Dunmore #2, and Dunmore #3. Under them all lay the Pottsville Conglomerate, bedrock. Explaining how the beds ran, our guide talked fast, and didn't ask for questions.

"C'mon," he said.

Striding along the gangway, going deeper into the mine, he sang out, "When the pillars start talking, miners start walking."

After uneasy glances at the walls, we followed, quickly.

Geological faults, our miner-guide told us, were a big problem; big coal producers, but risky to mine. We stopped beside a cathedral-like room. Inside, a hand pushed through the debris of a cave-in; when our miner pressed a button, the hand waved. Amused, a few people laughed, but the wounded mannequin guarding the room looked on, impassive. The space was too much, our guide pointed out: the folding earth had shoved a vein twenty-three feet straight up, raising a column of anthracite but also creating a dangerous mine prop problem.

How do you take so much and not get buried?

Gawking at such spaces is no recent phenomenon; curiosity seekers have strolled through coal mines near here since at least the 1840s. The final report of the First Geological Survey of Pennsylvania (1858) includes two full-color lithographs of mines near Wilkes-Barre, considered by at least one observer to be "outstanding examples demonstrating geology and artistry."[19] In volume 2's frontispiece, "The Baltimore Comp. Mines, Wilkes-Barre," rock strata dwarf three tourists who have come to wonder at the Mammoth vein, the largest coal seam in the northern field, in some places forty or more feet thick. The lithograph depicts no markers of industry or technology, other than a fence and three tunnels, which might pass for natural caves. The tunnels on the lithograph's left side mirror gaps in the rock columns on the closer right side; all the gaps open into mines. Cliffs of coal and rock, topped with evergreens, overwhelm the ghostlike and easy-to-miss people who stand at mine entrances. The immensity of the Mammoth vein made the Baltimore mine, which first shipped coal in 1814, a popular tourist trap three decades later.[20] But why? Were people awed by the coal or by its disappearance?

Maybe by its disappearance. An emphasis on the vast interior space rendered in the other lithograph, "Interior of Baltimore Co. Old Mine, Wilkes-Barre,"

Fig. 1 Miners propping workspace, 1916. Courtesy of the Lackawanna Historical Society.

suggests that the absence of coal is the site's main attraction.[21] Inside the mine, the viewer looks across a gigantic room, through two more rooms, toward the mine entrance, a distant sphere of light colored with green trees and blue mountains, a summer scene. A well-dressed man stands just inside the opening, chatting with two brightly dressed women: one in a red shawl, the other in a blue dress. Making the colors stand out, the rest of the scene wraps them in black and gray. Dwarfed by the interior space, the only other figure, an indistinct miner on a small shelf inside the largest room, blends with his surroundings. The scene offers no trace of mining equipment. It's as if the space has been hollowed without effort. As if by magic.

Three years ago, I discovered that coal may not be the only fossil fuel beneath my house. I happen to live above the Marcellus, a swath of shale under much of Pennsylvania that holds what may soon become one of the largest natural gas fields in the world. Thickest in eastern parts of the state—Susquehanna County is a current center of attention—Marcellus shale formed during the Devonian period, just over 360 million years ago, a time that saw a major mass extinction, mainly of marine life. As layers of organic material accumulated and deteriorated, they hardened to shale, and produced natural gas, which eventually created enough pressures of its own to fracture the surrounding rock. Not long after, just over 300 million years ago, Iapetus, the shallow sea separating the ancient continents of Laurentia and Gondwana, rapidly closed. As the continents came crashing together, a "promontory in the vicinity of New York City locked Gondwana and Laurentia at a pivot point," which swung Gondwana clockwise, slamming it into Laurentia and thrusting up the central and southern Appalachians, which buried the shale and rolled beds of anthracite. The collision, which lasted about 15 million years, determined not only the pitch of coal seams but also the direction of Marcellus shale fractures.[22] In other words, what played out over millions of years millions of years ago has led major corporations to think about whether they want to drill—read, mine—under my house. Again.

Long after the drilling ends, oil and gas people may well remember alongside I. C. White the geologists Terry Engelder (Penn State) and Gary Lash (SUNY Fredonia), who started the recent corporate stampede to northeastern Pennsylvania. In early January 2008, the scientists pointed out that "the Marcellus would become one of the world's top super giant gas fields." They soon spurred on the resulting rush to sink unconventional wells when they claimed that "Marcellus Shale weighs in with more than 500 trillion cubic feet of gas in-place spread over a four state area."[23] Engelder calculated that there's enough gas in Marcellus shale to satisfy all U.S. energy needs for at least twenty years, at current levels of consumption.[24] Although Marcellus gas may reduce the nation's carbon emissions and could cut U.S. dependence on foreign oil, one thing is certain: tapping it puts in play billions, if not trillions, of dollars.

To strike it rich, rig operators must drop their drills six to seven thousand feet, turn them at right angles, bore in a NNW or SSE direction several thousand feet more, and inject at high pressure sand and water to fracture further the rock.[25] Gas then squeezes through the resulting fissures toward the pipe, which carries it to the surface . . .

Working Away

To help me understand what's happening at home, I wrote *Here and There* as narrative scholarship.

The description of the 2011 Modern Language Association Convention theme, "Narrating Lives," omitted how narrative informs scholarship in the study of language and literature. Although MLA president Sidonie Smith acknowledged in the description that the association "assembles membership stories of the professional lives of language and literature scholars in changing times," she left no room for how the interweaving of personal stories and traditional scholarship "exposes the work of the humanities in the world."[26] This interweaving, however, has become a major practice of ecocriticism, a fairly recent and expanding subfield in the discipline.

In a paper delivered at the 1994 Western Literature Association Conference (WLA), Scott Slovic, a founder of the Association for the Study of Literature and Environment, used the term "narrative scholarship" in urging "ecocritics to 'encounter the world and literature together, then report about the conjunctions.'" Slovic's term caught on. At the following year's WLA, nineteen ecocritics offered position papers about narrative scholarship. Since then, several prominent writers have published important examples of it.[27]

Although ecocriticism is not alone, of course, in introducing the personal into scholarly work, narrative scholarship does occupy a unique position within ecocritical practice, so much so that one critic claims that narrative scholarship is "how ecocritics write." This is not surprising, given the subfield's roots in nature writing, which privileges representations of individual interactions with the wild; as Terry Gifford notes, "Narrative scholarship has, in a sense, been an assumption behind American nature writing since John Muir's first published essays." In this context, it is noteworthy that when ecocriticism was organizing itself as a distinct subfield in the 1990s, many literary scholars who had "significant academic reputations as theorists" were turning to the personal, a fact that 1998 MLA president Elaine Showalter noted in her presidential address.[28]

As is the case with personal criticism in general, ecocritical narrative scholarship is not without critics. In a 2004 essay in *Environmental History*, Michael Cohen characterizes some versions of narrative scholarship as a "praise-song school" of criticism, which, he argues, is "not sharply analytical but gracefully meditative." Cohen claims that such scholarship is "fraught with dangers": it too easily becomes "travelogue," "clichéd," or "sermonizing." Two years later, Eric Ball accuses narrative scholarship of avoiding "many of the political aspects of environmental and ecological discourse." Asserting that narrative scholarship "could only have come out of the U.S. tradition of nature writing and its related ecocriticism," British academic Terry Gifford, a writer of narrative scholarship, points out that "this kind of writing is generally frowned upon in the United Kingdom with the suspicion that such personal narratives are probably too self-indulgent and uncritical."[29] Ouch.

Questions about the legitimacy of narrative scholarship affect not only eco-criticism, but also every discipline within the humanities. Any scholar concerned with the relationships among writer, text, and world must address issues related to the use (or not) of the personal in scholarly writing. In addition to literature and language studies, the disciplines of anthropology, history, and sociology struggle with the use of the personal in their scholarly practices.[30] At a time when the humanities seek connections with wider audiences, personal criticism has emerged as a major form of outreach. Azar Nafisi's *Reading Lolita in Tehran* (2003), for example, has been a runaway best seller.

Narrative scholarship should especially interest, and trouble, literary scholars, who now confront questions about the value of their work. Reporting about the 2009 convention session "Why Teach Literature Anyway?" the *Chronicle of Higher Education* observes that "one could argue that the real story of MLA 2009 was a quiet but urgent one: how literary scholars can justify what they do nowadays."[31] Writing about literature using a form all understand—narrative—is one way to go.

Fields of Play

Six chapters, plus a coda, follow. The literary texts I examine are from the region, or fit with the book's themes, and they address issues that are both local and national in scope. The problems that people confront in northeastern Pennsylvania, including problems related to water quality, resource extraction, and waste management, are problems that confront people across the country. In *Here and There*, I examine not only how everyday nature gets represented in literature, but also how literature has helped me to understand my connections to home.

Confronting a natural gas rush in northeastern Pennsylvania, I think in chapter 1 about water, a central concern of many of my neighbors, who fear groundwater contamination. The chapter examines how the region treated its water sources in the past, and asks what it would mean to live with bad water. The landmark Pennsylvania Supreme Court case *Pennsylvania Coal Company v. Sanderson* (1886), Mary Austin's sketches in *The Land of Little Rain* (1903), Robert Frost's poem "A Brook in the City" (1923), and Leslie Marmon Silko's novel *Ceremony* (1977) create a context for understanding how the Marcellus gas play may play out.

Chapter 2 acknowledges that to write about the region is to record trauma, both human and environmental. Miners faced the constant threat of injury or death; cave-ins, floods, fires, roof-falls, asphyxiation, and machinery accidents took their toll of lives and limbs.[32] Although coal mining here has all but ended, strip mines still scar mountainsides, culm banks dominate former patch towns, and streams run stained with acid. Coal mining has irreparably damaged a quarter of the region's 484 square miles; it's no wonder that the U.S. Environmental Protection Agency defines the Wyoming and Lackawanna valleys as a distinct ecoregion.[33] Exploring how writers have represented this trauma, I use as points of departure the work of Scranton poets W. S. Merwin and Jay Parini; I read Merwin's "Luzerne Street Looking West" (1956), "Burning Mountain" (1960), and "The Drunk in the Furnace" (1960) alongside Parini's "Anthracite Country" (1982), "The Lackawanna at Dusk" (1982), and "A Lost Topography" (1988).

Thinking through how maps shape how we know a place, the third chapter, "Fixing Fence," investigates the life of Jason Torrey, a central figure in Wayne County history, a Massachusetts man who first settled in northeastern Pennsylvania on land later owned by my family. In addition to the family connection, Torrey interests me because he worked as a surveyor, someone who created many of the property lines that we live with today, lines that a bioregional consciousness blurs, if not erases. In 1814, Torrey drew the earliest U.S. county property map that shows landownership.[34] Robert Frost's "Mending Wall" (1914) helps me to think through issues raised by Torrey's work.

"Barn Razing" meditates on the history of the farm by tracking the erection and erasure of its barns. Our dairy farm evolved in the mid-nineteenth century near enough to a rail line—initially laid to transport coal—to move from participating in a local market to contributing to the New York City milkshed, a fact manifested in the farm's barn building. I end this chapter with a recounting of my razing of a three-story barn, on a Memorial Day, no less, that signaled a loss of this history.

"Other Places" argues that it matters where you learn. Within the context of my experiences as student and teacher, I wonder how different types of schools prepare people for the moral issues implied in land use. I place beside Marywood University, my nonprofit employer, the for-profit University of Phoenix and the Scranton-based International Correspondence Schools, which was founded to educate anthracite miners. The chapter concludes with an analysis of Robert Frost's "The Pasture" (1914), a lyric that taught me how to see the land anew through poetry, which I define as a collection of other places.

The final chapter, "Rendering the Mounds of Home," reflects on the Lackawanna Valley as a palimpsest of unstable ground: layers of mines that brought to the surface underground wealth now haunt people as an underground menace. Land subsidence, caused by the collapse of mine pillars, has long plagued the valley, a fact I explore in studying celebrated incidents in the context of the major U.S. Supreme Court case *Pennsylvania Coal Company v. Mahon* (1922). Not only is mine subsidence a metaphor for the region's present economic instability—and the instability of all things—but so is strip mining, which mauled the valley from the 1920s to the 1970s. The underappreciated film *Wanda* (1970) and the Pulitzer Prize–winning play *That Championship Season* (1972) link these instabilities to ironies in the circulation of waste. Mining created mountains of inferior coal and slate. Once a chief supplier of fuel to East Coast cities, the Anthracite Region now imports the same cities' municipal garbage, creating even more artificial mountains. (One local landfill runs excursion tours of its facilities.) Reflecting on the A. R. Ammons poem *Garbage* (1993), I place mine subsidence and mountain building within the context of current debates about what to do with the remains of our creativity.

The coda briefly examines reclamation and restoration projects at Marywood University to understand how people help to heal human-inflicted damage to the natural world. After reading Wendell Berry's "The River Bridged and Forgot" (1982) as a way to reconceive our relationship to the rest of life, I end the book with a glance again at the gray dawn of natural gas drilling in northeastern Pennsylvania.

A major political force in the 2004 and 2008 presidential elections, a recent flashpoint in controversies over immigration, and a potential East Coast energy supplier (once again), northeastern Pennsylvania stands at a crossroads in its history. But it stands there perplexed, I believe, looking for a story that not only transcends but also incorporates the narrative of decline that others have pinned to it. As I look at my home, I see that although dark sites remain, some brown fields are, in fact, greening.

The uniqueness of a place's geology, culture, and history denies the global economy's demand for an interchangeable-parts definition of human experience. To assume that every place can be any place is to endanger all places. What works here does not often work there, so the best way to understand any place is to see it in the context of other places, other times. All I can offer people who want to understand this one place, northeastern Pennsylvania, is my perspective as an insider with an outsider's point of view. Overlaying my lived experiences with my experiences reading literature and history, *Here and There* shows how the region connects to and shapes the world beyond home. I'm from the place I write about, but the more I think about it, the more mysterious it gets. What I keep discovering is more than I could have imagined, more than I can absorb, more than I can say.

How have you been at work in the world?

1

Working Watersheds

Thales says that it is water.

—Aristotle, *Metaphysics*

At the same time that my neighbors and I are learning new words—Jis, muds, and fracking, for example—we confront new acronyms such as MCF, MER, PIG.[1] And the terms, the terms keep coming. I discover that to drill on air is to sink a bare bit through the water table. A Christmas tree, I hear, is a collection of pipes on a well top. Someone mentions that horizontal drilling has revolutionized oil and gas production, and an expert reminds me that "all energy requires water; water requires energy."[2] Even as I struggle to sort words and terms, big companies—Exxon, Hess, Chesapeake—bandy about big numbers: $6,000/acre and a 20 percent royalty. Two thousand drilled, four thousand permitted, maybe one hundred thousand more: a gas rush.

Searching for some clarity, I signed up for the August 2010 Marywood University forum "Marcellus Shale: Opportunities and Challenges." Industry terms, numbers, and names dominated presentations about energy extraction, community impacts, and water quality. I heard my then representative in the U.S. House, who was up for reelection, declare that the "gold rush is here," that "Marcellus

Shale is a second chance," and that "we can have it both ways." A little more cautious, thankfully, one of my representatives in the U.S. Senate told me that "we need to invent the future in the right way" and that "we can't repeat the mistakes of the past." The president of a coalition of gas companies—its logo a water droplet encasing a green leaf—pointed out that Marcellus shale is a "long-term play"; when fully developed, by about 2020, it will have put tens of thousands to work and will have added billions to the state economy. On the other hand, the head of the Pennsylvania Department of Conservation and Natural Resources (DCNR) reported that the state's conservation efforts suffered a major setback in October 2009 when the state swiped money from the DCNR budget to shore up its general fund. If Pennsylvania wants a model for what might happen as the rush runs its course, a Penn State professor suggested, it should look to Texas and other shale areas; experience in these places has shown that boomtowns are not better off for the boom.[3] He urged communities to ask a question that too many in the Anthracite Region failed to ask 150 years ago: "What happens when it's over?"

I walked away as bewildered as before. Strolling across campus toward home, I realized that I had no category to absorb the immensity of what might happen. Like a slowly approaching hurricane might, the size of what was coming posed questions I couldn't begin to answer. How does one person prepare? How do people "invent the future"? When the storm breaks, how do communities "have it both ways"? And the question I couldn't shake: How do we keep the powers at play from wreaking havoc on us and the land?

Past is prologue, they say, which may be why at least two forum speakers urged me to think about the rush to drill within the context of the region's history of resource extraction. In her opening remarks, for example, Marywood president Sr. Anne Munley insisted that we "recall our regional history at moments such as this." What's at issue, she asserted, is "balancing an economic opportunity with stewardship of the land for future generations. In a region long used to economic hardship, this is a difficult balancing act to resolve." Citing acid mine drainage, U.S. senator Bob Casey reminded me that the region's "history is instructive"; we've "been there, done that." Both urged me to read attentively, think deeply, and act carefully. Amen to that, I said. But then again, how well can I read, think, and act when I'm in a rush?[4]

A lot has happened since land men began knocking on people's doors. By mid-2010, they had leased one-fourth of Pennsylvania. Facing a 2009 budget crisis, the state allowed drilling on large blocks of state forest and game lands, much of which, we were later told, the state owned no mineral rights to anyway. During the same budget battle, Pennsylvania, unlike most states that have oil and natural gas reserves, refused to impose a "severance tax, a tax on natural resources 'severed' from the land."[5] Meanwhile, my brother, facing falling milk prices, signed a lease allowing Houston-based Southwestern Energy to drill on the homestead. A few miles to the south, at the Matousheks' farm, Louisiana-based Stone Energy dropped the gas rush's first drill in Wayne County, creating a well that joined seventy thousand others that dot the state, reminders that drilling is not new to Pennsylvania, which is, after all, the birthplace of the oil and gas industry.[6]

The terms, numbers, and names fade when someone mentions water.

People fear that natural gas drilling will contaminate drinking water. Sinking a gas well requires about three million gallons of water, which must be sucked from rivers, streams, or water wells. Once the water and its toxic additives have shot through shale, they resurface as wastewater that must be either treated or recycled. It doesn't help to know that water from a fracked well is three to five times saltier than seawater, or that in 2007 scientists discovered that gas wells capped in 1920 have contaminated nearby water wells.[7]

Accidents happen. The Pennsylvania Department of Environmental Protection recorded between 2005 and 2010 "hundreds of examples of spills at natural gas drilling sites." In March 2009, for example, DEP fined Cabot Oil and Gas for "allowing methane to escape into [Susquehanna County] residents' drinking water." Later that year, in September, a "spill of a hydrofracturing lubricant" in the same county may have contaminated Stevens Creek. An environmentalist's aerial photographs sparked a 2009 state investigation of a Wayne County well; a preliminary report found that a "'weathered petroleum product' of unknown quantity was discharged . . . into a forested area." In June 2010, a Clearfield County well on a private hunting club's property in the "middle of a state forest" spewed for sixteen hours a "geyser of gas and wastewater."[8]

Slapping firms with small fines and short stoppages, Pennsylvania has gone easy on gas companies. I would have expected a state with three major watersheds—the Delaware, Susquehanna, and Ohio, whose waters touch millions of lives—to exert a little more force. The Susquehanna, for example, drains

27,510 square miles, supports a population of over four million people, and makes up 43 percent of the Chesapeake Bay watershed.[9] The Ohio watershed, draining the west end of the state, contributes water to the largest river system in the United States, and sends its waters to the Gulf of Mexico. With more miles of streams than any other state but Alaska, water-rich Pennsylvania suddenly must rely on the federal Environmental Protection Agency to initiate a "study of hydraulic fracturing that would consider . . . the whole life-cycle of a well."[10] Why?

Not everyone agrees with Pennsylvania policy. In August 2010, the New York Senate overwhelmingly approved a moratorium on gas drilling in that state. Aware of the fifteen million people who drink water from the Delaware rivershed, which supplies New York City and Philadelphia, the Delaware River Basin Commission effectively declared in May 2009 a drilling moratorium.[11] Fearing that chemicals used in fracking wells would contaminate the city's drinking water, Philadelphia City Council in March 2010 "unanimously approved a resolution that asks the Delaware River Basin Commission to conduct an environmental impact study of natural gas drilling in the Delaware River watershed prior to approving any permits." At the time, the Commission was mulling a request from Stone Energy to draw water from the West Branch of the Lackawaxen River in order to frack the Matoushek well, an application the Commission approved on 14 July 2010. Water withdrawal from the Lackawaxen has brought "the City of Brotherly Love and this predominantly agricultural county much closer than ever imagined."[12]

In November 2005, I stood 282 feet below sea level, looking out across the salt flats of Death Valley, thinking about Frank Norris's McTeague handcuffed to a dead body. The moment expressed all I knew about deserts: hot, dry, deadly. Out on the flats, people appeared and disappeared in heat waves; I ventured not so far, studying what surprised me, the presence of water, as bad as it is, in Badwater Basin. Native to a humid place, I missed the sight of a good spring; I had no working category for knowing arid land. But then again, I was a tourist there, so I concentrated on the awful beauty: distant mountains, sharp rocks, sandstone colors. And I had a bottle of water, the van—not far—had air conditioning, and the paved roads in and out had signs. Glancing back at Badwater, I could imagine staying awhile, a day maybe. What I couldn't imagine was living there.

West of Badwater, between the Sierra and Inyo mountains, stretches the Owens Valley, home for a time to Mary Hunter Austin; here she wrote *The Land of Little Rain*, essays about Death Valley and the Mojave, Lone Pine and Independence, land she named the Country of Lost Borders. A transplant from the Midwest, Austin kept her senses alert, for years, as she slowly came to know the country; only after she had "summer[ed] and winter[ed] with the land and wait[ed] its occasions" did she begin writing. As she wrote, she thought a lot about water, which keeps that arid land alive, no matter how "dry the air and villainous the soil."[13]

Reading her essays in well-watered Pennsylvania reminds me of what I and many of my neighbors have for too long taken for granted: our access, so far, to good, clean, abundant water. With water at its heart, *The Land of Little Rain* pays careful attention to "precise place-based knowledge," because getting right the details matters as much for one's survival as for one's aesthetics.[14] As Austin points out, "Not the law, but the land sets the limit" (3). Accustomed to where they are, for example, western cattle "drink morning and evening," and protect themselves by lying at night on "exposed fronts of westward facing hills." At home in a water-starved world, they so closely resemble less domesticated animals that in "these half wild spotted steers the habits of an earlier lineage persist" (15).

Water drives desert dwellers: if you can't find a sip, you're dead. As Austin matter-of-factly points out, "To underestimate one's thirst, to pass a given landmark to the right or left, to find a dry spring where one looked for running water—there is no help for any of these things" (5).[15] People cannot depend on springs, "for when found they are often brackish and unwholesome, or maddening, slow dribbles in a thirsty soil" (4). For a human to get around, she insists, requires a sophisticated awareness of weather and wind, plants and animals, elevations and the position of the sun. If you don't know the country, well, it might kill you. This is land that "forces new habits on its dwellers," not the least of which is where to find water (7).

Close reading can help. Animal tracks lead to springs, which are few and far between, and cattle die with their noses pointed toward water holes.[16] These are not the only signs of water, however: Austin describes a circle of stone with an arrow pointing toward a spring, a mark Shoshone made "near where the immemorial foot trail goes up from Saline Flat toward Black Mountain" (17). Another arrow sign, of an "older, forgotten people," built closer to the spring, instructs the thirsty: "In this direction . . . is a spring of sweet water; look for it" (18).

People war over scarce water. In the Country of Lost Borders, upstream farmers defend irrigation ditches in dry years, holding water for themselves before it flows on to others, assuming any remains (86). Austin recounts that at the end of one summer, Amos Judson, for example, shot up Jesus Montaña, who dared contest Judson's right to all the water in Tule Creek (87). A dozen or so years later, however, Mrs. Diedrick, Judson's latest downstream neighbor, held Judson off with a long-handled shovel. These incidents lead Austin to point out, prophetically, that "some of the water-right difficulties are more squalid than this, some more tragic" (87).

Not a few years later, a more squalid and tragic difficulty afflicted Owens Valley when Los Angeles started stealing the heart of the country, siphoning its water to expand into what the city has become, a place where streams have gone underground, springs have been built over, and water trees run in concrete sluices. Grown beyond its place, Los Angeles stands at the end of a more than two hundred mile ditch that drains water "east away from the Sierras, south from Panamint and Amargosa" (3). For otherwise arid Los Angeles, it's not land that sets limits; it's law. The lesson: if a large number of people want what's at your feet, they'll take it, one way or another, whether it's water, coal, or natural gas.[17]

Ditches keep no one for long.

A ditch bisects the farm. Well-meaning, I'm sure, the Soil Conservation Service engineered the gash in 1973 to catch runoff from the sidehill and divert it from racing down the driveway or coursing through the pasture behind the house to the Flat, where it had already carved a shallow channel. Steering the flow from one side of the farm to the other, the Ditch dumped water into the woods, out of sight. Before the bulldozer raised the bank, no one, I bet, walked among the hemlock and beech to find where the water would go, how it would get there, or what it would do as it found its way to Johnson Creek. Maybe the site supervisor assumed that trees and rocks would disperse the force of the water, or maybe he assumed eroding a woodlot a lesser sin than eroding the pasture, an old apple orchard. Or maybe no one thought about it. So now in the woods, the flow cuts deep gullies, in some places a dozen feet down through Lordstown stony loams. And no grass has reclaimed the gullies, which would blunt the loss, as grass had in the water's former course. Between ditch and creek, a handful of hemlocks have lost their footing, and heavy rains plug the sluice pipe under the road near my brother's house. The Ditch didn't solve an erosion problem; it moved it, and maybe made it worse.

From Honesdale to the state line, a ditch once cut a path parallel to the Lackawaxen River. Prior to 1849, the Delaware and Hudson Canal ended at the edge of the Delaware only to begin again on the other side, but after the construction of the Roebling aqueducts, Lackawaxen water went on to empty into a second river, the Hudson, eighty-four miles to the east.[18] One hundred and eight total miles, the Delaware and Hudson Canal measured in 1851 six feet deep, forty-eight to fifty feet wide at the top, and thirty-two feet at the bottom.[19] To float boats, canal tenders had to maintain its depth; to save its sides from erosion, canal traffic and water flow had to maintain walking speed. Opened in October 1828, the D & H, a symptom of the early nineteenth-century canal fever, carried for seventy years Lackawanna Valley coal to New York City markets. For seventy years, water from the farm, located along Johnson Creek between Hankins Pond and Miller Pond, fed four rivers that supplied industrial America: the Lackawaxen, the D & H, the Delaware, and the Hudson.

Water worries determined where the canal began. Fearing that local landowner Jason Torrey, who operated a sawmill on the river, "would not guarantee an adequate supply of water for the canal," the D & H cut him from their plans to create a canal head. In August 1827, Torrey had contracted with the D & H to donate to the company half his land at the forks of the Dyberry for the canal terminus; in return he expected his remaining land to jump in value with the rise of the town that would support the canal's operation. In September, however, D & H founder Maurice Wurts crossed the Dyberry and swindled Torrey's neighbor, Samuel Kimble, convincing him that his land was worth little because the canal would begin on Torrey's property. As historian Vernon Leslie notes dryly, "The brothers Wurts were not known for their generosity or integrity in regard to land deals."[20] Early-day land men, I imagine.

Water supply was a serious and chronic issue for the new river. Constructed "during a season of unusual drought" in 1826, the sides of the canal had to be watered and allowed to settle before the basin could be filled. Hacked through sections of "porous, stony soil," the waterway sometimes leaked, which meant

Fig. 2 Delaware and Hudson Canal, 1898. Courtesy of the Lackawanna Historical Society.

lining the bottom with clay. Operating only from May to December, the ditch had to be refilled every spring, which meant that engineers put to work springs, creeks, rivers, and swamps.[21] Despite raising reservoirs all along the route, including Belmont Lake, Hankins Pond, and Miller Pond, the company couldn't keep boats afloat in 1851, 1854, 1870, 1883, and 1895.[22] Finding enough water even after a flood could be tough; in recharging the canal following an 1862 flood, canal overseer Russel Lord, "in effect, attempted to pump dry the Lackawaxen."[23]

Along the canal's feeder streams, water-intensive tanneries sprang up, each feeding not only on water but also on the area's hemlock, whose bark produced tannic acid, a necessary component in tanning hides. The tannery that stood between Pleasant Mount and Belmont, along the West Branch of the Lackawaxen, was part of an international business that by 1860 accounted for two-thirds of the value of Wayne County manufacturing, a stat in large part attributable to the canal offering access to New York's port. Supplying tanneries with hides from as far away as South America, in 1872 the canal floated 1,690 tons of leather and hides and 729 tons of tanners' bark.[24] It's a good bet that tanners simply dumped used vats of tannic acid into streams like the

Johnson; a mix of acids, blood, and offal cannot be good for water quality.[25] By the mid-1880s, however, the industry, making mainly shoe leather, collapsed across the county after it exhausted the supply of hemlock.[26]

With railroads delivering coal at an ever-faster clip, the canal lost ground. In 1880, D & H president Thomas Dickson approached the company board of directors with three reasons to shut it down: (1) it's "expensive to maintain . . . liable to damage, and can be used a portion of the year only"; (2) the "question of a water supply is becoming more serious every year"; and (3) "traffic cannot be moved upon [it] as cheaply as by rail."[27] At the end of 1898, the D & H finally closed the canal, and the Lackawaxen, Delaware, and Hudson rivers reclaimed their waters.

As the weather warmed in 1899, the canal became a "stinking, unhealthy ditch." One seventeen-mile section sold to the Erie Railroad "bought the Erie considerable abuse over sanitary problems" because people feared malaria outbreaks. When operations ended, life along the canal banks changed almost instantly; mules disappeared into D & H mines, workers left for jobs elsewhere, and many of the busy towns that had sprung up along the towpath withered and died.[28]

Our house sits on a lake we've never seen. As large as a Finger Lake and about one hundred feet beneath us, neither ice nor rain created it. An orphan of anthracite mining and a brainchild of the state Bureau of Mining and Reclamation, the Acid Mine Lake names a basin beneath a basin, a watershed of pollution cupping the watershed I glimpse from my front door. Not good.

To mine coal below the water table, companies continually pumped water from their mines, even when mines were idle due to labor strikes, accidents, or money troubles. Owners, strikers, non-miners: everyone respected the pumps because they knew that if the pumps stopped mining would end, forever. In 1960 the pumps stopped.[29]

In January 1959, Knox Coal Company miners chipped away at a coal seam near Pittston to within six feet of a buried valley under the Susquehanna River. Left by the Wisconsin ice sheet, "water-bearing, quicksand-like sediments" broke into the mine, pulling the river with it, sweeping away twelve men, and sending seventy more scrambling for the surface. The resulting whirlpool, 120–50 feet wide, defied for days all attempts to plug it, including running into the abyss thirty or more railroad cars loaded with coal. By the time the river surface smoothed, ten billion gallons of water had been sucked into Wyoming Valley mines.[30]

A massive pumping and propping operation cleared the mines, but by then the three major coal companies had discovered that deep mining here was no longer profitable. Deciding to pull out, Glen Alden, Moffat, and Hudson agreed among themselves that the last outfit left would shut down the pumps. After the last switch flipped to off on 1 November 1960, water gradually collected in mine gangways and rooms, crosscuts and hoisting sheds, its level rising by January 1962 to 609 feet above sea level. Mine water soon gushed "from numerous bore holes and seeps along the Lackawanna Valley," coursing down hillsides and collecting in basements.[31]

Called in to solve the flooding problem, the state decided that siphoning off the water would relieve the underground pressure. Near Old Forge, where the river spills over the Moosic Saddle anticline, workers drilled down four hundred feet, creating a hole that "drains all of the flooded mine tunnels from Olyphant through Scranton and Taylor."[32] The resulting gush daily spews into the river one hundred million gallons of water laced with a ton and a half of iron oxide (i.e., rust), along with "iron, aluminum, manganese and sulfur." If you wanted to stab a river in the heart, this would be one way to do it; from Old Forge to the Lackawanna's confluence with the Susquehanna, no "fishery or any significant aquatic community" survives.[33] The river rusts, lifeless, in its last three miles, its water and rocks a surreal, bright orange. The price for my dry basement is a long stretch of dead river.

Scranton and its river have always had an uneasy relationship. In the early 1850s, the river may have, just may have, "flowed deep and strong, with an abundance of water, that came sparkling pure from the thick forests and wooded hills of the upper valley," but this, the Scranton family knew, would not last. In 1854, the Scrantons, scrambling to supply their growing village with water, organized the Scranton Gas and Water Company, which began four years later to pump water from the Lackawanna River, near today's Scranton High School, uphill to a reservoir at Madison Avenue and Olive Street.[34] By 1866, the year of the city's founding, the river was officially "declared unfit for public water supply." With river water undrinkable, in 1867 the company dammed Roaring Brook, a Lackawanna tributary, but in 1870 these waters so corroded flues at the

Lackawanna Iron and Coal furnaces that an explosion killed eleven workers.[35] The water company quickly retreated farther up the mountain, making reservoirs as it went. Meanwhile, garbage, industrial waste, mine runoff, and sewage smothered the river, so much so that by the 1920s much of the Lackawanna was dead, and, aided by state and local government, remained so for years. A 1937 Pennsylvania clean streams law "exempted coal companies," and as late as the 1960s local officials resisted state and citizen efforts to clean up the river, arguing that "pollution from the mines neutralized the health threats from the sewage." For too long, the city knew only a wasted waterway.[36]

Despite its troubles, the Lackawanna is beautiful. Sixty-two miles long, it drains 350 square miles, flows through twenty-three municipalities, and passes through an area populated by nearly 250,000 people. From sources atop the Moosic Mountains, the river drops "an average of 39 feet per mile" on its trip to the Susquehanna, cutting rock that was once the "ocean floor in the Devonian period, the great swamps of the Carboniferous period, [and] the folded and uplifted sedimentary rocks of the Permian age." The river rises from glacial ponds in Wayne and Susquehanna counties: Lake Lorain, Bone Pond, Independent Lake, and Dunns Pond feed the east branch; the west branch carries water from Fiddle Lake, Lake Lowe, and Lewis Lake. Through parts of Scranton, just north of the Old Forge borehole, the river has recovered enough in the last thirty years to offer excellent trout fishing; north of the city, a section between Jessup and Jermyn—and many people refuse to believe it—the Pennsylvania Fish Commission classifies as Class A Trophy Trout waters. Despite this resurrection, more than a dozen major outfalls still empty mine acid into the watershed.[37]

As I worked on this chapter, I followed the "cleanup" of the largest oil spill in U.S. history. When the BP *Deepwater Horizon* drilling rig exploded on 20 April 2010, killing eleven workers and gushing millions of gallons of crude into the Gulf of Mexico, I couldn't help but see it as a larger version of the Old Forge borehole. Every day, long into July, oil washed ashore along the coast, crippling the Gulf economy, all for a few barrels more. *Guardian* writer Naomi Klein put it exactly right when she noted that the spill was less an industrial accident than a "violent wound in a living organism."[38] The Earth bleeds, we watch, and little changes but the scale of disaster.

Every other day, usually, I run up Richmont Street, sprint across North Washington Avenue, jog up Electric Street, swing around the Oral School, and pass through the gates of Forest Hill Cemetery, where I wind my way among the dead. With the original cobblestone roads paved, thankfully, running in the cemetery is less dangerous than it might otherwise be. The six mausoleums look like cottages, with maples shading their front doors; two of them, Barnes and Lucas, back into a hillside. Along my route, I glimpse marble stumps and vases, Egyptian towers and sleeping lambs. I cross a stone arch bridge, pass beneath towering oaks where owls nest, and duck mountain laurel that hangs over the way. Although enticed to linger and listen, I head home, my running shoes slapping pavement between the stone and wrought iron entrance.

Civil engineer J. Gardner Sanderson designed Forest Hill as a rural cemetery, a parklike escape from the work world.[39] In the post–Civil War era, when the rapidly expanding industrial economy shifted into high gear, "rural cemeteries represented society's desire for stability." With more people alienated from their work, they needed a place to rest, relax, and recreate. An important part of the rural cemetery, water "not only provided a natural break in the scenery but also encouraged meditation and relaxation." Its life-giving symbolism suggested the mid-nineteenth-century shift from the colonial fear of fiery damnation to an assurance of "happy eternal life."[40]

In the late 1860s, west-running Meadow Brook left Gypsy Grove swamp, meandered through the woods, and flowed into Forest Hill, where it spilled through three eye-shaped ponds; leaving the cemetery, the stream slipped across new house lots, pooled in another pond, and then slid off an esker to find the river. The clear running brook, then home to trout, is now no more than a ditch funneled into a concrete pipe. Already forced underground as it entered town, Meadow Brook lost its water in 1962 when the federal highway system built Interstate 81.[41] Except for storm runoff, these days Forest Hill is bone-dry.

Robert Frost writes about the hubris behind a similar channeling in "A Brook in the City," a poem that opens with a farmhouse, once nestled in the stream's "elbow-crook," now swallowed by a "new-built city" (4, 24). Representing a dying life that hangs on, the farmhouse sits in town off-kilter, cockeyed to the street, a reaction against the expectation that it must adjust to an artificial order, one that pins it down with a number and no name. Although the house may have once freely used the stream as a water source, the city system must now pipe a metered supply indoors. Unlike the farmhouse, which had conformed to the land, the city demands that the land conform to its idea of itself. A farm—at least the better ones, these days—works within nature's seasons, but a city refuses to accept such limits, imposing on the ground an out-of-time grid.

To extend the grid, planners pave meadows and burn apple trees, but a brook is another story: "How else dispose of an immortal force / No longer needed?" (13–14). Flushing "cinder loads dumped down," the speaker notes, cannot stop the stream "at its source" (14, 15). A living thing, water will find a way, planners know, so instead, "The brook was thrown / Deep in a sewer dungeon under stone / In fetid darkness still to live and run" (15–17). But, as the poem's central line wonders, "Is water wood to serve a brook the same?" (12). How many gardens must go? Are we not mad to channel the brook after we've burned the orchard? To cut up an apple tree may be a sin, but to straiten a brook is to erode our being.

Out of sight, the brook is, however, not out of mind. Its absence haunts us because a built environment doesn't help us to answer ultimate questions about being and knowing. We made the city, we know, but the brook that we cannot destroy is not of our doing. Despite its current "kept forever under" streets, the water leads us to "thoughts . . . that so keep / This new-built city from both work and sleep" (22, 23–24). The fact that the stream can now be found only on "ancient maps" tells us how far we've come in separating ourselves from nature, the wellspring of life (20).

We may demand that the brook "go in fear," but, deep down, we know our own bluster: we can never discover all the answers (19). Poetic imagination, however, leaps beyond the handmade; it checks our hubris by placing our work within larger patterns, wider contexts. Nodding to this idea, the speaker, a poet who once knew the long-gone brook's "strength / And impulse," dips his finger in the stream to make "it leap [his] knuckle"; afterward he tosses into the "currents where they crossed" a flower, an aesthetic object, an emblem of art (5–6, 7, 8). Symbolic of inspiration and creativity, the brook's energy—unpredictable, uncontrollable, unstoppable—challenges our rage for order with the intimation that there are forces beyond reason. All we can make within life's flow is a momentary stay.

Can buried brooks inspire?

Can wastewater sustain us?

Without water, Forest Hill desiccates hope. When Meadow Brook ran free and clear, the place represented transition, life to come. Without living water, the cemetery stockpiles bodies with nowhere to go. Although designed to balance "civilized dominance of nature and sublime wilderness," Forest Hill long ago lost its wildest thing, erased in favor of easy travel, leaving us only a fake wild, as nice as that may appear. Accumulating moments in time, Forest Hill once gave place to community memory, but with its water gone, a key link in that memory has evaporated.[42] Meadow Brook, the most natural and ever-changing tie between the cemetery and its community, was thoughtlessly destroyed, making the cemetery not for the living but for the dead. Although the stream once knitted, in time and space, the cemetery and its neighborhood, from the start mine acid tainted the link.

On 30 July 2010, I interviewed Forest Hill superintendent Norma Reese. Her office occupies the west end of her long and narrow house, which sits tucked under a row of trees a hundred feet inside the cemetery gates. Baskets of flowers hung from the front porch and stood in pots on the front steps; inside, wind chimes hung from the ceiling, cemetery files lay open on the desk, and a 1915 map of the grounds hung from a wall. A collector of angels and unicorns, Norma sat behind George Sanderson's bank desk, her graying hair pulled back. She wore a "Merry Christmas 2008" T-shirt, silver-wire glasses, and clogs. Having overseen Forest Hill for twenty years, she's become part of the place; she's not only its caretaker but also its defender and historian. She's fond of the Forest Hill sassafras tree, the hemlocks and ground pines, and the red and white oak; not long ago, she discovered something she'd never seen in the cemetery, a red berry elder. Recognizing me as someone who runs in the cemetery, someone she had long ago named the pusher for helping her to get a riding lawnmower unstuck, she now had a name for the face.

Norma informed me that in the mid-1860s J. Gardner Sanderson and his father, George, convened their next-door neighbors to form a cemetery board of trustees, which included Elisha Phinney, two doors to the east; J. Atticus Robertson, who lived next to Phinney; and C. Dupont Breck, who owned the parcel directly opposite George. In 1868, the board bought land from the Pennsylvania Coal Company to found Forest Hill because culm banks were quickly overshadowing the city's Pine Brook cemetery.[43] Not only fears of being twice buried, but also the hilltop ground's geology may have guided their purchase.

Cemeteries tend to occupy moraines, glacially deposited piles of earth and stones that are often "steep and hummocky, with erratics and boulders. Yet it's easy ground to dig in, and well drained."[44] And the topography didn't invite culm dumps.

In the same year that the association bought land for the cemetery, J. Gardner and his wife, Eliza McBriar, purchased property along Meadow Brook, about three blocks from where Bridget and I live. Drawn by the purity of the water, which they traced to its source, the Sandersons built an impressive house on Meadow Brook's north bank, excavated a fish pond—similar in size and shape to the Forest Hill ponds—and piped water into their home.[45] Surrounded by flower gardens, a fountain, and an arcing drive, they had a sweeping view of the river as it curved gracefully along the valley floor, a view soon interrupted, however, by new-built homes, the billowing smoke of a D & H rail yard, and the black breaker at Centennial mine.[46]

At about the same time, maybe in the same year, the Pennsylvania Coal Company opened the Gypsy Grove mine, two miles upstream from the Sanderson property. Water pumped from the mine coursed through a company ditch into Meadow Brook, polluting it. Corroded pipes, dead fish, and undrinkable water forced the couple to abandon brook water sometime in 1874; in November 1875, they sued Pennsylvania Coal for damages. First heard in the Luzerne County Court of Common Pleas in 1878, the case reached the Pennsylvania Supreme Court, which in 1886 ruled in favor of the coal company.[47] Ruling against water quality, *Pennsylvania Coal* turned property law on its head.

Pennsylvania Coal advanced several arguments. The company asserted that water pumped from its mines was natural—"its impurity arises from natural, not artificial causes"—and that it reached Meadow Brook by natural means, gravity. Company lawyers discovered no one else in Scranton complaining about water, and, besides, the Sandersons were "supplied with abundant pure water from other sources." The company conceded that Meadow Brook water may be impure, but its impurity comes from elsewhere: prior mine openings, barnyards, or the old section of Dunmore Cemetery. Advocating fairness to all, the company claimed that if it cannot use its "land for the natural purpose of mining coal because our neighbor cannot keep his tame fish in his pond, the same rule should apply to him. He should not be allowed to maintain a fish-pond so near our mine that we cannot use it."[48]

What is natural? Pumping water from a mine is not a natural act, I believe, but neither is raising a "large dam" across Meadow Brook to create a pond. From the pond, the Sandersons also built a fairly elaborate "water-works" that included two hydraulic rams, one "for the purpose of raising water from a lower to a higher level," in this case from the pond to a storage tank in the house's attic, the second to force "water upon the lawn for the purposes of irrigation there, and for the purpose of supplying a fountain."[49] Drinking directly from Meadow Brook is a natural act, I suppose, but I enjoy drinking water piped into my house as much as I like electric lights and a heated home. At what point do my accumulating preferences undermine their sources? When does my land use rob others of their use?

The Pennsylvania Supreme Court had to choose between coal and clean water. They chose coal. In a 5–2 decision, the justices ruled that the Sandersons suffered a "mere personal inconvenience," which "must yield to the necessities of a great public industry, which although in the hands of a private corporation, subserves a great public interest." Scranton, after all, had prospered solely because of coal. And this was a mining region, the judges reminded everyone; the Sandersons simply should have known that mines poison "mountain streams." Pointing out that the couple has benefited from the wealth mining has created, Justice J. J. Clark found "no great hardship, nor any violence to equity, in their also accepting the inconvenience necessarily resulting from the business."[50]

The court also agreed with the company that mining is a natural operation with natural consequences. Polluting—destroying—Meadow Brook was simply one result of a natural process, mining. Writing for the majority, Justice Clark asserted that "the defendants introduced nothing into the water, to corrupt it; the water flowed into Meadow Brook just as it was found in the mine; its impurities were from natural and not from artificial causes." It didn't matter that the company pumped the water to the surface or that sulfuric acid killed the stream. Clark simply noted that a miner "may upon his own lands, lead the water which percolates into his mine, into the streams which form the natural drainage of the basin, in which the coal is situate, although the quantity as well as the quality of the water in the stream may thereby be affected."[51] This reasoning gave coal companies a green light to mine with abandon.

A closely watched case at the time, *Pennsylvania Coal Company v. Sanderson* has come to symbolize how nineteenth-century courts struggled to meet legal challenges created by the rise of new industries and technologies. Had the decision gone the other way, coal companies may have faced scores of lawsuits based on the effects of their mining operations, but with its ruling in favor of Pennsylvania Coal, the case signaled that the law was moving from protecting individual property rights to protecting corporate property rights. The Sanderson case marks the culmination of a movement in property law from an agrarian to an industrial point of view; after *Pennsylvania Coal*, "property law was no longer about the right to remain undisturbed in one's lawful use; it was now chiefly about the right to use land for maximum gain."[52]

The dispute wasn't a big guy/little guy battle. The Sandersons were well known and well connected; they and their neighbors were not innocents swallowed by urban and industrial life. An 1877 map of our neighborhood shows that J. Gardner and his father, the original developer of our Green Ridge suburb, occupied stately homes on three-quarters of a city block on Seventh Street, which was soon after christened Sanderson Avenue. Depicting the pond that the Sandersons created to trap Meadow Brook water, the map shows the stream as a thin, nervous line lost among the Sandersons' ruled and numbered lots, which wait for buyers and builders; after leaving the pond, the brook passed under four rail lines, crossed two city blocks, and skirted the Centennial breaker before escaping into the Lackawanna River.[53]

George Sanderson, Sr., C. Dupont Breck, and Elisha Phinney laid those gridlines and actively promoted coal and railroad interests. Sanderson, a Pennsylvania Senate colleague of George Scranton, "with whom he co-operated in securing needed legislation," founded the city's first bank, made a pile of money in downtown real estate, and built a railroad to his suburb.[54] Breck represented the Duponts in the local manufacture of mine explosives, and Phinney ran flour and feed operations that supplied "food to the industrial city's expanding population."[55] Powerful men connected to powerful people, these guys understood land as money, not life. Like the rest of us, they were both creators and destroyers.

I confront this fact about myself in Leslie Marmon Silko's *Ceremony*, a novel whose lessons about land use I'm still learning. The story depicts a Native American farmer coping with an acute awareness of the world's suffering, vividly symbolized by the first atomic explosions, which a local uranium mine fueled. Tracing his healing process, the novel follows Tayo, a traumatized World War II veteran, as he gropes toward wholeness through remembering his and the Laguna Pueblos' stories, patterns at whose heart rests human oneness with the land. As he recovers, Tayo learns that his life tells one part of a single, communal, human-and-land story, one that others want erased. To remember, to put story and place back together, Tayo must relearn to pay attention to the land, its flora and fauna, its rocks and waters.

Tayo's troubles—and his healing—have much to do with water. Early on in the narrative, he flashes back to the scene of his psychic wounding, the Bataan Death March: as he and a corporal struggle to carry the former's wounded cousin Rocky, an effort that an incessant storm makes more difficult, Tayo damns "the rain until the words were a chant . . . he could hear his own voice praying against the rain" (12). If Rocky dies, Tayo thinks, "it would be the rain and the green all around that killed him" (11). To save Rocky, he "made a story for all of them, a story to give them strength," its words like "pebbles and stone extending to hold the corporal up" (12). But the words fail: the corporal falls, Rocky slips from their grasp, and a Japanese soldier clubs the wounded man to death.

When he returns to his Laguna Pueblo home, Tayo believes that his curse has caused a long drought, although similar droughts had afflicted the area after World War I and in the Roaring Twenties (10). Droughts happen, Uncle Josiah had taught a young Tayo, "when people forget, when people misbehave" (46). His stories teach the boy that if people forget that the land is "where we come from . . . This sand, this stone, these trees, the vines, all the wildflowers," the earth—the "mother of the people"—will get "angry at them for the way they [are] behaving. For all she care[s], they could go to hell—starve to death" (45, 101). Warning Tayo against killing another fly, Josiah tells him, "Next time, just remember the story," the story of the "green-bottle fly who went to her, asking forgiveness for the people" (101, 102).

Trading war stories, the adult Tayo and his veteran friends substitute Coors beer for the waters of home. Realizing they had just served as pawns in another's story, in "defending the land they had already lost," they get drunk because beer is "soothing . . . The sky, the land were distant then"; the past lost "its impact and seemed like a vague dream" (169, 241; see 159). Just as they had accepted U.S. Army appeals to patriotism, they accept the image of purity that Coors peddles: to assure customers that its beer is brewed with "pure Rocky Mountain spring water," the company labels bottles with an outsized—fake—spring (55). To feel whole again, Tayo must first vomit beer, sweeping from his insides the lie on the Coors bottle, and with it the ritual of telling war stories, which had crowded from his mind the life lessons in Josiah's stories (168, 200, 250).[56]

Instead of beer, Tayo must drink the waters of home, which heal. On the way to a bar, he and his friend Harley stop beside a spring that flows "even in the driest years" (45). Kneeling at the water's edge and closing his eyes, Tayo "tasted the deep heartrock of the earth, where the water came from, and he thought maybe this wasn't the end after all" (46). Even within times of deep despair, the kind he experiences, such springs represent hope: "The people relied upon them even when the sky was barren and the winds were hot and dusty" (94). As he watches a spider drink from one spring, Tayo recalls the life-affirming stories of Spider Woman, who "had told Sun Man how to win the storm clouds back from the Gambler so they would be free again to bring rain and snow to the people" (94). Spider Woman, the "universal feminine principle of creation," reorients Tayo to his home (94).[57] It is Spider Woman, in the form of Ts'eh, who asks him the central question that Silko asks us: "What are you doing here?" (176).[58] In other words, are we destroyers or creators?

Creators.

I mean, I create. I plant a vegetable garden, I teach English, I write. Don't I?

I forget how young I was, but I know I was old enough to know better.

In for the morning milking, the cows drank from their water bowls, the pipes pounding.

"Didn't you count 'em?" my father said.

"For what?"

"That second-calf heifer. She's not here," he said. "Go look on top of the hill; between the gates."

I'd just come from there with the rest of them; my work shoes were soaked with dew.

"I didn't see her," I said.

"She had trouble calvin' the first time," he said. "I don't wanna lose her. Look again."

He turned away, heading for the milk house.

"What about feedin' the calves?" I called.

Over his shoulder: "Do that when you get back."

I hiked back up the hill, looking neither right nor left. She'll be all right; cows have calves all the time. And they're better off having them outside, naturally. In the barn, sometimes a new calf slips into the gutter and drowns, or smothers.

I crossed through the first gate and looked around. Nothing. Keeping to the road, I reached the ledges on top of the hill. I could see no black and white against the brown. Annoyed she wasn't there, I wheeled toward the woods, glancing through the trees. There weren't too many places she could be; the woodlot was small, the dry pasture pretty open, except for clumps of thorn bushes here and there. On the other side of the trees a lane divided the meadow from the Miller Road; from there I could see the hilltop above the barn. Nothing.

On the way down, I ducked in and out of the woods along the fence, checked the far side of the Ditch, and came back to the barn.

"Didn't see her," I said.

"Jesus Christ," my father said, pulling a milker from a cow. "What're you back for? She's hidin' somewhere."

"I looked."

He stood at the door and named places she could be. I said I'd checked every one.

"I don't know why you didn't bring her with the rest," he said. "It doesn't take long for somethin' to happen."

"She'll be all right."

He shook his head at me. "You feed these calves and get those milkers hung up. I'll go goddamn look for her."

Before I finished feeding the calves, he was back, coming down the walk like he meant it.

"Goddammit all to hell," he shouted. "She's right against the wall inside the first gate. How could you miss her?"

"I . . ."

He slapped his cap across his thigh.

"She needed help!"

"I . . ."

"Dead. Her and the calf both."

"But . . ."

His look jumped at me.

"You gotta start payin' attention!"

As with each of us, a capacity for destruction lurks within Tayo. When he breaks a beer bottle and attacks his buddy Emo, shoving the shards into Emo's belly, Tayo "got stronger with every jerk that Emo made, and he felt that he would get well if he killed him" (63). Later, hating whites for "what they did to the earth with their machines," he assures himself that "he was not one of the destroyers," even though he "want[s] to kick the soft white bodies into the Atlantic Ocean" (203–4). If killing promotes the magic that seeks to destroy the world, the ultimate sign of Tayo's healing is when, at the end of the novel, he refuses to succumb to the cycle of violence and decides not to attack Emo, who is torturing and killing their friend Harley (252, 253).

Emo represents the story of the destroyers; he carries a tobacco bag filled with human teeth. During the war, he "fed off each man he killed, and the higher the rank of the dead man, the higher it made Emo," whose name suggests his self-centeredness: o, me (61). Destroyers like Emo want to "gut human beings," to empty us of all feeling (229). Attempting to erase creation, they "work to see how much can be lost, how much can be forgotten" (229). To end our common story, to separate people and place, they "choke the life away . . . the killing soothes them" (232). Tayo has witnessed this evil at its worst, "the dismembered corpses and the atomic heat-flash outlines" (37).

Emo kills Harley at a uranium mine.[59] No more appropriate place represents the destroyers: here men mined rock that ushered in our era of mutually assured destruction, a "monstrous design" drawn within Tayo's homeland, at Los Alamos, a design that threatens all grounds, all homes (246). When subterranean springs flooded the mine in 1943, the U.S. government pumped it dry (243). But by the time it flooded again that summer, the Manhattan Project had had its fill, though "guards remained until August 1945," when bombs exploded over Hiroshima and Nagasaki (244). As the horror of wholesale slaughter comes home to him, Tayo recognizes that "from that time on, human beings were one clan again, united by the fate the destroyers planned for all of them, for all living things" (246).

Storytelling connects our stories with those of others, and places all stories within the context of the human story. It teaches us that we're not alone. This is why only storytelling can save us: stories are "all we have to fight off / illness and death" (2). Clutching a stone "streaked with powdery yellow uranium," Tayo cries at seeing this pattern, "the way all the stories fit together" (246). Affirming the time immemorial link between story and world, he sees this design written in the stars, which had witnessed "mountains shift and rivers change course and even disappear back into the earth" (254). Reoriented by this long view, he can now embrace Ts'eh, who weaves a creation story, one that makes "the Universe / this world / and the four worlds below"; in her story, "There is life here / for the people. / And in the belly of this story / the rituals and the ceremony / are still growing" (1, 2).[60] After turning his back on the uranium mine, Tayo plants for Ts'eh the seeds of a "tall dark green plant with round pointed leaves, deep veined like fossil shells," a living offering he knows will "grow there like the story, strong and translucent as the stars" (226–27, 254).

By the time he recounts his story to Laguna elders, "Tayo has come home, ordinary in his being, and they can get on with serious business, the day-to-day life of a village, which is what the land, the ceremony, the story, and time immemorial are all about."[61] Tayo's serious business, a realization of his Uncle Josiah's dream, is to raise cattle, spotted cattle that "could live in spite of drought and hard weather" (187). Able to adapt to changing conditions, his cows can eat cactus to survive, unlike white-faced Herefords, which "would not look for water" and would die expecting it to come to them (10, 79). Instead of raising "weak, soft Herefords" to conform only to a distant market, Tayo breeds "special cattle" that are, first, one with their place; his animals descend from "generations of desert cattle, born in dry sand and scrubby mesquite, where they hunted water the way the desert antelope did" (74). A mixed breed, his spotted cattle represent "everything that the ideal cow was not"; they could "tell a good place when they found it: springs and good grazing" (75, 225). Hill country, pastureland.

In late July, my mother and I picked my father's headstone. We chose a square marble piece, rough edged, set on a simple base. An engraved name, dates, and a Celtic cross were all the ornamentation. The wake was in Forest City, a town undermined, its pillars robbed. While we were at the funeral home, waiting to make the trip to the cemetery, the undertaker received a call from the church. The gravesite was occupied. Where should he go? Next to the family plot was a swale, the ground sometimes wet. I chose the spot, despite the undertaker's caution. I thought, my father was a farmer, for Christ's sake; he understood wet years and dry years, loams and gravel, life in death. I wanted to say, if you accept what we're doing, a wake and a burial aren't about warehousing something; they're about transition and transfiguration.

St. Cecilia's, at Hilltop—the mission church of St. Juliana's at Rock Lake, where an Irish settlement grew in the 1830s—closed in 2009. Constructed in 1865, St. Cecilia's may have been built to serve a rising population of tannery workers at Tanner's Falls. Positioned on a plateau, the Hilltop churchyard sits on solid earth; no mining here. The Morris and Wellsboro loams have slow permeability, the water table in wet times rises to a depth of twelve to twenty-four inches, and erosion is a concern when the ground gets disturbed.[62] Among the stones, Irish names (McCormick, O'Neill, McGraw) predominate. Touched little by the rural cemetery movement, ironically enough, the ethos of this rural cemetery is vastly different from that at Forest Hill; Hilltop reminds one that death is an awful, sublime calamity. Bound by stonewalls and the Bethany Turnpike, the graveyard huddles tight to the little clapboard church. No mausoleums, no obelisks, no Ozymandian blocks. No shade trees, no flowering shrubs, no gently curving roads. No one runs here. Once a congregation of farmers, the dead at Hilltop knew no separation of work and home; rest, relaxation, and recreation were homegrown, work related. One with the fields that back it, this field, the vacant half still cut once a year, doesn't invite one to linger; it waits for you to stay, to turn its soil, to plant and grow.

For too long, I've occupied space and called it living in a place, but, like a lot of people, I don't really know much about my home or even fully realize that I'm from here, and there. A reorienting experience, paying closer attention to home helps me to see what I'm doing in the world. These days, I find myself relearning my home grounds, their histories and soils, their tendencies and possibilities, and the arguments about them, which has been an education unlike that promoted in the institutions I've attended, K–12 and B.A. to Ph.D., which have taught me to leave home, even at home.

With yet another reworking of this place underway, I have to ask, when we drill, do we create or destroy?

2

Merwin and Mining

what he does / All his life to keep alive
gets into / The grain of him

—W. S. Merwin, "The Miner"

I first read "The Drunk in the Furnace" in an English class at the University of Scranton. The instructor led us through a close reading and then asked if anyone knew where the poem was set. No one did. "Here, in Scranton," he said. Most people in class were out-of-staters, mainly from New Jersey and Long Island, so they knew nothing about the furnaces. I didn't know much about them either, I confess, beyond their location. It never occurred to me—or anyone else, I imagine—to visit them, despite the fact that the furnaces were no more than a few minutes' walk from where we sat. Looking back, I see that I was being taught what most literary critics are trained to do: to keep my head down and pay attention to the text, only the text. Readers should put the ordinary world aside: you cannot get there from here anyway, after all, because a poem offers a perception of the world, not the world.

But these days, I cannot get the world off my mind.

Had we walked along Monroe Avenue, stepped across the railroad tracks behind the Lackawanna Station, and made our way down into the hollow to read the poem in the shadow of the furnaces, would our reading of it have changed?

I think so. If nothing else, we would have asked, in the open air, under the sun, a different set of questions, because we would have been reading the poet's experience of the place in light of our own experience of it. We would have seen it, the poem and the place, from a new angle.

When I finally did visit the furnaces, many years later, the first thing I noticed was how big—and castle-like—they really are.

Literary scholars analyze poems and write about poems, and they require their students to write in response to poems, but they often don't experience the places to which the poems respond.[1]

Few, I bet, have rebuilt a stone wall, farmed in Kentucky, or shoveled coal. Poets may do those things, but scholars? I don't think so. They have enough to do in reading, writing, and teaching. Texts take a lot of time and attention.

But this is changing, I know. Debates about the environment have led some scholars to do fieldwork, to see a text against the world it represents. A place-based study examines a literary piece in the "exact location about which the text being studied or used was written." Stepping out of the office and into the field, a scholar traces the "correspondences . . . between the text and the place" in order to offer new readings of each.[2]

I tried this at home with some W. S. Merwin poems.

Studied alongside the places they portray, Merwin's mining poems describe a shattered landscape populated by people who cannot see the damage around them, despite the fact that the damage haunts them. Here in the Anthracite Region, mines burn, "Smothered and silent," as "Burning Mountain" suggests, and retired miners find that a life's work "at last cannot / Be washed out, all of it, in this world." Intimately exploring this "inexcusable / Unavoidable" ground, Merwin gropes for answers to a question I've been asking myself lately: what are we doing to the world—and to one another?[3] If poetry—and any literature, for that matter—has any use value it's that it leads us to rethink what we think we see. Merwin's mining poems show us that we have an infinite capacity for making the unnatural natural.

The work we do shapes, for better and worse, the world and its inhabitants, both human and nonhuman. Coal mining landscapes may be an extreme and obvious example, but they are often out of sight, out of mind. With mines usually located well outside major population areas, Americans have the luxury of not seeing the "hard places" where the nation's "dirtiest work" is done. Mine-scarred landscapes repel most people, I think, because they represent the "unfinished, crude, and imperfect; perhaps they are too honest a depiction of how we have treated the environment and each other."[4] One of those hard places, the Anthracite Region, has been described as a "lunar landscape," as "one of industrial America's sacrificial zones," and as "grievously scarred."[5] Within the region lies Scranton, Merwin's boyhood home, a city of mines.

Son of a Presbyterian minister, Merwin moved to Scranton with his family in 1936, and he remained there until 1944, when he left for Princeton at age sixteen. In 1948, he sailed for Europe, returning in 1956 "to go back to Pennsylvania, and write about it."[6] His homecoming, I believe, shocked him, mainly because he saw his old neighborhood anew.

The years Merwin lived in Europe coincided with the final collapse of the anthracite coal industry.[7] While the postwar economy boomed in much of the United States in 1946–1960, the Anthracite Region slid into its steepest economic decline. By 1956, strip mining was widespread, unemployment topped 10 percent, and most deep mines were idle.[8] Although coal mining may have all but ended by the year of Merwin's return, culm banks burned, abandoned breakers dominated former patch towns, and streams ran orange with acid. Its wounds raw in the mid-1950s, Scranton's cityscape made visible the long history of environmental exploitation that made possible mid-century America's political, economic, and military power. Merwin probes the damage that human work has inflicted on the Lackawanna Valley.

As others have noted, *The Drunk in the Furnace* (1960) marks a break between Merwin's first three books of poems, which were "so objective, so mythic as to be anonymous," and the next collections, within which one hears Merwin's "personal poetic voice." A "master-poem," the title piece "radically recasts the material Merwin has been sifting over and over," material that examined family history and place. Merwin later admitted that he was attending to one place in the last third of *The Drunk in the Furnace*: "The focussing on one place in that way was deliberate, and it led me to see how limited the possibilities of that way were, for me, then."[9]

Written in December 1957, "The Drunk in the Furnace" describes a particular place. Scholars mistakenly read the poem as referring to an "empty iron furnace [that] rusts" in a junkyard at the edge of a town.[10] In fact, the poem depicts the Scranton Iron Furnaces, a structure of locally quarried stone that resembles a "bad castle" (14). Originally, the furnaces used anthracite to heat iron ore; later the company imported anthracite's rival, bituminous coal. A nineteenth-century description of the furnaces notes that "one large coal mine opens directly between the stacks of the furnaces, and you pass into it through the buildings."[11] In visiting the site and studying early photographs of it, one realizes that the furnace in the poem is a "hulking black fossil" because it represents a remnant of a large industrial complex that was dismantled in 1902 (4).

Large corporate interests and New York investors dominated the Lackawanna Valley almost from the beginning of white settlement. Scranton grew up around the furnaces, which produced rails for the railroads that made anthracite coal mining profitable.[12] During their sixty years of operation, the furnaces were "the single most significant factor in the economic, social, and industrial life of Scranton"; they helped to fuel nineteenth-century industrial development in the United States, which prepared the ground for many of the ecological problems we confront today.[13] Lodged, then and now, in the heart of the city, the furnaces are today a tourist attraction beside a cleaned-up Roaring Brook Creek.

"The Drunk in the Furnace" depicts a place damaged by the ravages of coal mining. Early drafts of the poem describe the final version's "naked gully" (2) as "stripped," a word that echoes the strip mining and deforestation that denuded the surrounding landscape. The revision underscores that the hollow is defenseless against erosion, even that caused by a tamed Roaring Brook. The "poisonous creek," which once powered the furnaces' hot air blasts, is venomous with mine acid, a common problem of the region's waterways (6). One draft's description of the furnaces as "unregenerate" recalls the words "unacknowledged," "unreclaimed," and "unavoidable" in an earlier poem, "Luzerne Street Looking West" (30, 31, 39).[14]

The poem contrasts the drunk in the "unnoticed" furnace with nearby churchgoers, who assume better days ahead. In singing, the drunk nudges them to pay attention to what they have "added / To their ignorance," the ground around them (5, 6–7). Self-closeted inside the furnace, "behind the eye-holed iron / Door" (12–13), the drunk's intoxicated state is a metaphor for the toxic state of the land. A captive audience, the churchgoers are confined inside the church, asleep, or with their attention riveted to the abstract landscape of hell, which they don't realize the furnaces' "stoke-holes" have made manifest on earth (23).

In a 1969 interview, Merwin notes about the drunk, "I wanted to invent a figure who to me was absolutely sensual and who belonged completely to that part of the world. . . . And then this one turned out to be like an invented myth for the place . . . he was a man who probably couldn't exist, but if he did, the place then had its man." The myth he makes is that of the singer/worker; the poem alludes to Orpheus and Phaeton, which many scholars have noted, but also, I believe, to Hephaestus, the ugly, lame god of fire, the craftsmen of the gods, whose forge is located under an active volcano. The Orpheus myth, Merwin reminds us, "evokes a harmonious relation with the whole living world"; Phaeton, he explains, is a "myth based on ego, envy, and exploitation, in which you try to take the chariot into the sun and drive it whether you can drive it or not, and you end up by destroying what you drive over and being destroyed yourself."[15] A welding of these myths, the drunk represents the region's people, who have retreated into their history and armed themselves with heroic accounts of building the nation that has forgotten them. Like the drunk, they cannot see straight.

A once-abandoned workplace, the furnaces become, under the drunk's direction, a new workshop, one that takes work as its subject. A "twist of smoke like a pale / Resurrection" signals the drunk's relighting of the furnace; at the sight, people are "astonished," literally *a stonied*, driven to fear and wonder (9–10; 8). Announcing a new kind of work in "Hammer-and-anvilling with poker and bottle / To his jugged bellowings" (17–18), the drunk's music calls the churchgoers' attention to the gully, reminding them of human transgressions against the hill and the creek, both poisoned and junked, a damage supported by their "tar-paper church," a weatherproof haven underwritten by the abstract fears of sin that the reverend paints in his sermon (22). Instead of fashioning rails, the furnace, at the city's heart, will now, with the drunk at its heart, shape songs

Fig. 3 Scranton Iron Furnaces, 1970. Courtesy of the Lackawanna Historical Society.

that teach "agape" (i.e., love) to the sober churchgoers' "witless offspring," who "flock like piped rats to its siren / Crescendo" (26–27). Unlike the adult towns-people who nod off in their church pews and "hate trespassers," the children "on the crumbling ridge / Stand in a row and learn," gaping in rapt attention at what they hear and see, recognizing what they had been taught to ignore: the story of a careless destruction written into the world around them (24, 27–28).

The children, who will make their own mark on the land, can change the course of that history. Ending with the word "learn," the poem asserts that our thoughtless wasting of the world is not natural. It can be unlearned. The genius of the poem asks us to remember what we've done in the world, never mind the next.

In September 2008, I attended at a local university a workshop about sustain-ability that was devoted to the writings of Wendell Berry. When discussion turned to practical ways to create a new relationship with the natural world, a political scientist wondered how such a relationship could be created in a landscape as damaged as that of the Anthracite Region. I wanted to say, you need to love it, critically love it. But even living here is suspect in some eyes. In discussing the poem, literary biographer Frank MacShane remarks, "One must be mad to live in such a place."[16] Maybe, but what MacShane refuses to see is that we all already live here. We may not be aware that we do, but we will soon be all too aware. The only madness is assuming we can escape the hard places.

The furnaces—and this lesson—have still not reached everyone. The next October, students and I gathered at the furnaces to hear art historian Darlene Miller-Lanning explain the site's industrial history. We read the poem at the opening of one of its stone arches, before a grate that still contained pig iron. Of the half dozen students, who had all grown up in Scranton, only one had been to the place before, and then on an elementary school field trip. The other students had never set foot there and knew nothing of it; two of these students were women in their late sixties. No one had heard of the poem. Sad, I thought. If we don't pay closer attention to our work in the world, all worlds will be lost. We pay a steep price for our inattention to places and poetry.

Like "The Drunk in the Furnace," "Luzerne Street Looking West" (1956) and "Burning Mountain" (1960) are parts of Merwin's "homecoming sequence."[17] As a set, they explore the diminished and forgotten landscape that anthracite mining left between urban and natural environments. This postindustrial landscape bears silent witness to industrialism's lingering effects on people and places. These poems' appearance coincided with a key moment in local history, one that challenged Scranton residents' faith in material progress: the disappearance of deep mining in the Lackawanna Valley. The poems imagine the region's human and environmental trauma, even as they acknowledge the region's rapid deindustrialization, one of the first in U.S. history.[18] In probing the region's injuries, both literal and figurative, the poems gesture as much inward toward the local environmental legacy of coal mining as they do outward toward the universal human urge for order in the face of death's inevitability.

"Luzerne Street Looking West" invites literary fieldwork. The poem places the reader on an actual street in Scranton and names a neighborhood cemetery, the Washburn Street Cemetery, and a stream, Lucky Run. To look west from Luzerne Street is literally to turn one's back on the site of the Washburn Street Presbyterian Church, where Merwin's father served as minister.[19] To look west from Luzerne Street is to confront the human and environmental damage that mining leaves in its wake, damage done to land "that no one had known to save" (14). Moving from school to mountain, the poem asks us to think about how the space between them came to be.

Exploring the aftermath of mining, the poem depicts a postindustrial landscape of "unrelieved waste" (13) that lies between the city, nodded to in the opening phrase "Some blocks" (1), and "the real mountain with its / Four undisturbed seasons" (28–29). This in-between world, without people, stripped of vegetation, hacked open, and trashed, represents what human work has wrought in creating and sustaining built environments. An indeterminate space, this place divides two orders: the wholly human and the completely natural. This space demands our attention because "It is, above all, the unacknowledged, / The unreclaimed, the entirely / Useless, that will not be forgotten nor / Disowned, but follow us to spread / Their shapeless variety at the edge / Of all we have made, and give us / No peace" (30–36). A silent presence, this ground cries out, reminding us of the war waged against it.

If a pastoral landscape represents the middle landscape between city and wild environments, the negative version of this middle is a mining landscape, a sterile ground of massive upheaval. As much as a pastoral landscape may represent a positive link in a continuum between the urban and the wild, the in-between world that mining creates registers the negative picture, the absolute disconnection between city and wilderness. The pastoral may face in two directions, but mining turns away from both town and mountain. After all, mine land cannot renew itself the way farmland can, at least ideally. And no families live at the colliery. Mine land requires reclamation.

The land at the end of Luzerne Street has changed some since the mid-1950s. Instead of open space, there are two junkyards (ah, sorry: "auto recyclers"), one on either side of the street, a moving company, and no culm banks, although their remnants constitute the ground across which spread junk cars and trucks in various states of dismemberment. The street now extends beyond the railroad tracks, where it suddenly becomes Dalton Street. To one's left, an abandoned boxcar sits alongside the tracks, forming a section of one junkyard's enclosure. The area is still a blank spot on city maps. In fact, most of the blank spaces on Scranton city maps were once the locations of collieries. The blanks remind one of no-man's-lands in war zones.

Those who wage this war graduate from the "new high school" of the poem's opening line, West Scranton High, whose mascot is the Invader. "Some blocks beyond" the school, Luzerne Street ends in a "weedy tract / Of shale and cinders . . . / Too indefinite to be called a field" (1, 4–6) that stretches between the city, below and behind, and Bald Mountain, above and ahead. Bordering this space is the Hyde Park breaker, whose "disused mine-shaft, full / Of water, leads under the graves" (18–19) of the Washburn Street Cemetery, where the victims of the Avondale disaster are buried. Human-made, the graves and the shaft direct one's attention to the underworld, the realm of the dead. The cemetery's potter's field, which "spills out / From among [the cemetery's] trees," points to the poor, the unknown, the unmarked, who are simply numbered to lie forgotten beside the community's named dead (16–17). These lines, in their focus on death, echo what Merwin said in a 2009 TV interview with Bill Moyers: "It's the dark, the unknown side that guides us, and that is part of our lives all the time. It's the mystery. That's always with us, too. And it gives the depth and dimension to the rest of it." In the same conversation, Merwin later claimed, "I think poetry always comes out of what you don't know."[20]

What the speaker knows is a human-made ruin. The graves echo the "canyons left over from / Strip mines" (20–21), which the landscape's "shallow stream," Lucky Run, fills with "bottomless basins, shoes, and [its] stained / Deposits" of mine acid (22–23). Beyond the canyons rise "Symmetrical mountains / Of culm," orderings of waste whose mimicking of the real mountain calls attention to their sterile artificiality (24–25).

Studying "Luzerne Street" on Luzerne Street is a good idea, sure, but doing so raises issues of interpretation. Does one study the place as it was when the poet was writing about it? This would demand a historical approach that is itself a stew of questions (e.g., what can we really know about that spot in that time?). Or does one study the place as it is when the reader reads the poem? (Does it matter whether the reader is already familiar with the place?) Both poem and place are new moment-to-moment; connotations and contours change. But the poem and the place change independently of each other. Then again, each also expresses continuities; the poem's words don't change, we hope, and the place's location remains constant, sort of. If it's true that the grounds of interpretation shift over time, how does one build a case for a place-based interpretation of the poem, even an open-ended interpretation? You cannot, but you can try.

"Luzerne Street" adds another layer of complication. Merwin wrote the poem in February 1956, six months *before* he left England to return to the United States.[21] The poem imagines, then, the landscape he remembers experiencing in his teens a decade and more before. Its deliberate imprecision in distance and description suggests, to me anyway, a remembered familiarity with the place. If so, the poem's concluding lines—"I never missed it when I went, / And never knew I loved it until now" (41–42)—are about the anticipation of going back, and not about the satisfaction of being back. The lines point ahead to the end of "Flight Home," the journal Merwin kept during his return, where he asserts that Americans "couldn't hate [the land] as fiercely as we do sometimes without there being something honest in our attachment to it. But there is always the sense of surprise, of inarticulate awkwardness, at discovering that the name for what you feel is love." The journal shows Merwin comparing American and European ways of "regarding" the land. Americans have "used the place, wasted it. It has made us prodigal, restless. And we are attached to it in still-raw ways that we aren't aware of, most often."[22] Sounds like he's talking about himself.

His return changed his mind. Although he witnessed firsthand mining's effects before leaving the United States, his travels in Europe offered him a standard by which to judge the ground he grew up knowing. He learned that in Europe "generations and generations having worked out a way of regarding the place, taught them where to fix the feeling, what to see and how to communicate with it." Confronting anew the scarred world of the Anthracite Region, Merwin discovers with a shock the diminishment of its land and lives, evidence of the "squalor, waste, ugliness, injustice" that its people don't see.[23] In effect, he observes the ground of his growing up from another perspective; he encounters it as an outsider might, emotionally, as if for the first time. His reseeing of a familiar Scranton landscape may be the reason why he decided not to include "Luzerne Street" in a published collection. The poem's tension between love and repulsion resolves into disgust when he stands on the ground the poem foresaw. The speaker may love the land he remembers, but the poet recoils from the same land newly seen.

This love of a remembered landscape defines many lives in the Anthracite Region. People who have migrated out of northeastern Pennsylvania since the 1950s have often retired here, despite the long winters and relative lack of amenities.[24] Communities in the region have become so accustomed to mined land that it has become natural to them, so much so that they are "loyal to this overtly inhospitable landscape." Their positive view of the region, however, depends on a "highly selective viewing of the land, based more on its historical significance than on its present form . . . they are deeply rooted to the land.[25] In contrast to the resident's view, "The land and the towns have repeatedly struck outsiders with their grim bleakness." Recent local public narratives about the region's history don't discuss the "visible destruction of the natural surroundings."[26] During land reclamation efforts, people sometimes express displeasure at the disappearance of nearby culm banks.[27]

This schizophrenic view manifested itself at a public hearing I attended on 2 July 2009. PPL Electric Utilities had decided to run power lines from its Berwick nuclear plant into and across the Lackawanna Valley; horseshoe shaped, the 102-mile line was to sell reliable electric service to New York and New Jersey. In opposing the building of twenty-story towers across the valley's ridgetops, several citizens noted that the region had already been "raped" enough by coal and waste disposal companies; the same speakers would often then point to the "pristine" landscape that the towers would mar. Add to this widespread apathy. When asked why no public hearing was held on the valley floor, in Scranton, from which the towers would be all too visible, the presiding judge noted that no one in the city had expressed interest in holding a meeting. The line, in my view, is another example of powerful interests taking full advantage of a shell-shocked people.

In the past, maybe people didn't really know that coal mining was destroying the valley. If that's so, to what extent did people turn a blind eye to what they were doing? Look at the region's visual art. George Inness's painting *The Lackawanna Valley* (1855), commissioned as an advertisement for the Delaware, Lackawanna, and Western Railroad, portrays industry in harmony with the land. William Cullen Bryant's *Picturesque America* (1874), published after mining had become widespread in the region, includes a pastoral vision of life along the Susquehanna River. The self-taught George Clough and the twentieth-century breaker painter John Willard Raught also blink at the damage around them, although Raught was courageous enough to decry it in letters to the editor. The visual arts may have refused to see, but as early as 1866 a guidebook was asking why it's necessary to "mar (and it would seem to have been done almost wantonly in many instances) the face of nature by stripping the hill and mountain-side of the growth and grove of trees." A few years later, Horace Hollister in his *History of the Lackawanna Valley* (1869) laments the damage done to the region's "unresisting hills and valleys." But then again, astounded by the technological advances of the Industrial Revolution, American tourists flocked to industrial sites, including coal mines, to marvel at human efforts to improve nature.[28]

These are curious reactions, given the violence done to people and places in the region's history. Sparsely settled, even by Indians, the region hardly knew itself, culturally, before coal was mined: "Unlike the bituminous coal fields of Appalachia where the imprint of a distinctively American culture is so strong . . . the anthracite fields had little premining settlement." The dominant industry, coal mining, shaped the region's worldview, and the "coal business was industrial feudalism." Until the mid-twentieth century, the majority of people in the Lackawanna Valley who were employed in mining and its attendant businesses worked for the coal cartel that had dominated the region since almost the beginning of the industry.[29] By the turn of the century, the region was well on its way to becoming "one of industrial America's sacrificial zones, an area scarified by generations of coal mining and then abandoned to economic decline when the mining ceased." When anthracite mining collapsed, the coal companies left, one by one, leaving the region to shoulder the crippling effects of deindustrialization. By the time of Merwin's return, the number of people streaming from the valley had accelerated to a flood.[30]

In returning to the Anthracite Region, Merwin revisited a place and a people reeling from posttraumatic stress. According to sociologist Kai Erikson, trauma can result from "acute events," such as a flood, an earthquake, or an industrial accident, and from "chronic conditions," such as drinking toxic chemicals that have leaked into groundwater, living near a nuclear reactor that is suspected of emitting radiation, or breathing fumes from industrial sites.[31] In addition to the Anthracite Region's labor strikes, political assassinations, and often-deadly tensions between successive waves of immigrant groups, more than thirty-five thousand miners died on the job, and thousands of others were maimed—on an almost daily basis. "In the last three decades of the nineteenth century," wrote historians Dublin and Licht, "the Bureau of Mines recorded more than 24,500 injuries, for an average of 846 per year. . . . These figures definitely underreport the dangers of mining." Maybe worse than the reality of injury and death was the anticipation of them. An analysis of one major coal company's records has led Dublin and Licht to conclude that in that company "virtually all miners could count on being injured at some point during their working lives." This was when miners worked, but most mine workers were underemployed, leading to a chronic household gap between wages and expenses, which likely added to people's anxiety.[32] In the region's 150-year coal mining history, men

Fig. 4 Miners working on tracks in gangway, 1925. Courtesy of the Lackawanna Historical Society.

died not only in major, headline-grabbing disasters such as the Avondale fire (1869), the Baltimore Tunnel explosion (1919), and the Knox Mine flood (1959), but also in daily, little-publicized rock falls, machinery accidents, and electrocutions, a fact Merwin, a minister's son, could not escape knowing.

The title character of "The Miner" is a man who yields to an uncertain, precarious existence, long before he physically must: "Even his dreams soon / Are untroubled by the oppressive / Weight of the earth, and it comes to close / Over him every morning like a habit" (12–15). He has become used to a way of living that will eventually kill him, if not because he's in the mine, but because the mine is within him: not only does he dream about the mine, he breathes its "damps," a word that denotes both moisture and noxious gases that can kill (16). Spending his working days in the dark, he lights his way with a single lamp as he moves through the trapped sunlight around him, sending to the surface chunks of it that others will burn for heat and light. "[I]f he lives to retire" (21), a big if, he will sit "bathed / By the innocent sun," the source of the coal he mines (22–23). Although the mountain "may not crush him," he will likely die from within, from black lung; his work has gotten into the "grain of him" (16, 25). He would not be alone: "Public Health Service studies in the 1920s and 1930s found that roughly 20–30 percent of employed miners suffered serious disabilities due to black lung," which was not recognized in Pennsylvania as a disability worthy of worker's compensation until 1965.[33]

A companion poem to "The Miner," "Burning Mountain," written in February 1957, reminds readers of the mine fires that plague the Anthracite Region. Although fires in culm banks eventually burn out, fires in mines persist. And although spontaneous combustion starts fires in culm banks, human error causes mine fires. In 1946, while Merwin was attending Princeton, a fire at a municipal dump in the city of Carbondale, fifteen miles north of Scranton, spread to local mines.[34] This fire forced my mother and my grandparents to abandon their home in 1961, following years of their neighbors being "nauseated or knocked out" by the fumes. Attempts to extinguish the fire by flushing it with "silt-bearing water" only served to spread the flames. Ultimately, the fire had to be dug out, a project that took more than a decade to complete.[35]

The forgotten ground of "Luzerne Street" reappears in "Burning Mountain." As in "The Miner," people get so accustomed to the danger that they forget that the mountain is burning; the opening stanza's phrases "if you listen" and "if you pause to notice" suggest that it takes a conscious effort to know that the fire burns, despite its proximity to the "chimneyed city" (6). After a while, the mountain "practically seemed normal" (34), with its pastoral landscape obscuring the industrial upheaval hidden at its heart. But the farms won't last; their "wells of good water, / Still cold, . . . should last us, and our grandchildren," but beyond these generations, who knows? (35–36). The fire, after all, will "outlast / Our time and our grandchildren's" (24–25).

Despite years of "worrying" and "old-womanish / Precautions," a miner forgets his lamp in a mine shaft and causes a fire that burns for generations (17–18). He puts into motion a catastrophe that no human can call back. The best we can do is to attempt to contain it, but even this is a belief founded on "trust," not certainty (23). Evidence of the dissipation of all things, the mountain's disaster, its holocaust, is written in the heavens' falling stars: "The meteors burn out in the air to fall / Harmless in empty fields" (32–33). In the same way that humans cannot stop the earth's "molten core" from cooling, despite "all the fires we light" (28, 30), no precautions can stop the mountain's "[w]asting" (21). And the fire is not "unique; there was always one of these / Nearby," no matter where the speaker moved (26–27).

The Carbondale mine fire covered 120 acres, destroyed approximately 500 homes, businesses, and other buildings, and displaced more than 1,000 people. The fire originated in the city's dump, which was located in an abandoned mine pit on the west side of town.[36] Whether the fire started due to someone's carelessness or whether the city set the garbage afire is still an unanswered question. Not until 1959 did the federal government step in, declare West Side an "urban redevelopment district," and offer "fair prices"—that is, slum prices—for people's homes. The tight-knit working-class neighborhood—my grandfather was a conductor on the D & H Railroad—did not think to fight the label or the home prices until too late.[37]

A slow-moving, invisible danger, the fire didn't worry anyone at first. Only after carbon monoxide killed retired miner Patrick Collins and his wife, Elizabeth, inside their home in 1952 did residents see the fire as a serious threat. Afterward, people slept all year, winters and summers, with their windows open. They kept their cellar doors unlocked so that mine inspectors could check twice a day for coal gas. As the fire burned, another menace emerged: mine subsidence, which occurred at least twice. A supply of coal disappeared from one home when its basement collapsed, and residents Santo Perri and his young son narrowly escaped falling into a pit that opened in their backyard.[38] National media covered the fire; *Pageant*, for example, ran an article in July 1957, the month before Merwin returned to the United States. It's no stretch to believe that he read this and similar reports, but unlike news pieces, which describe the facts of human work, his poetry reimagines our work so that we can see it anew. In making the familiar strange, he asks us to pay attention, to look closely at where we are and what we do there.

Merwin believes that a right relationship between humans and the natural world is not hierarchical. People live in and with the world beyond us; we're not creatures set apart, no matter how powerful we think we've become. Poetry reminds us of our place in time, because its subject, as Merwin points out, is the "living context that we have been born into; our responsibility and whatever gift we may have is driving us toward trying to address that context and speak for the time we live in, the moment we live in." One aspect of our moment, one that Merwin would like us to change our minds about, is the "assumption that human beings are different in kind and in importance from other species," which, he claims, is a "dangerously wrong way of seeing things."[39] By patiently reclaiming for the last thirty-five years several acres of a former pineapple plantation on Maui, Merwin has been practicing an uncommon way of seeing. He dates his own change of mind to the mid-1950s, the time when he returned home to the United States.[40]

In his latest collection, the Pulitzer Prize–winning *The Shadow of Sirius*, Merwin returns to Scranton. "Empty Lot" describes the Delaware and Hudson property directly across Decker Court from his boyhood home at 1115 Washburn Street.[41] The poem imagines the land "before there were houses / when bears took their time there under trees they knew / now we were told that it belonged to / the D & H Coal Company and they / would do nothing with it but keep it" (15–19).[42] The land has been so altered that the speaker cannot imagine what it was like when it was forested and inhabited by wildlife, but even this alteration is not the whole story. The company will ignore the ground it owns until it needs to tear it open to rescue miners trapped below, where the company keeps incessantly busy, destabilizing the world above. The coal company cannot be bothered with other meanings of the word "keep": to be faithful to, to protect, to tend. A transition, the poem's central line—"as it had been for so long"—suggests that, compared with the bears' time, our time will be short (14). Underscoring this, the speaker hears below, during the night, explosions and "picks ticking in the dark," which also mark the passing of time and echo the clinking of the irons in the game of quoits, which the men play in the lot (27).

The poem "No" explores how we refuse to imagine. The speaker stands in the Washburn Street Cemetery, looking west over tombstones toward the abandoned entrance to the Hyde Park mine.[43] He stands among the dead, originally mainly Welsh, in a place where many miners are buried, men who likely worked in the mine. Alive to the place, the speaker personifies the tombstones, which "wept on" (3), and he imagines the shaft entrance as a passage to another world, but "they" tell him "no . . . it was not the entrance / to the underworld or anything like that" (10–11), though they likely believe in the gates to a Christian heaven. In their minds, they have sealed off the entrance to the world below in closing a "black / iron gate" (5–6) that shears off the "rusted tracks" that emerge from the idle mine (5). They have buried a history that the speaker imagines still breathes in the "unbroken sound of pure darkness / that went on all the time under everything" (7–8). Refusing to see any poetry in the place, they stick with the prosaic, the facts they know, which include that their houses were paid for by others' work, in a past recalled only through "negatives of the pictures" (14). A photo negative produces a positive picture, which is a selection and framing of a moment in time. The mines, with their rooms and passage-ways, are a negative, a dark version of the sunlit world the houses occupy. This underworld and its shades are the source of the city in the same way that the unknown is the source of poetry. In both, death gives shape to life. As Merwin says, this is the shadow of Sirius.

Sirius, the Dog Star, is the brightest star in the heavens. Merwin defines the title's luminous shadow as "pure imagination"; we cannot see the shadow, the star's negative picture, though it's there. We are the shadow of Sirius, he asserts; we are the unknown, which is the source of poetry.[44] The known doesn't spark our curiosity the way the unknown does. What we know places us at rest; what we don't know, including ourselves, pushes us to seek answers.

On a sunny June day, Bridget and I took a walk in the Washburn Street Cem-etery. The place is not well kept. Most of the two-part marble stones have been toppled, other stones stand tilted, and the grass is halfheartedly cut. A few trees huddle to the left and to the right of the main entrance; on the left is the Old Welsh section. If you go straight, take the first left, and walk halfway to the next intersection, you'll see, on the right, the graves of the Avondale dead, buried in three rows, most of their stones vandalized or made illegible by time. If you go right at the first intersection, you'll walk to the top of a hill, its crest bare of trees but studded with markers. Look west from among them and you'll see the ground Merwin describes in "Luzerne Street."

Others have put their minds to this place. Poet, novelist, and biographer Jay Parini grew up on the West Side of Scranton, a few blocks from Merwin's former home. Parini attended West Scranton High School and, like Merwin, lived abroad for several years, experiencing a long-settled landscape in Scot-land from 1970 to 1975 while earning his Ph.D. Coming of age a generation after Merwin, Parini experienced a landscape where active mining had virtually dis-appeared. In poems such as "The Lackawanna at Dusk" and "Anthracite Coun-try," he walks the same ground as Merwin, a postindustrial landscape alive with loss. Commenting on *The Shadow of Sirius*, Parini claims that Merwin "makes the past present for us. His past becomes ours as we read, and reread."[45] Parini could as easily be talking about his own work.

"The Lackawanna at Dusk," for example, describes a "river lost to nature" (1). The phrase "dead canal" points not only to its lifelessness, but also to its artificial state (2). The tamed river has been killed by the mine acid "scumming its banks" (3). On an old railroad bridge at day's end, the speaker adds his "spits" to the river's "swill," a small—but representative—act in the watercourse's degradation, a history underscored by the speaker seeing in the river below "odds / of garbage and poisoned fish" (7, 10–11). Breathing the "homely smell" and "fumes" around him, the speaker has become used to the damage he describes (8, 9). The line "A ripe moon cobbles the waters" may imagine the light of a full moon repairing the river's wasted waters, but light and night only hide at a distance the trash that they reveal close up (13). Further, the word "cobble," as a noun, means a lump of coal, which suggests that the water looks black, like the source of the river's death, anthracite. The poem concludes with explicit reference to the origin of the river's end: "Mounds of culm burn softly into the night" (14). Underscoring its unflattering picture of the river, the word "swill" appears in the poem's center, in terms of the number of syllables, words, and lines.

The collection's title poem, which immediately follows "The Lackawanna at Dusk," focuses on the subject of the prior poem's last line, a burning culm bank. The slag in "Anthracite Country," however, "smolders like moments almost forgotten" (3). As in Merwin's "Burning Mountain," this culm is "unwatched / by anyone living near. The smell now / passes for nature. It would be missed" (8–10). Here again, people have naturalized a human-created toxic atmosphere. The poem alludes to deindustrialization in its description of the "Rich earth-wound, glimmering / rubble of an age when men / dug marrow from the land's dark spine / it resists all healing" (11–14). The poem ends with the line "Its luminous hump cries comfortable pain," which suggests that people have become used to a damaged land (15).

In Parini's collection *Town Life* (1988), the poem "A Lost Topography" depicts "backhoes leveling / the once-bright culm that filled the air / with reek of memory" (3–5). In the poem, the adult speaker, returning home after an absence, remembers walking "this way from school, / imagining the lives ploughed under, lost" (7–8). Loss in the poem includes the speaker's youth, miners' lives, and the familiar landforms of his childhood. The backhoes are, in effect, erasing a history. The leveling of culm banks, which included returning the waste to the mines from which it came, signaled the demise of coal mining. In the 1960s, for example, workers crisscrossed downtown Scranton with pipes that directed culm into mines, an operation called flushing. It was as if the city sought to hide what it had done to itself. This pattern of wasting a wasted landscape has continued in the present with the establishment in the region of landfills that accept out-of-state garbage and the dumping of Philadelphia harbor sludge into open pits.

Parini may or may not be recalling Merwin's poem "Lackawanna," which appeared in *The Carrier of Ladders* (1970), Merwin's other Pulitzer Prize winner. Merwin's poem compares the Lackawanna River with the River Jordan, where John baptized Jesus. Baptizing himself in a dead river, the speaker enters into history, into an adult awareness of time, which he "shrank from" as an "obedient child" (13, 12); the river "flowed from under / and through the night the dead drifted down you / all the dead" (32–34). About the speaker's fear of the river, the poem describes the water as "black," moving under gases (perhaps the smell of sulfur) (9). The stained buildings may simply be soot-covered, but they may also point to the stained glass in churches.

The Lackawanna River has been nursed back to health in recent years, but its last three miles are still dead. The Old Forge bore hole, which still drains Lackawanna Valley mines, flushes daily into the river millions of gallons of water laced with a stew of metals, making the river here "very acidic and extremely low in dissolved oxygen."[46] It's rust-colored.

These poems refuse to see Scranton as the site of an urban pastoral. The Invaders of "Luzerne Street" and the raiders of Wall Street have triumphed, time and again. We need to heed the drunk/poet when he calls us to mind our work. Then maybe we can imagine a new relationship with the land.

3

Fixing Fence

The land was ours before we were the land's.

—Robert Frost, "The Gift Outright"

April meant fixing fence, which meant walking the line between us and others. Some afternoons, it'd be warm, a spring heat; other days, cool breezes blew. In the woods where the tractor couldn't go, we'd carry posts and wire, hammers and staples. Echoes of the sledgehammer driving posts and nail hammers striking staples mingled with the buzz of flies and the caw of crows. All around us, in every direction, lay silent, overgrown farms, evidence of a worn-thin land.

We'd come upon places where whole sections were down, barbed wire twisted, the fence posts snapped; sometimes we'd find a tree across the line, the wires taut beneath. We knew that snow drifts snap posts and stretch wire, so we accepted that fences would fail, but we'd curse and complain when we found that a hunter or snowmobiler had cut his way through.

Inevitably the fence that crossed the creek would be ripped away and tossed ashore, broken weeks before by blocks of ice riding spring floods. Sometimes the wires would be buried in the creek bed; other times they'd be lost, swept somewhere downstream.

"Go the other side," my father said, pointing with a nail hammer, "and throw those damn wires back."

I looked at the water sweeping by. He simply nodded upstream, at the spot where the cows went over.

We'd just stepped from the woods below the Flat, where the cows would lie in late summer afternoons, among the hemlocks, the ground beneath them blanketed with brown needles. The sun didn't shine in there much, so no brush blocked our way, but the fence was old, the barbs small, the wire brown with rust. In spots, strands stretched from tree to tree, the bark grown in grimaces over the steel.

What went unsaid: that I might soon be in Maryland, at the university.

The water wires had been washed onto a fan of gravel. Here and there they were buried; in other spots they lay covered with grass, stones, and sticks. I tugged.

"C'mon," I heard, "you can do better than that."

I pulled again, walking the strand, raising it until I found the end. Two years ago this had been new wire.

"Now toss it over here," he shouted, throwing his hammer across.

I hooked the claw behind a barb, bent the wire around the head, and threw the hammer in an arc back across the creek. It splashed at his feet.

"Jesus Christ!" he said, jumping back. "What'd you do that for?"

While I resurrected the second strand, he tacked the first to the tree, just to hold the end there. The wire hung half in, half out of the water.

The line crossed the creek just as it flowed into Cimahoskys' woods. Upstream, a strip of bare ground, scrubbed flood-clean, separated the woods from the Flat, which unrolled a quarter mile to the line fence opposite.

I grabbed the first wire with fence pliers and pulled it from the water, the wire winking and dripping. Holding the pliers against the tree, I pushed them back, stretching the wire taut.

"More!"

I pushed harder.

Where the tree had been gouged, my father furiously drove a staple behind a barb. Next to it, he drove another.

"Wrap it," he said.

Fig. 5 Con-Acres, ca. 1970. Photo courtesy of the author.

On a strand that tied the tree to the fence, I wound the end, twice.

"Again," I heard.

We put up two strands across the water, using no posts, just wire to mark the line. A ten-minute job.

"That should hold for a while," he said, turning his attention to the wire and post ahead.

The creek swept along, cool, undisturbed . . .

A dictionary tells me that "to fix" means to "make firm or stable," to give a permanent or final form to.[1] At best a half-truth. To fix fence is to know that the fence is never permanent, stable, or final—no matter how finished it looks after you've fixed it. Stitching time and place, a fence only patches up past and present, here and there.

My father and I stood at the end of a long line of fence fixers.

The fences that marked the place framed how we saw the world. And we fixed each fence, every year. The line along the south side, bordering Silas Kellogg's original patent, ran east in a straight shot across Johnson Creek, up the hill, across Baxter Road, and through the woods behind the barn, over the Miller Road, and down along the Big Meadow, Woodchuck Grove, the Orchard, and the Gregory Pasture, half of which touched Miller's Swamp. From the corner where peppermint grew, the line ran to a right angle and then went west across the top of the Gregory Pasture, along the Piece Next to Curley, over the Miller Road, down to the Twenty-Acre Lot. Pasture and woods but mainly meadow, the Twenty-Acre Lot was its own rectangle, perpendicular to the main box, its line running north, west, and south. From there, the line dropped down behind the house, across Baxter Road, the Flat, and the creek, to the final right angle. Running south from there, it cut through woods to the start. Inside the rectangles lay lands originally warranted—in the eighteenth century—to Richard Van Fleet and to Walter and Elizabeth Kimble.

In the mid-eighteenth century, most Americans would have known this part of Pennsylvania as blank space on a piece of paper. For example, in his 1776 map, Thomas Pownall, who bases his work on the 1755 map of Lewis Evans, depicts northeastern Pennsylvania as largely empty. Bound by the New York–Pennsylvania line, the Delaware and Susquehanna rivers, and the Cushetunk ("low land") Mountains, the region is represented as white space, with a "Great Swamp" hatched in and the word "Mountains" marching across the center.[2] Incidentally, the swamp is drained by an unnamed river, maybe the Lackawanna. The Lackawaxen, spelled *Legheiwacsein*, which Pownall locates farther south than we know it today, gets his attention because Edward Scull "has lately laid out some great Tracts of Land on this Creek." Scull, commissioned by the Pennsylvania proprietors, made his surveys in 1749, in the year after the colony purchased the land from the Iroquois Confederacy, "lands from the 'Kekactany Hills to Maghonioy Mountain,' and between Susquehanna and Delaware on the north side of 'Lechawachsein Creek.'"[3]

But in the 1790s, a "fever for the back lands of Pennsylvania" infected Philadelphia investors. In April 1792, the state legislature, believing that all vacant land in the state had been purchased, dropped the price of unimproved lands from twenty-six cents to six cents per acre.[4] Cheap land, revolution in France, and overinflated expectations led land speculators to pour money into buying up northern Pennsylvania land. Most investors never ventured near the place, but to trade the space for cash they had to name what they were looking at as this or that square of ground, with so many acres here, so many acres there.[5] The surveyors they hired to walk the woods got familiar enough with the land to make it knowable—in the abstract—by bounding it on paper with inked lines and on the ground with marked trees. Line fixers and mapmakers, the surveyors arranged space into alienable places. To landowners at a distance, the paper patterns made the blank make sense, but their surveyors' sketches, which largely ignored natural features, didn't help buyers to know the place. To know, to see, the land would take lifetimes of labor, generations of settled people turning their attention from lines on a map to details on the ground.

Unfortunately for investors, the northern Pennsylvania lands they purchased between 1780 and 1800 didn't sell well, mainly because "the supply of land far exceeded the demand for many years." The speculative bubble soon burst, breaking the fortunes of many prominent men, among them Robert Morris, "financier of the Revolution," and leading Constitutional scholar James Wilson. Within six weeks in 1796 one hundred fifty Philadelphia investors went bankrupt; in a single two-week period sixty-seven were jailed.[6]

Surveying and selling land sometimes ended in other kinds of confusion. For example, the land downstream of the water wires, Cimahoskys' woods, was once owned by Silas Kellogg, who amassed 2,370 acres, for which he received a patent in 1798.[7] But his warrant locates his property not on the Lackawaxen, but on "Lackawanna Creek," located one watershed away. More often than not here, surveying led to prolonged lawsuits, burned homes, and open warfare. When Americans rushed in, their confusion about where they were created no end of trouble.

"Mending Wall"

In "Mending Wall" Robert Frost explores what it means to fix fence. The poem depicts two farmers engaged in an annual ritual; they right the wall marking the line between them (13–14). Since their last meeting, the speaker has worked alone to repair human damage; hunters, rovers who ought to know better, have torn apart whole sections, leaving "not one stone on a stone" (7). This deliberate destruction, which makes for a lot of work—believe me—Frost sets beside nature's knock at the wall; frost has tumbled the "upper boulders," creating gaps in the line that "even two can pass abreast" (3, 4). The neighbors "walk the line" to fix, if only for a moment, the inevitable: the natural decay of all things (13). But in rebuilding the wall, they also renew their relationship, which, like all human relationships, requires constant attention.

At first divided, the neighbors come together, only to divide again. In line 12, the speaker is I; the neighbor, "my neighbor." Over the next eleven lines, however, as the men work at piling stone, speaker and neighbor unite as we and us. Line 24, "He is all pine and I am apple orchard," marks a break, the first clue that we shouldn't put complete faith in the voice we hear. When the speaker declares "My apple trees will never get across / And eat the cones under his pines," he seems not to realize that pines have the power to shade out apples (25–26). The neighbor, I think, chooses not to remind the speaker-farmer what he ought to know, but, being neighborly, "only says, 'Good fences make good neighbors'" (27).

The poem reminds us to pay attention. Feeling a sense of "mischief," note, the playful speaker tests his neighbor's awareness of the constancy of change, although he descends into arrogance, I believe, when he "wonder[s] / If [he] could put a notion in his [neighbor's] head" (28–29). Refusing to be baited, the neighbor repeats, "Good fences make good neighbors" (45), which keeps the speaker's mischief from doing damage. Of course the neighbor is aware that things fall apart; if he weren't aware, he wouldn't have answered the speaker's call, ever (35). The good fences line stays confusion: mending the wall makes vivid to these men what divides and unites us all, our shared isolation. Working in the gap brings us together. The speaker knows the problem, but assumes that the neighbor doesn't see the stopgap remedy. It's no accident, though, that the neighbor offers his line in the act of repairing the wall; as he speaks, he's "Bringing a stone grasped firmly by the top / In each hand" (39–40). Although the neighbor, we're told, is "like an old-stone savage armed . . . / [who] moves in darkness," the line's next phrase—"as it seems to me"—underscores that this is the speaker's perspective, not necessarily the only perspective from which to see the neighbor (40–41).

Students sometimes read the poem as a criticism of the neighbor's ignorance. All walls should be ripped down, they say. Didn't Thoreau claim there should be no separation between us? Didn't Whitman shout, "Unscrew the locks from the doors! / Unscrew the doors themselves from their jambs!"?[8] Sure, I answer, but how would you know yourself in a world without borders? Where would I begin and you end? Don't we constantly negotiate, probe, and rework the in-between space where we interact and come to know one another? Tending to that space clarifies us; only with others' help do we remake ourselves. The poem isn't about the wall; it's about the neighbors' ritual reconciliation of their differences. Everyday heroes, they battle back the chaos that threatens to overwhelm them.

Jason Torrey

The farm's first fence fixer was Jason Torrey, a Massachusetts man who arrived here in 1793.[9] After exploring for a month, he "selected a lot of land for himself, and having hired a man for a week . . . he commenced clearing his land." A squatter, he meant (so it seems) to farm, to build a "log house and fix his dwelling there." His years living at the farm, 1794–1801, were ones of "extreme poverty . . . he was often absolutely penniless, and well nigh foodless, and burdened with debt, and several times had his oxen and other items of property attached by the constable, and was often greatly discouraged and depressed."[10] I wonder: How desperate was he, early on, this sometime farmer but mainly a surveyor, the man who laid many of the property lines that we live with today, lines that have divided and joined people for over two centuries? What kind of liner was he?

In Torrey's life I see a pattern I recognize in my own: arranging maps and words, leaving the farm's work to a younger brother, and defending the place after moving away. Familiar with farm and town, here and there, he pursued interests, as I do, that combined the abstract and the concrete. We may be different kinds of surveyors, but our stories of the farm share some of the same lines.

Surveyors such as Torrey framed many Americans' first glimpses of the ground they settled. Even if someone built a home and planted a crop, he wouldn't gain title to his farm until he and the land office could locate it on a map. In fact, many people saw the property they hoped to farm on paper long before they saw it in person. Making a land office map required someone

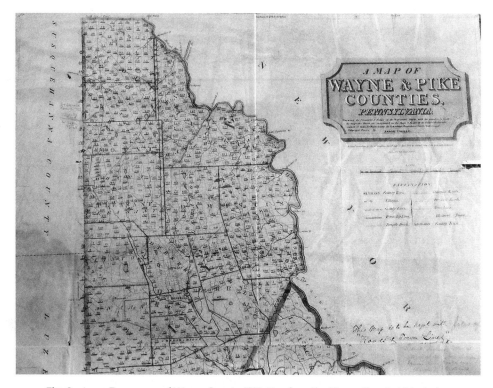

Fig. 6 Jason Torrey map of Wayne County, 1814. Map from the Wayne County Historical Society's Archives.

to walk the ground it represented; someone had to reduce the clutter of three dimensions to a cleaner two. Coined as a word in 1551, the year of the first English translation of Thomas More's *Utopia*, "surveying" measures space in terms of time; a surveyor determines degrees of distance in minutes and seconds.[11] To lay a straight line, a surveyor needs to know where he is on a spinning globe by locating a point of beginning and then determining its relationship to magnetic north, using compass and chain, or to the North Star, using transit and tape. Equal parts art and science, surveying requires precision and imagination, but early surveyors were as error-prone as they were exact.

A few days into cutting trees, Torrey was approached by Samuel Baird, a "surveyor and agent for capitalists in Philadelphia," who offered him a job as a surveyor's assistant, at eight shillings a day.[12] Baird likely heard that Torrey had learned the "Art of Surveying . . . [and] Studied English Grammar" at the forerunner of Williams College.[13] The good pay and easier labor, I imagine, made Torrey's decision a quick one. On his twenty-first birthday, 30 June 1793, he began working with Baird, and they laid lines for fifteen days. The fifteenth day, 16 July 1793, found them surveying a tract along Dyberry Creek, a branch of the Lackawaxen, near land claimed by a Walter Kimble.[14]

Possessing "an instinctive habit of reducing details to system," Torrey soon proved himself a capable mapmaker. Through the summer of 1794, he again worked for Baird in the Beech Woods, and then wintered with his boss in Pottstown, closer to Philadelphia. While there, he realized he could make a fortune if he could find unappropriated lands to sell to Philadelphia speculators. To locate such lands, he "needed to be familiar with the maps at the land office as well as with the wilderness country in which the lands lay, and with which he was already becoming well acquainted."[15] On 30 May 1795, Torrey and Baird signed an agreement to split the profits on their discovery of "between fourteen and fifteen thousand acres" of vacant land.[16] Unfortunately, the state land office was closed; with the office's reopening date uncertain, they could do nothing with what they knew. In the meantime, Baird introduced Torrey to several Philadelphia land barons, who soon employed him to make "maps and drafts of their lands" and to prepare "papers connected with the titles and conveyance of lands."[17] It seems reasonable that Torrey would have investigated whether the lands on which he was making a farm were, in fact, available. Among his papers are surveys that describe parts of the farm as vacant (i.e., claimable).

In 1796, when the land boom went bust, surveying went slack. By June, Torrey was back in Wayne County, apparently ready to farm, which may be why on August 13 he purchased from Walter Kimble the warrants he would use to gain title to the place.[18] After an extended stay in Massachusetts that fall and winter, Torrey returned to the farm with a horse, two oxen, a cow, and his brother Samuel, but left almost immediately, on April 2, for Philadelphia. While in town, he renewed his ties to "the land owners and the officials at the land office."[19] In between business trips to the city, he kept busy around the farm, planting potatoes, clearing land, and building a log cabin. But farming was not his passion. As early as May 1795, he was writing his farmer-father to say that his "constitution will not endure one-half the fatigue which some people undergo with pleasure."[20]

If knowledge is power, Torrey became—at least locally—a powerful person. He soon knew more about land titles in Wayne County than did anyone else.

His writing ability made him the "secretary of almost every public meeting," and he wrote many of the "public papers by which the Courts or the Legislature were addressed." Perhaps most important, people in the region "came to him with their land business, not only when they needed surveying done, but when they needed advice in respect to perfecting their claims and securing their titles." He also possessed an "acquaintance with the laws concerning land titles and the ownership and control of real estate . . . [that] was hardly surpassed by any lawyer in the State."[21] What he knew, if he chose to use it, put him in position to move from squatter to landowner.

Maps

Torrey's maps masquerade as windows on a stable world. Each names and puts into relation parts of the land; each shapes space into a place. By placing a place among other places, a map shows us that we're not there, we're here, which is there, on the map. By presenting to us the place in time and through time, a map offers us the illusion of seeing a place all at once.

A topographical map may locate and order ground, but it's no window. Like writing, it represents, which means, literally, to make present again. And like a narrative, a map, an abstraction of space, is made up of marks—signs—and the meaning of the signs depends on the interrelationship of the map's maker, reader, and purpose. The lines of a township topographical map, for example, tell one story to a dairy farmer; they tell another to a land developer. It's no accident that topography and topic share the same root, *topos*, meaning place.[22] Topography literally means to write a place. To draw well a topographical map, one must know the land's surface in some detail. To write well about a place, to bring a place alive, one must get immersed in all its details. A good map may allow us to imagine being there, but good writing lets us imagine living there. Like maps, stories make spaces into places.

The place-writing connection runs deeper, however: into argumentation, the very ground on which, I believe, the republic stands. To take a position, to persuade others about how you see the world, you need to find good arguments. Read Aristotle. In his *Rhetoric*, for example, he explores common sources for arguments, which he calls *topoi*, places from which to argue (see book 2,

So too with images

chapters 23–24). If you find yourself in a running debate with someone about, say, property lines, Aristotle's commonplaces—definition, testimony, and comparison, for instance—can help you to be heard. To argue well is to keep your place. But if you lose your place, can you argue at all?

When we read maps, we take on faith that what they show us is really there. I look at an 1872 map of Mount Pleasant Township, and I see a stream that runs by the Cronons' place. If I hadn't lived there, I'd assume that that stream is south of the Cronon house. If it's the one I assume the map means—which is the only one there, at least today—the reverse is true: the Cronon place is south of the stream, which is a trickle, really. Close enough, I suppose, and it may have been drawn this way just to make room for people's names.

But we have faith to the point of fantasy. We say New England or the Mid-Atlantic, regions that exist only in our minds. New England and the Mid-Atlantic are collections of states, after all, which are no more than lines on a map, which we believe determine those spaces on earth. On the ground, states are no more than arbitrary divisions marked by stones set here and there to signify where one state ends and another begins. Even regions defined by natural land formations—the Mojave, for example—expand and contract more than maps can suggest. If maps are windows on the world, we tend not to see the frame.

I reveal my fascination with maps in "The Essay as Literature," a creative nonfiction course I teach every year or so. Reading essays, memoirs, and reportage, we trace the line between fiction and nonfiction, which is not as easily fixed as we usually think.

The second day of class, I walk around the room showing each person a Portolan Atlas, published in France in 1547.[23] A rich green populated by figures of people and animals, the map depicts the Gulf of Mexico and Central America from the perspective of European explorers. As I circumnavigate the room, no one can tell me what in the world the map represents. When I turn the map upside down, though, everyone easily sees the map they've always known. One's orientation to the world, I point out, changes depending on how one looks at it. Where we stand frames what we see.

Unfolding a Mercator projection, I ask whether anyone sees anything interesting. A few quickly note North America and Europe in the center, but no one knows that the graceful lines that crisscross the oceans represent trade routes.

The Mercator map distorts land masses in adjusting for the earth's spherical shape; that's why it's frequently shown with a series of cuts at the poles. It's no accident, I mention, that the Flemish Gerardus Mercator, whose name means "merchant," made his map in 1569 to help ship navigation, in a period when global trade by sea was flourishing.

I pull out the Gall-Peters Projection, an equal area map, which ignores the fact that the earth is a sphere. As we compare the size of landmasses in each map, we see big differences. On the Gall-Peters map, Africa and South America are larger; Alaska and Greenland smaller.

Three maps. None, I say, reproduces what's there. Each has a point of view. Each interprets the world based on a separate set of assumptions.

So, what does the world look like? There's one Earth: a rough sphere of rocks and trees and things. But what it looks like—what it is—depends on one's perception and maybe why one's looking in the first place. Even the photo from Apollo 8 caught only half of our vulnerability. Is there a reality that we can point to and say, there it is? Maybe all we can do is point. Maybe, as Wordsworth knew, we "half create" the world we see.[24]

Before maps were widely available, church members in England would turn out on Rogation Days to walk the parish line to fix in their minds its boundaries and to repair its markers. People would use willow switches to beat boundary stones, priests would pray for good harvests, and boys would be whipped to remind them where the lines lay.[25] In *The Country Parson* (1652), George Herbert encourages pastors in the practice because it involves: "First, a blessing of God for the fruits of the field: Secondly, justice in the Preservation of bounds: Thirdly, Charity in loving walking, and neighbourly accompanying one another, with reconciling of differences at that time, if there be any: Fourthly, Mercy in releeving the poor by a liberall distribution and largesse."[26] All reasons to fix fences, yes, but despite what Herbert says, the custom reminds me how often we interweave memory, righteousness, and violence.

Yankee-Pennamite War

During one of my first hunting seasons, I took a stand along the fence between Ayoubs' and the big pasture at the Other Place. Distant shouts, a few shots: the

Rock Lake Hunting Club was driving Miller's Swamp. Along the ridge above Ayoubs' pond stood a spot of blaze orange, a stander, one of theirs. As calls from the swamp drew closer, deer, in twos and threes, trotted across the broken ground before me, but they were too far away, running among too many thorn trees. I heard three shots, close, but none fell.

My brother and three friends had posted themselves in other parts of the Other Place, well behind Rock Lake's men but close enough to see the deer they missed. We weren't happy that day: Rock Lake had already that morning driven deer from hunting grounds we considered ours.

The drive over, I turned to find my brother, but instead I saw beside the fence, not fifty yards away, a doe, looking at me. Heart racing, I raised my .243, found her neck in the crosshairs, and tripped the trigger. She whipped around, jumped the fence, and disappeared among the trees. I was pretty sure I'd missed, but when I stood where she had stood, I found spots of red fanned across the snow.

It wasn't long before a Rock Lake hunter emerged from the woods, saw me, and made directly for me, his rifle unslung.

"See anything?" he said, getting closer.

"Wounded one right here," I replied.

He stopped, red in the face.

"You guys comin' 'round here!" he said. "Poachin' on our drives! Who do you think you are?"

A shiver ran down my back. When I didn't reply, he came at me.

"This is our land to hunt, not yours! I'm sick of it!"

Three other hunters gathered behind him. Another walked beside the fence.

"I—I'm on my land," I stammered, pointing at the land beyond them. "We rent that land."

"Bullshit!"

"He's right," the hunter at the fence said. "They rent it."

The first hunter pushed past him, shouting over his shoulder. "You track that deer down in that swamp and I'll have the game warden on you!"

The others followed him along the line, and soon their orange jackets disappeared.

Five or so minutes later, after we heard truck doors slamming, three of us tracked the doe through the swamp, but we never found her.

For a long time I assumed that the farm had no history. The family had a history, sure, but the farm? No. The Other Place was just a name. I didn't really see the story there, at my feet, the house and barn foundations, the remnants of an orchard, and the lane that connected them to the Miller Road. But every farm has a history. The house and barns, the walls and fences, the fields and even the woods have origins. Building a wall or a barn, clearing a meadow or a pasture, or planting an orchard or a garden is an event, something defined not only by space but also by time. And none of these actions is ever completed. The barn and wall need repair; the meadow and pasture need to be cut, the orchard trimmed, the garden replanted. Each object carries traces of the acts that made it. Making sense of the traces tells a story of the place.

Writing history imposes on the past a stable surface, a pure narrative that fixes what's come before as this way or that way. Dig beneath the surface, however, and one finds instability: pillars of a narrated past stand amid huge gaps. With its beginning and end, its causes and effects, historical narrative implies a predetermined progress whose outcome is evitable. It's hard not to write history this way, but doing so eventually crowds out some people who helped to write it. In the final draft, failed arguments, for example, get short shrift.

A discontinuous history, on the other hand, a series of stories that moves from one event, person, or place to another without inevitable links, reveals the gaps in march-of-progress histories. Essayist Richard Rodriguez coins the term "brown history" to describe a shadow history that confuses the traditional narrative of U.S. history. He describes brown as "mixed, confused, lumped, impure, unpasteurized, as motives are mixed, and the fluids of generation are mixed and emotions are unclear, and the tally of human progress and failure in every generation is mixed, and unaccounted for, missing in plain sight." Discrete stories accrete in such discontinuous histories. Discrete, which comes from the Latin *discretus*, the past participle of *discernere*, means "individually distinct, but not different in kind."[27] A narrative of discrete parts unfolds less through plot than through story. Suspicious of boundaries, it opens out into complexity, ambiguity, and messiness, which makes it akin to daily life. When one seeks answers to the question, how did things really happen, one begins and ends with another: who knows?

Although I gradually became more aware that the farm told a story, one I knew only in bits and pieces, I was still surprised to learn that the place had a contested history. Located where lands of the Iroquois Confederacy, to the north, folded into the land of the Munsees, to the east and south, the farm was a handful of acres in the tribes' hunting grounds. As far as I know, neither group raised a village between the Susquehanna and the Delaware, though several tribes did settle along the banks of both rivers at different times, in different places. The Iroquois, who lumped together the Munsees, Unalachtigos, and Unamis as Delawares, defined all three as subordinate tribes, though the Confederacy was "not particularly successful in managing" them.[28] It's not hard to imagine one tribe poaching on another's hunt.

In drawing its lines, Torrey started the farm's story near the end of a border war. In 1768, an often-overlooked battle about boundaries broke out over possession of the Wyoming Valley, and erupted here and there across northeastern Pennsylvania before, during, and after the American Revolution, pitting against each other European immigrants and Native Americans, Revolutionists and Loyalists, and Connecticut and Pennsylvania settlers. Although similar wars raged all along the American frontier during the Revolution, this particular conflict, the Yankee-Pennamite War, was not about divided national loyalties but about a land feud between Connecticut, Pennsylvania, and Iroquoia. Over a fifteen-year period, violent arguments over property lines sometimes ended with one or two people killed, but more than 225 died in a pitched battle in the Wyoming Valley in 1778.[29]

The Yankee-Pennamite War reminds me that colonists did not put aside their everyday concerns during the Revolution to fight a disinterested battle for freedom. After the colonies declared their independence, Connecticut settlers labeled Pennsylvania claimants Tories, a label that soon became a self-fulfilling prophecy. At the Battle of Wyoming, Pennsylvanians who had been displaced upriver fought with the British to avenge the loss of their valley lands to Connecticut people. Connecticut settlers were no better. In addition to pushing out Pennsylvanians by hiring Lazarus Stewart, who led the Paxton Boys in their infamous massacre of the Conestogas, the Yankees were motivated during the Revolution by "land hunger for the lush upriver property of Pennsylvania claimants and their numerous Indian neighbors, not independence from the Crown."[30]

The trouble began with bad maps. In March 1681, Charles II, wanting to pay off a debt to the Penn family, granted William Penn a charter for Pennsylvania.

Of course, the king may also have wanted to rid himself of Quakers, who were no end of trouble, including Penn, a member of their inner circle.

I picture Charles in an ornate room, surrounded by aides, studying a map, which was likely no more than a sketch at best, at worst a bad guess. At a distance, both literally and figuratively, Charles couldn't see the land the map represented, nor could he imagine it. Its details escaped him. Paying scant attention to what he could see, he gave land to Penn that he had already granted to Connecticut in 1662. The drawing of the colonies' crisscrossing lines set in motion a chain of events that created a web of violence in the next century. Like all maps, the king's conjured the illusion of a linear connection between here and there; this particular illusion, unfortunately, spilled blood when others tried to draw it on the ground.

In the mid-eighteenth century, someone in Connecticut dusted off the colony's charter and noticed on a map that just beyond a strip of New York State, Connecticut continued on to the Pacific, at least theoretically. In June 1754, at a conference in Albany, a Connecticut company bought much of northeastern Pennsylvania from the Iroquois, a "purchase" that began at a line ten miles west of the Delaware River, a few miles east of the farm. The Iroquois, however, insisted that they hadn't sold the region to anyone; they claimed fraud.[31] Despite the Confederacy's cries of crime, Connecticut people started moving into the Wyoming Valley, which brought them into direct conflict with Delawares and Pennsylvanians. Alarmed by what it saw as a Connecticut intrusion, Pennsylvania purchased the same land from the Iroquois in 1768.[32] Undeterred, Connecticut settlers ignored Pennsylvania's claims and kept arriving, which led to periodic shootouts. The killings stopped in the 1780s, but the dispute wasn't fully settled until courts decided individual cases in the early 1800s.

Until then, land titles were unclear and uncertain, and the threat of violence hung in the air all across northeastern Pennsylvania, including Wayne County and Mount Pleasant Township. As late as 1796, Connecticut sympathizer Walter Kimble expressed "no confidence in the Pennsylvania title, and would not give a damn for all of them, for the land was not taken up legally, and might be held by possession." In 1799, Connecticut claimants "mobbed, burnt in effigy, and insulted" an emigrant from Long Island who dared to accept title to township land under Pennsylvania law. In "the spring of 1803, Wayne County officials reported an end to settler opposition, yet surveyors working for state landholders still encountered hostility in parts of that county the following fall."[33] Determining who owned what land ended in a legal nightmare of competing claims founded on a misplaced faith in maps.

Kimble v. Torrey

The Yankee-Pennamite trouble touched the farm through a series of lawsuits that began in 1809, when Walter Kimble accused Jason Torrey of fraud. Kimble, who sold Torrey the warrants he used to gain title to the farm, accused the surveyor of "concealing from [him] the fact that the warrants could be laid on other land." In response, Torrey argued that it wasn't his responsibility to remind Kimble that he could use his warrants elsewhere. As Sam Baird's assistant, Torrey knew the status of Kimble's warrants. As someone with access to the paperwork on vast landholdings, he also knew where to find vacant land, and he surely knew that a market existed for lost warrants. The story of the farm, in short, may have begun with a cheat.[34]

―――――――――

August meant haying, so in a meadow miles from home, John Schoonover and Walter and Ben Kimble bent to their work: John pitching, with Ben raking after, and Walter making the load. The sun was high; it must've been about two o'clock.

Hearing hoof beats, they paused. A dark roan.

Jason Torrey reined up beside the wagon and swung from the saddle. Wiping his forehead with a shirt sleeve, he looked flour white, out of breath. He nodded at Ben and at John, who went on working. Walter vaulted from the wagon, still clutching a pitchfork.

"Now, Jason," he said, "isn't that Jirah Mumford's horse?"

Torrey held a handful of paper. He smiled. "And as thick-headed."

"Looks like him, too," Schoonover called, gathering hay.

The brothers laughed.

Torrey said, wheezing, "I come to see what you'll do with these warrants."

He held them out, but Walter hardly glanced at them.

The horse tossed its head and licked Torrey's shoulder, leaving a string of spittle.

"Don't know what to do with them," Walter said. "They're lost. There's no land to lay them on, they tell me."

Nodding, Torrey studied Schoonover, who was tossing hay onto the wagon.

"I'll give you what they cost," Torrey said. "The first cost."

Walter raised an eyebrow.

"As there's no land to lay them on," Torrey went on, "they would answer me to turn into the Land Office." He coughed into his sleeve. "Them and some money I owe there."

"Sure," Walter said. "First cost. I don't give a damn for them."

Torrey fumbled a wad of paper money. "I—I'm a bit unwell."

"Jirah's workin' you too hard," Ben said.

Torrey held the money out to Walter, who took it.

"I have the deed poll . . ."

Walter shook his head. "Come 'round to the house in the morning. I'll sign then."

Torrey nodded, and swallowed.

"It's the heat," he whispered.

He caught the reins and labored into the saddle.

"Tomorrow then?" he said, touching his hat.

Walter tossed his chin and watched horse and rider cross the field, splash through the creek, and vanish into the trees.[35]

———————

Two and a half years before this, on 23 February 1793, Walter and Elizabeth Kimble (Kimball) bought the warrants as a reward for finding lands for the sellers. The warrants described land along the "North east Branch of Lacke-waxin," which, depending on where you stand, could refer to Johnson Creek or to Dyberry Creek. The Kimbles believed that they had warrants for eight hundred acres, or four hundred apiece, the maximum allowed by Pennsylvania law. In October 1794, Torrey contacted Kimble about surveying land along the Dyberry, but after he completed the survey Baird discovered on his maps that Kimble's land had already been claimed. Baird declared Kimble's warrants "lost," and Kimble believed them to be so.[36] I suspect that Torrey discovered during his 1794–95 winter in Pottstown that he could buy Kimble's warrants and use them to obtain sooner the land on which he squatted.

A squatter had first rights to buy from Pennsylvania the land he occupied, as long as he spent five years "improving" it—clearing land, planting a crop, building a home—but he was not to claim land already warranted. To be certain he wasn't squatting on someone else's land, the squatter consulted the district's surveyor, who had the sometimes-conflicting "responsibility of upholding squatters' rights and protecting the warrantees' interests."[37] A surveyor squatting on vacant land, Torrey faced, I believe, a difficult ethical choice when he purchased Kimble's warrants. As a surveyor, he had inside knowledge about warrants in the area, he knew Kimble's warrants were dead, and he knew they could as easily describe land on the Johnson. Enriching himself, Torrey chose, in my view, poorly.

Ahead, snow filtered through the hemlocks. A dozen paces to the left, the Dyberry trickled by, iced up along the edges.

Thirty-six-year-old Moses Killam balanced on his right shoulder the rifle he'd carried at Minisink. As he fingered a nick in the stock, he heard a snap, glanced back, and for a second he lay again on the hot, treeless hill, piling stones to protect himself, hearing Brant's Iroquois rush an angle in the line.[38]

Moses squinted at the sun and sighed. Despite stepping in Jacob's tracks, Walter moved with a heavy tread. Any game was long gone.

"Walter, where we goin'?" Moses said.

Kimble stopped and pointed with his rifle. "Here. Here was that land."

"Yeh?"

Moses wanted to go home. His feet were cold.

"Ah." Kimble shook his head. "Gone. . . . Damn surveyors."

"What about the warrants?" Moses said. "You didn't sell yer warrants, did ya?"

"I did." Kimble spat in the snow. "Damned land jobbers got it all." He tossed his chin at the woods and went walking. "That bastard Mordecai Roberts. Cheats. The lot of them."

"At's a pity."

Kimble turned. "What's that?"

Moses adjusted his spectacles and looked upstream. "Well, ya mighta got other land for 'em."

A cloud crossed Kimble's face. "With those warrants? I got my money for them. And glad of it."

"Ya coulda took 'em . . ."

"If I couldn't have this," Kimble said, stabbing a finger at the ground, "I'll not have any!"

"I just . . ."

When Kimble leaned closer, Moses took a step back. A few paces ahead, Jacob watched.

"If I took land with them, it'd be at the North Pole or the Devil's Arse!" Walter said, stepping into the track again. "I don't want it!"

Moses didn't know when to let go. "But with titles up in the air . . ."

Kimble swung around, blocking the sun. "I don't give a damn for Pennsylvania title," he groused. "The land was taken up illegally. Possession, that's owning."³⁹

————————

In his *History of Wyoming*, Charles Miner tells us that Walter Kimble "presented a singularly interesting specimen of the manners of his age. His appearance must have been striking and imposing. He is described as having been a tall, strongly-formed, athletic man, of a dark complexion, grave, even saturnine in his disposition, of great vigour of mind and force of character. . . . Resolute, determined, brave, he was uncompromising, obstinate and rash." Not a man to cross. And he wasn't fond of surveyors. While having breakfast with Killam and Torrey at the latter's Mount Pleasant home in 1798, Kimble didn't mention the warrants, "but he frequently said hard things against Surveyors and Land Jobbers generally."⁴⁰

The trouble began "when on the map [Kimble] was shown that the Land on big brook [a branch of the Dyberry] was taken he berated and without ceasing continued to berate poor Mordecai Roberts," the man who ended up with the land Kimble wanted. But Kimble's anger may be understandable. His warrant points to "400 acres on the headwaters of the North east Branch of Lackewaxin," but the 1794 survey is, ironically, vaguer than the warrant in describing the land as "situate[d] on the waters of Lechawexin."⁴¹ Torrey's patent follows the survey in simply describing the land as located on the "Waters of Lackawaxen," which, by the way, drains two-thirds of Wayne County.[42] In effect, the survey locates the land anywhere along the Lackawaxen, allowing one to claim land almost anywhere in the watershed. Underscoring this, the survey map, which depicts a rectangle of property lines, names the adjoining property owners; curiously enough, the same rectangles and names show up in maps of lands along both the Dyberry and Johnson creeks. If nothing else, it's an interesting coincidence, given that Baird and Torrey made the surveys and drew the maps. So, does the Kimble survey describe lands on Dyberry Creek or lands on the Johnson? Both, I'm afraid.

If Torrey could move the warrants from the Dyberry to the Johnson, so could Kimble, who had all along cited his warrant's description of an open meadow, a valuable space in the middle of any woods. In his suit, he simply asserts that there is a meadow along the Johnson, whose existence would mean that those lands were originally warranted to him. The testimony of Eliphalet Kellogg, Silas Kellogg's brother, backs him up: "I know the Lands in question. [I]t lies on small Branches of Lekawaxen [Johnson Creek]. . . . There is an open Meadow near the line. The Meadow was included in an old Survey."[43] Theoretically, one applied a warrant to a particular place, but in practice, or so it seems, one could apply a particular place to a warrant.

Dry stuff, maybe, but it underlines a dangerous assumption that too many of us unthinkingly share with Torrey and Kimble: land is only a commodity, an abstraction. Absent from the Torrey/Kimble case is any discussion of the details of the land itself, its stones and soils, contours and trees, probably because neither side knew them well enough. Both men assume that lines can be fixed and that once drawn they mark the permanent boundaries of a new thing, some-one's property, in this case a farm. But arguing over a map encourages one to detach its lines from the ground they've been sketched to represent; each parcel of land then becomes separable from its many contexts. The lines could then enclose land here or there, land on the Dyberry or on the Johnson. To locate the lands they argue over, Kimble and Torrey put their faith in maps, so much so that it reaches an absurdity: Kimble asserts that Torrey hid his possession of the land. In answer, Torrey points out, rightly, that it's tough to hide a farm, especially one Kimble visited on at least one occasion.[44] But if the farm's not on a map, is it there?

What goes around comes around. Not long after Torrey used the warrants, a new survey found that he had less land than he thought. An 1802 resurvey revealed that Elizabeth Kimble's warrant yielded 286 acres, "being the residue of the tract originally surveyed thereon, after excluding the prior surveys"; Walter's warrant ended up encompassing even less land, 86 acres.[45] Six years after leaving the land to his brother Samuel's care, Torrey finally gained title to the farm, on 25 January 1808, not long before Kimble sued.[46]

How could Torrey know what he had? He didn't spend much time farming. Making surveys and drawing maps kept his attention. For example, on 7 August 1800, he "finished his map of the [Bethany] village plot at this cabin in Mt. Pleasant, and started, by moonlight, at 3 o'clock of the morning of August 8th, for Wilsonville, where he arrived at 10" to act as clerk for the sale of Bethany lots. In the mid-1810s, he worked summer and fall in the woods, surveying land into hundred-acre parcels, and then in winter finishing each tract by making "drafts and maps" of the surveys. At the same time, he kept investing in Wayne County land, but by October 1828, as he greeted the first passenger boat to travel the Delaware and Hudson Canal, he saw the nation's history flowing away from him, heading west, over the Moosic Mountains, to the coalfields in the valley beyond.[47]

I find myself so caught up in books and maps here that I need to remind myself that the lines Kimble and Torrey argued over define the farm, not the land. Running at right angles, the farm's fences ignore the curve of the creek, the sweep of the hill, and the extent of the woods. Lying at the edge of the Pocono Plateau, within sight of the Moosic Mountains, north and east of the Wyoming Valley trough, the land is Basher silt loam on the Flat, Wellsboro channery loam above the barn, Oquaga channery loam on the sidehill, and behind the barn Oquaga and Lordstown extremely stony loams, with slopes varying from 3 to 75 percent. Populating the place are Eastern hemlock, sugar maple, locust, basswood, white ash, and American beech, along with timothy, brome grass, Russian thistle, dandelions, dogwood, and mountain laurel. White-tails and wild turkeys, barn swallows and red-winged blackbirds, killdeer and sparrows, bats, squirrels, woodchucks, and black bears . . . yellow jackets and bumblebees, mayflies and mites . . . pink eye and poison ivy . . . Conlogues and Weavers, Ayoubs and Nebzydoskis . . .

To make a place out of space, we remake the land, if only in surveys and memory maps, fences and poems. Even a jar placed in the woods can orient us, making an apparent chaos knowable; in "Anecdote of the Jar" (1919) Wallace

Stevens shows us that we make sense of the world through our own making. Our makings express our yearning for an elusive wholeness; we're forever trying to fix the existential gap between us and what's out there. What we make defines us. Do our makings separate us further from the land and one another, or do they lead us closer? Dividing land into parts, a property map tells us one story: that each of us can comprehend an alienable world. Reminding us that we inhabit a common world, a poem shows us that we're not alone and that what we know is, at best, partial.

After my brother Danny took over running the farm, an accountant advised him to raise money by selling stone. Walls were soon torn apart, the pieces loaded on pallets, and the pallets stacked on flatbeds bound for, I imagine, construction sites or maybe for golf courses and gated communities. Erasing the bounds of meadows made fields less knowable; with their margins gone, the views across them are longer. Several have disappeared into one. But the removal of walls signaled something maybe more sinister than a loss of bounds; it foreshadowed the foreshortening of the farm. Not long after, Danny sold off the Other Place, reducing the farm to less than half its size, which has only increased the uncertainty of its survival. The place is, I fear, being swept off the map.

I remember Whitman singing, "I know I have the best of time and space, and was never measured and never will be measured."[48]

Who knows?

4

Barn Razing

No one sees the barn.

—Don DeLillo, *White Noise*

Pinned to the bulletin board in my mother's kitchen is a photograph of my father with his mother, Katherine; his father, Walter; and his sister, Rita. My grandfather relaxes in a wicker chair in the front yard, my grandmother standing behind him, her left hand on the backrest. My aunt, who was probably ten at the time, leans against the chair, to my grandfather's right. To his left stands my father, six, maybe seven. It's summertime, and he's wearing short pants and a white shirt, his cock-eyed stance betraying a vague fear. A picture of kingly contentment, my grandfather—I never knew him—shirtsleeves buttoned, smirks at the camera. Caught glancing at my father, my grandmother, whom I hardly knew, says something to him, while Aunt Rita, eyes downcast, waits on the photographer. Looming above and behind the whole family, who are lined up just right of center, stand the barns, one behind the other.

When I look at that black-and-white day in the 1930s, I study the lower barn. With the doors closed, the planking in good repair, and glass in the windows, it's in great shape. No gaps, no cracked and concave cinderblock wall. Solid, tight.

The barn's appearance measures how well the farm was doing in those days, despite a world depression. With so many farms nearby, my grandparents could rely on neighbors for help, machinery, and company. No more. Most neighbors don't farm. Their barns wear away; their fields grow brush. Painted and repaired barns stand, here and there, on profitable places, but most barns, I've noticed, fall somewhere in between, in a gray area populated by farmers making a living and farmers who didn't make it.

A lot of Americans, though, look beyond the barn, no matter the shape it's in, to the life they take it to symbolize, a simple, happy, honest way of being in the world. A barn evokes images of family and community, hard work, and human ties to nature: the stuff of American self-identity. Despite how often it's pointed out that this is not how things are, the images persist, even as these symbols of rural life disappear. Of the thousands of barns that once defined rural spaces, most have been torn down, allowed to fall down, or worse, converted to second homes. As a nation, we'd rather literally leave our country past behind—too much work, mud, and manure back then—even as we keep a bucolic version of rural life alive in our collective consciousness. Few of us herd cattle or sheep, few of us live outside cities, and few of us encounter fruits and vegetables before they end up on supermarket shelves, but a lot of us love cute farm animals, country kitsch, and suburban homes with big lawns and John Deere mowers. The persistence of this pastoral perspective has become a kind of whistling in the dark.

Published at the height of the 1980s farm crisis, Don DeLillo's *White Noise* captures our inability to see beyond a mythic rural America. Early on in the novel, Jack Gladney and Murray Siskind, professors at College-on-the-Hill, drive out to Farmington to visit a "tourist attraction known as the most photographed barn in America." Along the way they pass signs telling them that they are approaching "THE MOST PHOTOGRAPHED BARN IN AMERICA." While at the site, they watch photographers snap shots from a "slightly elevated spot set aside for viewing and photographing." After a long silence, Murray turns to Jack and says, "No one sees the barn. . . . Once you've seen the signs about the barn, it becomes impossible to see the barn. . . . We're not here to capture an image, we're here to maintain one. . . . We've agreed to be part of a collective perception. . . . They are taking pictures of taking pictures." As, maybe, DeLillo's voice in the novel, Murray goes on to claim that it's impossible to know what the barn was like before it was photographed: "we've read the signs, seen the people snapping the pictures," we can't escape the barn's "aura" (12–13).

Murray explains to Jack that the barn that was is gone. All that we have are images of the barn, images that, in lifting the barn from its context, create a reality that erases the one that existed prior to the first photograph, a displaced reality to which we can never return, despite our yearning to do so. The technical term is simulacrum, an image divorced from its content, or, a copy of a copy of what's real. That Jack and Murray watch people photographing a barn and not, say, a church, is significant, at least for me, because the barn represents the myth of an agrarian America, one that Americans perpetuate, a myth of wholeness and solidity that leaves unquestioned our faith in food abundance.[1]

Underscoring this misplaced faith, *White Noise*'s supermarket, a latter-day cathedral, feeds our fantasy of living forever, in this life. A place "sealed off, self-contained . . . timeless," the supermarket reminds Murray of the Tibetan "transitional state between death and rebirth." Akin to a sealed room where a Tibetan priest might prepare the dead for entrance into the afterlife, the supermarket "recharges us spiritually, it prepares us, it's a gateway"—not, however, to "uterine rebirth or Judeo-Christian afterlife" but to our renewal as spendthrift consumers (37, 38). For example, after checking out, Jack reflects on the "mass and variety of [his] purchases . . . the sheer plenitude those crowded bags suggested"; in shopping he achieves a "fullness of being that is not known to people who need less, expect less" (20). Even the ascetic Murray, who searches for "non-brand items in plain white packaging with simple labeling," participates in a "new austerity" that is just as satisfying as Jack's buying; Murray is "not only saving money but contributing to some kind of spiritual consensus. It's like World War III. . . . They'll take our bright colors away and use them in the war effort" (18). The bright colors, the volume of goods, and the clean and well-lit aisles hide from these professors the industrial system that satisfies their hunger for stuff, a hunger that the system creates through its ubiquitous advertising images. The food chain may stretch from Jack's shopping cart back to Farmington's "most photographed barn in America," but no one sees the link between farm and shelf because the culture's white noise interrupts all attempts to tell the tale.

"MasterCard, Visa, American Express" (100).

If we took a close look, we'd discover an unstable food chain. An example: on 18 February 2008, the federal government demanded a record recall of

143 million pounds of beef that had been rendered at a California meatpacking plant and distributed across the country.[2] The recall was triggered, as you may remember, by a Humane Society video that captured workers using forklifts to prod downer cows toward slaughterhouse pens. A major sign of mad cow disease, the animals' unsteadiness prompted renewed fears of the disease's presence in the United States. This incident, which required an undercover operation to unmask, followed too closely Canada's December 2007 discovery of its eleventh case of the brain-wasting disease, which was brought to you by a food system that encouraged feeding cattle to cattle.[3] If mad cow doesn't make you a little uneasy when you order a Big Mac, nothing will.

The lower barn may not be the most photographed barn in America, but it's the only barn on the farm that's been preserved in two paintings, both by Jim Kilker, my uncle, a World War II tail gunner and retired General Motors manager. Against the wall in the room where I write is Uncle Jimmy's first lower barn painting, untitled, dated 1979. A summer-scene watercolor done in several shades of green and brown, it lifts the barn from its context; there's no cow barn, no fences, no machinery. The fissured cinderblock wall looks, improbably, solid, its concave masked by a plum tree. Gaps between the planks look like shadows, not damage or the wear of age. From this angle, from the house's front porch, one expects to see power lines and poles, but they're not there. The pasture, which should take up the middle distance, is all woods; the woods are, oddly, an inner ring of hemlock and an indeterminate outer ring, nothing like the mixed growth I know. Depicting an imagined barn, a barn only he saw, this squared-off watercolor repairs time and renders the barn as a solid stable. A wish fulfillment. An urban New Jerseyman's hankering for a black-and-white farm life.

Painted years later, during the deepening of the 1980s farm crisis, Uncle Jimmy's second watercolor, a winter scene, includes the cow barn, the sheep barn, the garage, and the silo. The house, it seems, has been deliberately crowded out. In its narrow, rectangular frame, the painting sets the barns at a distance, across a snow-encrusted field bound by a barbed wire fence. The barns huddle at an angle, and one has the sense of seeing them from below, as a visitor first sees them upon coming up the driveway. The gaps in the lower barn, in all the barns, are more obvious. Power lines crisscross between them; a telephone pole stands in the scene's center. The atmosphere is stark; the mood, cold; the tone, dead-on. He titled this one *An Endangered Species*.

Fig. 7 Painting of lower barn (Jim Kilker), 1979. Used with permission of Eleanor Kilker.

My first published effort looked at the lower barn. The essay talked about how the barn had a good roof and how it was always a point of contention in the family because we couldn't agree whether to fix it or tear it down. In 1984, *Pennsylvania Farmer* printed the piece, as a good laugh, though the running argument was no laughing matter to us. Published under my mother's name, the essay interests me now because it was, I think, a way of making public a private, family tension. I'm not sure, but maybe I thought that if we knew that everyone else knew we would be forced to make a decision. We didn't.

In the fall of 1988, my first semester away in grad school—at a land-grant university, no less—I took a class that explored contemporary fiction. We met at the instructor's house, three or four miles from campus. A major figure in her field, she was a commanding presence in person, and she attracted advanced, professionally minded students. Her husband was a major scholar, too, so meeting at their home made me uneasy; it suggested a melding of private and public life that I still wasn't sure I was prepared for.

Graced with hardwood floors, exposed beams, sliding doors, and skylights, their bi-level had a barn-like openness. One could stand in the foyer and see the kitchen, living room, and dining room, all separated from one another by islands surrounded by bar stools. What threw me was the microfilm reader in the middle of the living room; it dominated a folding table strewn with open books, notebooks, and bales of loose-leaf papers. I thought: these two are serious scholars.

We lounged in Morris chairs, under warm lights, which led one of us, Dan, to nod off now and then. As usual, I kept quiet during class, and, I admit, I caught myself a few times with heavy lids. Not a good way to impress the teacher, I know. During brief silences, I listened to someone, deep in the recesses of the house, tapping at a keyboard.

We read what I've come to know now as the usual suspects of the postmodern American novel: Robert Coover, Ishmael Reed, Thomas Pynchon, Don DeLillo. These writers played with language in ways that made me pause; my reading to that point had been focused on the modernists and their predecessors. As part of the course, we were required to offer an oral overview of a contemporary literary theory, which we would all then discuss in relationship to a given novel. My presentation on deconstruction was paired with *Gravity's Rainbow*. Yikes. My ramble about the ideas of Jacques Derrida went pretty well, I thought; I was speaking up, after all, until she interrupted to point out that, although I'd touched on the theory's key terms, I'd forgotten a key concept, *the* key concept: meaning is undecidable. I flushed, and went silent. Oh, yeah, that's right. I'm not sure now, but maybe my years at a Jesuit university had made it hard for me to accept that not every text had a single, correct meaning.

And I wanted to decide. Deconstruction struck a single chord in me, then: great, I get it, but now what? It was like these master theorists had brought me to a cul-de-sac. All they wanted to do was to drive around the circle so I could look at all the pretty houses. I wanted to say, this isn't my neighborhood; where I live is disintegrating while we congratulate ourselves on how sophisticated we are because we can't decide whether we're looking at a false colonial or a fake Victorian. Despite their own brand of arrogance, New Critics at least asked you inside before they gave you directions to the next development.

One August day, a shiny red pickup parked in the driveway. After climbing out, the driver, a big man in a black baseball cap, turned to look thoughtfully at the barns. He soon disappeared, but I could hear his heavy step on the back porch; a few seconds later, he came into the kitchen, a salesman's smile creasing his face.

"I was drivin' by," he said, closing the door, "and I couldn't help notice your barns need paintin'."

My mother shot a glance at my father.

"We'll get to it," he said.

"Mind if I have a glass a water?" the man asked.

My mother filled a glass at the sink.

"I'm from Georgia," he went on. "Thanks. Come north to paint every year, right after the Masters." He paused. "Ever been to a golf tournament?"

No.

"It's a nice thing. Anyway, my crew's paintin' a barn 'bout two, three miles from here. It'd be easy to get someone here to work on yours. They don't look so good."

"No," my father said. "They're all right."

I glanced at the newspaper spread before me on the table. My father was too polite, I thought.

"Wouldn't it be great to add a shine to those roofs and keep the rust from 'em," the Georgian said.

"We'll get to it," my father said, following the man's glance.

"D'you know Ed Brookin'?"

"Yeah, sure. Up Bigelow way."

"That's right. I painted his place last year. He's a reference a mine. Call him if you're not sure."

My father inspected his face. "How much?"

The Georgian stepped to the window. "Oh, I can do 'em for three hundred, I imagine."

My mother left the room.

I whispered, "Don't."

My father looked at the barns, folded his arms, and stared at the paper.

"Go ahead," he said, waving a hand. "Do the cow barn."

"The big barn?"

"Yeah."

"Sure. I'll have my man here in a few hours."

"I'll pay when I see it's done."

The Georgian stood at the back door.

"Thanks for the water," he called to the dining room, smiling at us.

The painter, a silent black man in his late twenties, arrived later that day in a color-splattered flatbed loaded with barrels, coiled hoses, and a rusty generator. Without fear, he walked backward, straddling the peak of the roof, spraying silver from side to side. The paint cascaded across the tin, drying in waves. The roof looked like it was melting. If you didn't get too close, though, the job didn't look half bad.

A few days later the Georgian returned.

"That Tinker is back," my mother said, going deeper into the house.

My mother inherited the word from my grandparents, who may have known Tinkers while living in Carbondale between the world wars. An itinerant Irishman, in the United States more often an Irish American, a Tinker is a member of a community more often known as Travelers, whose roots stretch back to precolonial Ireland.[4] Largely because Travelers were mobile and represented the unknown, settled communities greeted them with suspicion, sometimes with violence. The man in our kitchen was likely linked to the largest Irish Traveler community in the country, Murphy Village, a well-off suburb of North Augusta, South Carolina, itself part of greater Augusta, Georgia, home of the Masters Golf Tournament.

My father opened the back door.

"That barn there's spoilin' the look a the new paint job," the man said, stepping inside and pointing at the lower barn. "It just doesn't make your place look good from the road."

"It's all right."

The Georgian leaned against the sink, pushed back his Titleist cap, and studied the bulletin board.

"It just doesn't look good," he said. "I think you oughta let me paint that roof."

I glared at him, but said nothing, knowing all along that my father would say yes.

And he did.

Not long after, the same painter parked beside the lower barn. In a few minutes, we had an unsteady barn with a roof that looked great from the road.

One could trace the farm's prosperity in its history of barn building. On 12 April 1834, Thomas Cronon, a New York Irishman, purchased from Jason Torrey the land where the farmhouse stands, 151 acres all told. On 28 June 1843, he sold 74 acres to Dennis Baxter, mainly, I imagine, because he, Cronon, had too many mouths to feed; he and his wife, Ann, had four children, all girls. By 1850, Cronon owned one house, two oxen, four cows, 15 acres of improved land, and 74 acres of unimproved land, a combined value of $257. His county tax: $1.54. Good Catholics, the Cronons also had three more kids, two of them girls; a second boy and seventh girl would soon arrive.[5] No mention of barns.

The cow barn, at least, must have gone up during or just after the Civil War, when Cronon was making enough money—probably selling food and timber to the growing coal regions or, maybe, to an expanding New York City—to hire my great grandfather, Peter Conlogue, or McConlogue as he sometimes signed his name, who arrived from Ireland in 1860 as a fifteen-year-old. In 1874, Peter married Cronon's youngest daughter, Matilda, and moved to Warren County, where he worked in the lumber business in the aftermath of the oil boom there. The two purchased the farm from her brothers, Michael and Hugh, in 1878, and moved back to Pleasant Mount in 1884.[6] My best guess is that the Cronon brothers erected the lower barn in the 1870s, or maybe Peter put it up late in the next decade. Whoever they were, the builders followed a local pattern of barn building based on a model imported from England.

The English barn—the lower barn's an example—has changed remarkably little since its first appearance in medieval times, consisting usually of three bays, one on each side of a central driveway, often called the barn floor, a name originating in the days when farmers threshed wheat in the central space. The one-story layout came to the New World with the first English settlers, and made its appearance in New England, where it became known as the Yankee barn.[7]

Farmers here modified the Yankee plan to create a "basement barn."[8] Forty-by-twenty, the two-story lower barn took advantage of the sidehill's slope; on the upper side, a landing, framed with fieldstone and filled with rock and dirt, led to the second floor. Builders gathered stone from ground nearby, and the hemlock they used must have grown on-site or down along the Johnson. Either way, the logs were cut to lumber and left to dry before they were rigged at right angles with wooden pins into a frame that a crowd of neighbors must have helped to lift. Raising a post and beam barn signaled faith in the future, short-lived as good times often are.[9]

Whoever raised it hewed the beams by hand—the adze marks stayed fresh-looking—and the central beam had been taken from a tree whose likeness hasn't been seen here since. Later, a heavy cable, probably added when the cinderblock went up, ran under this beam to tie the sides together. Years ago, so my father told me, his father or grandfather stabled horses below and stored hay above. But the half story under the roof may have always held this and that.

The builders used *Tsuga canadensis*, Eastern hemlock, a once-dominant species here. Among the most shade-tolerant of all trees, a hemlock sapling can "grow even in the shade of a dense grove of the mature trees." The tree's bark produces tannic acid, which Native Americans used to staunch wounds to "promote healing." Euro-Americans used tannic acid to tan leather, big business here in the mid-nineteenth century. Tanneries, often themselves made of hemlock, stripped the region of its trees in service of an international hell-for-leather demand for boots and shoes.[10]

Sometime in the 1930s or '40s, my grandfather replaced the lower barn's ground floor frame with a cinderblock wall, which he placed on what must have been the barn's original dry-stone foundation. Not a smart idea. The building now rested on unsure footing; cinderblock is not as forgiving as wood. By the time I was six, the wall had cracked in several places, and I could move whole sections of it with a gentle push. All but my father thought that the barn was unsafe, and often enough my mother would complain that it ought to come down. But it never moved.

My father refused to hear of it coming down, and he had no money to repair it. A carpenter who came once to look it over recommended that a new barn be built. My father said no. End of discussion. The carpenter shook his head. Back at the house, my father went on about how the barn had a good roof and how he had plans to fix it so that we could store hay there. Never happened.

Of course, one could trace the farm's demise in its loss of barns.

In 1982, I ripped down the granary, whose wooden bins I remember filled with oats once, only once, in my life. Seven or eight years after that, Danny pulled over the silo with a John Deere 2510 and a heavy chain; the tube dropped, accordion-like, right across the foundation. When he put up the addition on the cow barn in '96, he tore out the sheep barn. With every razing, my ailing father protested, but with each loss his cries grew weaker as the place he knew slowly disappeared.

What we were sweeping away was the farm's legacy of mixed farming; chicken houses, sheep barn, pig barn, horse barn, granary, and silo all symbolized a farm economy that kept its eggs in different baskets. The slow disintegration of each structure signaled the farm's increasing specialization, to the point where today only the cow barn and a machinery shed remain. Along with the barns, however, has gone the know-how to run a mixed farm. These days, if it's not milk, it's not possible. Caught up in this, we're perpetuating the industrialization of "nature's most perfect food." And not just here on this farm; it's the same on almost every dairy farm in the United States, and soon it'll be the same across the globe and across crops.

Although milk offers the illusion that it comes straight from the cow, behind every glass of it stands an intricate and attenuated system of production, processing, transportation, and distribution. How else can a food so "utterly prone to contamination" get into your refrigerator so regularly? Twentieth-century innovation may have made the milking machine, but nineteenth-century industrialism created the urban habit of drinking fresh milk daily. To have milk with breakfast back then required a dense railroad network that linked city and country, an urban reform movement that sought to ensure a safe supply, and an advertising industry that sold nostalgia for country life and played on consumers' interest in "perfecting children."[11] To move milk, railroaders, reformers, and advertisers peddled a promise of purity, a promise that papered over how milk made it from cow to kitchen.

Much of the milk drunk in New York in the first three quarters of the nineteenth century originated from dairy barns attached to city breweries, where hundreds of cows ate "brewers' grain mush." The resulting blue milk killed kids; an urban child in the 1840s had only a fifty-fifty chance of living beyond age five, in part due to drinking bad milk As brewery barns gradually shut down, railroads shipped in from outlying farms more and more milk. By 1910, New York siphoned milk from six states; to ensure a safe supply, the city sent inspectors to examine work practices and facilities at far-flung dairies. New York's dependence on imported milk was total: testifying before the New York Milk Committee's 1910 Conference on Milk Problems, a Lackawanna Railroad representative reported that the city "derived its entire milk supply by railroad, most of it two hundred to four hundred miles away."[12]

Early milksheds followed railroads, which generally ran through valleys. The New York milkshed touched us a mile west of Pleasant Mount. If it was typical, this milkshed extended from the line five miles in either direction.[13] At the outer edge of the five miles, the farm's milk—as cheese early on—moved beyond Belmont, into the Lackawanna watershed, to meet the train this side of Herrick Center. For sixty years little changed. When I was a kid, my father still took milk in cans to the milk plant on the old O & W rail line. But for the truck, it might as well have been the nineteenth century. When the plant closed, he trucked to Honesdale his own and the milk of several neighbors.

This all ended in 1971, when state inspectors required us to install a bulk tank. Nowadays, a three-axle truck picks up Danny's milk every other day— every day in flush times—and takes it to a processing plant in Flemington, New Jersey, 130 miles away, before it's trucked to New York, another 50 miles.

The centrifugal force of the New York City milkshed is both blessing and curse. It's a blessing because fluid milk brings farmers more money than does cheese; it's a curse because slight fluctuations in a fickle market puts farmers at the end of a price yo-yo, despite strict government price controls. The Pennsylvania Milk Marketing Board, for example, determines minimum wholesale and retail milk prices for farmer and consumer, but its calculations don't include the cost of production, which for one farmer stood at $16.50/hundredweight in October 2009. In the months before he sold his cows, this farmer received for his milk $11.15/hundredweight. A hundredweight, by the way, is about 11.6 gallons. The consumer, meanwhile, bought a gallon of milk for $3.60. The price at both ends is outrageous. This is, I believe, a farm and consumer crisis. Consumers pay way too much for milk while farms go under. Forty-four percent of U.S. dairy farms disappeared between 1997 and 2007. The Scranton *Times-Tribune* reported in May 2010 that 80 dairy farms remained in Wayne County, fewer than half of the 175 that operated in 2000.[14]

Blaming the middleman may be easy, but it's usually true that in a crisis like this the middleman rakes in money. For example, on the heels of "$12.5 billion in 2008 sales of more than 2.4 billion gallons of milk," Dean Foods, the nation's largest dairy processor, "reported [in 2009] a 31 percent leap in second quarter profit of $64.1 million." Dean and Dairy Farmers of America produce and process a major share of U.S. dairy. A conglomeration of cooperatives—including Dairylea, where Danny ships his milk—Dairy Farmers of America sells its farmers' milk to Dean for processing; in 2008 DFA accounted for 40 percent of Dean's total milk output. It's no coincidence that the U.S. Justice Department launched in September 2009 an "antitrust investigation into whether milk-processing titans are shortchanging dairy farmers."[15]

Masking this crisis is the common perception that milk is a perfect food, one intimately tied to nature, an idea we've inherited from the nineteenth century, embodied most often, then, in the milkmaid. This nostalgia did not go unnoticed by U.S. writers. For example, Frank Norris mocks the image of the milkmaid in *The Octopus* (1901), a novel that depicts male California bonanza farmers battling the Southern Pacific Railroad. The gruff character Annixter, one of the state's principle bonanza wheat farmers, softens under the influence of Hilma Tree, a young woman who works in his ranch's dairy. She first comes to his attention when he finds her making cheese, "the sleeves of her crisp blue shirtwaist rolled back to her very shoulders." Despite his best efforts, he's unable to dispense with his attraction to her. His only frame of reference to understand her, however, is the agrarian myth. To Annixter, who is suspicious of women, Hilma represents "the natural, intuitive refinement of the woman not as yet defiled and crushed out by the sordid, strenuous life struggle of overpopulated districts. It was the original, intended, and natural delicacy of an elemental existence, close to nature, close to life, close to the great, kindly earth." When Hilma and her family suddenly leave the ranch, Annixter spends the night thinking about her, realizing just as a new day dawns that he loves her: "The little seed, long since planted, gathering strength quietly, had at last germinated." His awareness of love coincides with the fact that his wheat "in one night had burst upward to the light." As you can see, Norris doesn't go for subtle symbols: loving the milkmaid remakes the bonanza farmer. By extension, drinking milk remakes the city dweller.[16]

Milkmaids have disappeared and Danny, rather than our sister, Ann, milks cows, mainly because the sale of milk to factories in the mid to late nineteenth century displaced home cheese and butter making. As dairying became more

Fig. 8 The author's father, Bill Conlogue, 1998. Photo courtesy of the author.

capital-intensive and factory-like, women left the barn, which became "associated with men."[17] Extending this "masculinization of milking," in 1917 the company founded by Swedish engineer Gustaf de Laval marketed in the United States the "first widely accepted milking machine."[18] Creating a partial vacuum at the cow's teat, de Laval's machine, which Danny uses today, revolutionized dairying. As milking times decreased and herds expanded, even more men replaced women as milkers.

This replacement happened so quickly and completely in the United States that in *Barren Ground* (1925) Ellen Glasgow gets notice for depicting a female dairy farmer who employs only women to milk her cows. Working hard to industrialize her farm, Dorinda Oakley uses the latest and best technologies, including a cream separator, a "tractor-plough," and electricity.[19] Aware of her market, she sells the agrarian myth to urbanites by supplying "Old Farm" butter to hotels in the heart of political America, Washington, D.C.

These days, cows can milk themselves. DeLaval, for example, markets a voluntary milking system (VMS) that automatically milks a cow when she chooses to be milked.[20] This strikes me as the ultimate industrial system; the next step, I bet, is to get rid of the cow. A voluntary milking system saves labor, but like all labor savers it drives a tough bargain: installing such an expensive system may drive down labor costs and increase production, but increased production drives down profits, which forces farms with high labor costs out of business. With machines like voluntary milking systems, it's no wonder that tourists ride buses through some of the larger operations' barns, marveling at the technology, much as people in the nineteenth century toured coal mines and bonanza farms. Only the owner of a large dairy can afford a voluntary milking system, but he's already behind a desk managing shifts of milkers. If the system were affordable for Danny, who does his own milking, it would be a good thing; it would offer him a break from a grueling 24/7/365 round of work, work that I no longer know.[21]

We live—officially—in a post-farmer nation.

In Washington, D.C., in 1962, the Committee for Economic Development (CED), a group of government, academic, and "industry" leaders, declared war on American farmers when it decided that agriculture's main problem was that there were too many farmers. CED recommended that the federal government cut price supports on key crops in order to move, *drive* is more like it—within five years, no less—two million farm families from the land, a mass migration whose bonus would be lower urban wages.[22] The idea was that if you made it as difficult as possible for people to stay on the land, eventually they would choose to leave. And since they chose to leave, the government would be free to claim that farmers left the land to pursue "better opportunities" (i.e., urban jobs). No farmers, as far as I can tell, were invited to participate in CED meetings. The policy has worked spectacularly well. Across the United States, so few farmers produce food for American dinner tables that in 1993 the U.S. Census Bureau decided that it wasn't worth it to count them.[23]

The few farmers who remain must get big or get out. I remember attending with my father a Wayne County Dairy Day, sponsored by the Penn State Extension and held in the Honesdale High School auditorium. The first speaker represented the Pennsylvania Department of Agriculture. Saying what he'd likely said dozens of times before, he recited a litany of the state's farm production statistics. As he spoke, he made no eye contact with anyone, nor did he smile, or ask at the end if his audience had any questions. When he stopped, he simply turned and walked away, to sit in the last seat in the first row, his back to us. Throughout the rest of the program, he looked straight ahead, interrupting his stare only to smooth his suit or to cross his legs. I felt his contempt.

The next speaker was a farmer, probably in his mid-thirties, who talked about how the latest technology allows him to participate in Honesdale's social life. He encouraged farmers in the audience—and there were few; it was mid-morning—to invest in the latest gadgets. Those who refused, he claimed, ended up making less milk and selling out. It's a competition and only the strong survive. He was satisfied, so it seemed, in his own ability to make it. I thought about asking him what he wanted: a lot of high-tech tools or some neighbors.

A banker in the audience then stood up, not half a dozen seats away.

"There're no forty or fifty head dairies in Wayne County," he said. "They don't exist."

An extraordinary statement.

My father and I were there; he milked forty cows; he existed. This banker couldn't see us. What he meant to say was that forty or fifty head dairies didn't matter, because they didn't make him much money. Again the refrain, get big or get out. I felt that we were at the center of an agriculture that had gotten so big it couldn't see straight.

Industrial agriculture asks this question: "Why do small agricultural enterprises—either peasants in Europe and the Third World or family farmers in the United States—still exist?"[24] An answer: small farmers and their families are willing to exploit themselves to keep the farm alive. Distant cousins, friends of friends, in-laws, all will now and then help to fix fence, move cattle, spread manure, and put in hay, any of which can be just enough work for a small farm to make it from year to year, labor-wise.

The work can be wearing. Take manure spreading, for example. I remember standing calf-deep in shit, weeping in frustration at trying to load the manure spreader. I'd heap a wheelbarrow, wheel it to the sheep-barn door, and, with a slight shove, pop it up onto a plank that led to the spreader. Sometimes the wheel would knock the plank outside, more often than not bringing the wheelbarrow with it. If the wheelbarrow made it onto the plank, there was no guarantee that I'd get to the spreader, which, because of the slope, pitched at an angle.

A little moisture, whether from snow or shit, could slick the plank, causing it to slide, upending the wheelbarrow and sending me scrambling off one side or the other, not a few times into the spreader.

As an assignment in an "Introduction to Literature" course at the University of Scranton, I wrote a poem about cleaning the sheep barn. The instructor had asked us to write a parody of one of the poems that we'd read during the semester. I chose "The Red Wheelbarrow" by William Carlos Williams. It mentioned a wheelbarrow, I used a wheelbarrow, and that deep into the semester, cleaning the barn was one of the things I did when I wasn't reading or writing for class, so why not? I tried to put into words an experience I'd had all too often.

    it all depends
    on a blue wheel
    barrow
    beside the white calves
    and a plank
    slick with snow
    sliding
    on a shit
    spreader

Reading *Walden* back then stopped me cold. In the fourth paragraph, Thoreau described my father, an only male child, when he observes young men "whose misfortune it is to have inherited farms, houses, barns, cattle, and farming tools; for these are more easily acquired than got rid of." Who made my father a serf of the soil? Primogeniture, I assume, a father dying young, and a burdensome awareness of the work that had already been done to make the place. Thoreau's question, a barn at its heart, chilled me: "How many a poor immortal soul have I met well-nigh crushed and smothered under its load, creeping down the road of life, pushing before it a barn seventy-five feet by forty, its Augean stables never cleansed, and one hundred acres of land, tillage, mowing, pasture, and wood-lot!" I couldn't escape being my father's oldest son, despite my older half brothers. But I wasn't up to the challenge of shouldering a farm; I envisioned struggling with cultivating a "few cubic feet of flesh."[25]

When I was a kid, the lower barn was a dangerous place, an undiscovered country that fascinated me in an archeological way. I was always uncovering another piece of the farm's story: traces of bills and checks, fragments of newspapers, moldy machinery instructions. Over the years the barn had become the castoff spot for things that we weren't quite ready to toss. Most of what ended up inside slowly deteriorated. A lot was forgotten.

When I was in college, I sold most of what was in the barn to an antique dealer, effectively erasing the past; now whenever I visit a museum or stroll through an antique shop, I'm half afraid I'll happen on something that I first knew as a discovery in the lower barn. I not only sold memories, I destroyed them, treating them as unconnected pieces and scattering them into strange hands. Much of the stuff I just wanted to see survive, I reasoned, and no one was taking care of any of it. Now I wonder, would it have been possible to save it all? Was it worth saving? I sit here, and I cannot remember a quarter of what was there.

Memory is as much about space as time, an idea Wordsworth captures in *The Prelude* when he calls up childhood "spots of time." Such moments, he claims, can nourish and repair our "imaginative power," despite the fact that one may "need / Colours and words that are unknown to man / To paint" for others what one sees.[26] Too often, I think, memory refracts the light of the past and we color what we remember, dulling its sharp edges and blurring backgrounds. We tend memories as we might a garden, fencing and tilling, weeding and manuring, all to feed the narrative we know ourselves by.

The idea that memory is about space and time predates Wordsworth. In classical times, rhetoricians trained an orator to remember a speech by assigning to each part of it a room in the building where he would deliver his thoughts; just looking around would remind him of what he needed to offer next.[27] The building followed the speaker's line of reasoning. To think clearly, he had to know where he was, literally.

Curators structure museums this way. One walks through room after room, each often dedicated to a particular period; within each space, objects come into view according to a time line. The material history we touch allows us to feel the past, however briefly. We understand a cotton gin, measure the size of a slave's shackles, and examine how small the uniforms of long-gone armies are;

we heft a sword, load a muzzleloader, and wield a doctor's hacksaw. A tactile experience helps us to know what's gone, and what should be kept gone.

How do we remember what has passed? What is it that we recall when we write the past? Our names appear, maybe, buried in birth and death records, tax and bank documents, school and work papers, but even these signs mold away into an as-if-we-never-were anonymity. Even the material dry rots, the paper flaking, turning to dust. Once memory fails, what's left to tell that we passed this way but such "shards and remnants."[28] Given this, it's impossible, I suppose, to write a stable history—of anything. Beyond what little we can touch of the past, most of what we have to work with are what others have written, discourses, like this one, which are knowable only through other discourses, which have their own interests.

The lower barn stored much of the farm's memory: a horse-drawn plow and a horse-drawn McCormick corn-picker parked downstairs against the back wall; an early McCormick hay cutter, a cutter sleigh, and two sleds lay jumbled together upstairs; tossed on the bench were hand drills, blasting cap tins, and a shoe iron; nearby, milk cans stood next to a '44 Model A tractor; scattered in the half story: fainting couches, travel trunks, and a shattered spinning wheel. The barn accumulated stuff because someone thought that each piece might, just might, be used again; each thing was in decent shape when it landed there, but its usefulness slowly slipped into a past that awaited rediscovery, or oblivion.

Brought to the house, a few pieces survive. A claw-foot table—a long-ago gift?—now graces again the dining room; the French doors—their panes intact—hang nearby, joining dining room and parlor. A Dupont dynamite box collects magazines; a pair of opera glasses, found and lost once more, raises an unanswerable question: who in the farm's history attended the opera? Opera?

If you're not paying attention, the past can come back to haunt you. In 1970, the year Danny was born, we were putting the first addition on the cow barn. I was seven, the gopher who ran for hammers, nails, and bottles of beer. Neighbors would shout from the rafters what they needed and where it was. I'd walk the ladder a few steps and hand things up. After the frame was finished and the roof on, but before they poured the concrete floor, I used the dirt stalls to run my own construction site. I built roads and bridges and ran matchbox cars through two-inch pipes that would soon be linked as a vacuum line for the milking machine. One day, just before my quitting time, I backed half a dozen cars inside the pipes and left, abandoning my toy trucks and graders among piles of dirt and stone. A few days later, the floor was poured, the pipes put in place, the cars forgotten.

Around the time that the space shuttle *Challenger* blew up, in January 1986, the cars nearly wrecked me. At exactly the wrong time, they piled up in the milking machine's vacuum pump, cutting its capacity to almost zero. The milkers hardly worked; they fell from cows right and left, and it took hours, three times as long as usual, to finish milking. No one understood what was happening. My father had just had open-heart surgery, I had just started working on the obituary desk at the *Scranton Times*, and my oldest brother was working overtime as a pipe fitter. I'd milk the cows, drive an hour to work, record the dead, and come home to milk again.

I felt so frustrated that I couldn't think straight. The milkers wouldn't stay where I needed them to stay. They'd just fall. Or the cows would kick them away. The pulsators hardly made a sound. Cows got sick. Bobby and I accused each other of not milking right.

We pulled apart the vacuum pump: nothing. Then we uncoupled the pipe from the pump, and out popped a half dozen vintage cars.

On Memorial Day, 1989, I shattered a link between the land and us; I reduced a hundred-plus years of history to a heap of broken beams and roof tins.

I found in the garage two heavy chains and dragged them to the lower barn, where I wrapped one end around the post and beam at the joint of the first and second floors on the lower side. I dropped the other end outside through a gap in the planking. The second chain I hooked to the first and then to the underside of the tractor. I got on, hit the accelerator, and slowly let out the clutch. The chain tightened, and the barn stiffened, resisting; it didn't come tumbling down, as I thought sure it would. Tractor wheels dug into the driveway, tossing stone, raising dust.

My father appeared.

"What're you doing?" he said, anguished. "Get off that tractor!"

I didn't move, and I wouldn't climb down.

"Goddamn you," he shouted.

I looked at the horizon.

I popped the clutch, and the tractor lurched forward, bringing up the front wheels. The barn held. I did it again. My father ran, limping, inside the barn to the second story. While I maneuvered the tractor to pull from another angle, he undid the chain, and it clattered to the rock below.

"You're not gonna do it!" he called.

"It's coming down!"

I scooped up the chain, ran inside, and lashed it to post and beam. As I got on the tractor, I could hear the chain falling.

He stood at the gap, his face a mix of pain, confusion, and heartache. His hands shook as he lit a Lucky Strike.

During a silent struggle, with him pulling on my upper arm, I reattached the chain. By the time I got back to the tractor, the chain was hitting rock.

"This barn's coming down!" I screamed.

Four or five people had gathered on my brother's back deck, a few hundred yards away.

I grabbed my father's elbow and pulled him from the barn. He resisted, his old strength rising despite only six months since the triple bypass.

"Don't," he pleaded, tears in his eyes. "Don't."

I led him to the house.

"Stay inside!"

I slammed the door.

He sat at the kitchen table, watching as I pulled and pulled on the barn until the cinderblock gave way and the barn folded in on itself, broke apart, and collapsed.

My father sobbed. For a long time, years, he wouldn't talk to me. He would never say or listen to anything about the lower barn. When someone mentioned it, he left the room.

The cleanup took awhile. The tins were stored in the pig barn, and much of the scrap lumber was taken up the hill and burned. A few beams stretch across living-room ceilings somewhere. A bulldozer buried the rest right where the barn had stood. Back at school, I wasn't there to see it happen. A mound of grass marks the spot. The rock that had stood four feet high on its lower side is now level with the ground. The plum tree, once sacred: gone.

I think now that for my father saving the barn was more about the future than the past. He farmed when long-established assumptions about working the land were being tossed aside. Farming was caught up in a change that he knew was wrong, but he didn't have the arguments to assert how or why it was wrong. I stepped into this gap not knowing enough to save the barn, but I should have known enough to leave it alone. It meant something, at least to him, who would have known, more than the rest of us.

What world did I erase?

Was it black and white?

5

Other Places

Develop a critical awareness of the whole self, as well
as an understanding of the complexities of human
persons in diverse historical and social contexts.

—"Statement and Implementation of
Undergraduate Core Curricular Purpose"

Early on the first day of school in 1906, Bertha Conlogue, three months graduated from Pleasant Mount High School, left the house to walk the mile to Stone
School #7, where she would begin her first day as a teacher.[1] The walk was an
easy one: step a hundred yards down the hill, swing left onto Baxter Road, turn
right at the end, and walk two hundred yards along the Bethany Turnpike to the
one-room school. Focused on getting there—she had to open the place, light
the stove, and, well, worry—she didn't notice what she knew: that each side of
the road had been cleared of timber, hemlock mainly, the logs taken to prop up
mines in Forest City.

With no trees in the valley, Bertha may have been able to see the school
from the house: all that covered the ground on both sides of Johnson Creek
was a chaos of brush, briers, and stumps. Any other day, she may have shaken

her head at it and turned to glance at the backyard, where an ash shaded the woodshed. Beyond the stone wall that marked the yard stretched an apple orchard—about an acre of trees. Out front, beyond the lawn, stood a plum, a crabapple, and at least two McIntosh; nearby, tomatoes and squash ripened, dense with green. Along the stone wall on the lower side, between house and meadow, grew pear and apricot and rhubarb, roses and peonies. Up from the house, sheep grazed behind the garage; in the pasture beyond the barn wandered the cows, a half dozen, headed uphill, toward the woods. Haying had ended, thankfully. Summer, though, was all but over.

The school had been educating neighborhood children since its construction in 1840. Built of fieldstone and hemlock, likely collected on-site, the octagon-shaped school boasted wide-plank flooring and white beadboard walls and ceiling. During Bertha's time as teacher, her father, Peter, my great-grandfather, served off and on as a school board director, and she taught many of her neighbors' kids and her siblings Walter and Marie. A 1905–6 class photo captures the latter two among twenty-five other students of various ages lined up before the school's solid wood door.[2] Their surnames are familiar here today.

Bertha may not have willingly left teaching in 1911. In this year, when Pennsylvania revised its School Code, the state included a provision for "making qualifications for varying types of certificates."[3]

Bertha stepped into teaching when rural reformers, mainly urban Progressives, were demanding an end to the ungraded, one-room schoolhouse. Land-grant university educator Charles Galpin claims that the "social secret of the consolidated school" is that the "farm child socialized in the large school will break down the rough edges of the adult individualism and conservatism, as he goes back and forth from farm to school and school to farm." Folding the countryside firmly within the urban industrial economy, this re-education ripped less-progressive farmers from the land. A professor of agricultural economics at the University of Wisconsin, Galpin associates the reluctance to part with the small school with the mind of the "hoe-farmer," which is "ungraded, synthetic, massive, simple"; the "machine-farmer," however, is a "new cerebral type," who feels a "large range of intellectual intercourse, a constant enticement to a change of ideas," which meant purchasing the newest machinery and buying into the latest land-grant pronouncements.[4] School reform was farm reform.

Although anxious to undermine rural individualism and conservatism, Progressives like Galpin understood that erasing the one-room school would not happen overnight: "In all likelihood the little country school must be reckoned with for a generation, like the stove, the horse, the lamp, the candle."[5] In the case of Mount Pleasant Township, his prediction was on target. Of the township's twelve one-room schools in 1919, several, including Stone School #7, closed in 1928, a direct result of the conversion of Pleasant Mount Presbyterian Church into a public grade school. Consolidation of township schools took full effect in 1939, two years after a new high school opened in Pleasant Mount. The last one-room school, the Brick School, was shuttered in 1941, six months before the United States entered World War II. As schools closed, a pattern formed: the power to educate moved from the countryside to the nearest population center, in this case the village of Pleasant Mount, three miles from Stone School #7.[6]

Another wave of school consolidation broke in the early 1960s, when, to dismantle small districts, "sweeping organizational reforms were passed." In pursuit of "administrative efficiency," the state's Bureau of School District Reorganization "reduced the 2,056 districts with which it began to 742 by 1967, and to 501 by 1988." A result of this state mandate: the consolidated Pleasant Mount School merged in 1961 with Forest City area schools, five miles distant, to create Forest City Regional. Consolidation continues. In the wake of the 2008 economic meltdown, Pennsylvania governor Ed Rendell called for paring the number of school districts to one hundred.[7] The fewer the rough edges, the better . . .

When I was a first grader at Pleasant Mount, our teacher, Lourdes O'Neill, who also taught my father first grade, decided one March day that we should take a break from practicing reading and writing. She lined us up, marched us outside, and led us out of town on a two-mile trek to the Dix farm. Across the road from the Dix house and barn, under a rough lumber lean-to, with cords of wood stacked at each end, Ellis Dix explained how he made maple syrup. We looked into vats of clear sap, handled clear bottles of brown, and took bites of candy made in the shape of trees.

The Pleasant Mount School only went to fifth grade in those days; to start sixth grade I rode the school bus over the Moosic Mountains, a half-hour trip, to Forest City Regional, today still one of the state's smallest schools, population-wise, though it draws kids from three counties. Once there, I gradually turned to reading; soon I had earned a reputation as a bookworm.

Seventh-grade math class: I was squinting at the blackboard when Mrs. Marsicano shouted, "Well?"

She tapped a math problem, erasing spots of what may have been a two.

Sitting bolt upright, I looked at her, blank. She shot down the aisle, an open textbook pressed to her chest.

"Can't you hear?" she shouted, bending to catch my eye.

I stared at my hands.

"Well?" she said.

"I can't . . ."

"You'd rather read it in a book, wouldn't you?" She picked a paperback off the desk and slapped it back. "Answer me!"

I dropped my gaze, thinking I'd rather . . .

"Not everything's in a book!" she said.

Sick, I gaped.

"Listen, you," she said, lowering her voice. "I want the answer to that problem."

I squinted at the board. "I—I can't see it."

"Look!"

"I—I am."

Her face changed, and she stepped back. "You can't see that board?"

I shook my head.

She snapped shut the textbook. "You need glasses?"

I shrugged.

"Well, get them." She walked to the front, mumbling, "You better have them next time."

During lunch, we could step outside, into the parking lot behind the school. A pile of coal ash, for scattering in the lot after winter storms, stood to one side. The boys played king of the hill, the usual country kids versus city kids. Most country kids, like me, were farmers' sons; most of the city kids were sons of factory and construction workers, small-time businessmen, and teachers. In those days, the mid-1970s, the borough of Forest City had, maybe, 2,000 people, none of them miners. To put that in perspective: in 1906, the population topped 4,000, with more than 1,300 miners, all male, working the mines.[8]

The top of the heap, I knew, would be occupied by the powerful, but what I couldn't see then was that battling for a pile of waste distracted us from the damage at our feet: abandoned mines, coal strippings, culm banks, high unemployment, poverty, bare-bones schooling.

In those days, I saw reading and farming through the eyes of my family: as separate spheres, one active, the other passive; one about making time, the other about marking time. For a long while, farming and reading ran parallel courses; when I wasn't involved in one, I was actively engaged in the other. This never troubled me much, though I enjoyed reading more than milking cows and spreading manure. But when reading and farming began colliding, my view of things changed. I started seeing farming through the eyes of a reader; I started seeing reading through the eyes of a farmer.

I first read Willa Cather's short story "Neighbour Rosicky" in an American lit class at the University of Scranton.

The title character, a Bohemian tailor turned farmer, has a heart attack while clearing thistles from an alfalfa field; he dies the next day.

I recalled the story the next summer, when my father, out baling hay in mid-July heat, suffered his first heart attack. Later he said that when the pain started, he climbed under the tractor to escape the sun. Every time he heard me bringing an empty wagon, he pulled himself up and climbed into the tractor seat. I imagine him struggling up, one hand reaching for the wheel, the other clutching his shirtfront.

Everyone unloading hay at the barn kept complaining at me about how long it took for the loads to come in, so I noticed immediately that this next wagon was only half full. I pulled alongside.

"What's taking so long?" I shouted over the roar of both tractors. I pointed at the sky. "Supposed to rain tonight!"

"Pin's shearing is all!"

Not waiting for a reply, he eased off the clutch. The tractor lurched forward, and he turned to watch the baler eat the windrow.

He may have been gripping the wheel too hard or leaning too far forward in the seat, but I didn't notice. I parked in the shade along the stone wall and read, glancing now and then at the baler, which seemed to be working fine.

That winter, in a hospital room just before his open-heart surgery, I kept looking at his hands. I couldn't get over how white they were—nothing like the brown they'd always been. I thought of Rosicky's hand, a "warm brown human hand."[9]

Where you learn matters.

Before her death in 2007, poet Barbara Hoffman, who spent her work life teaching in the Marywood English department, regularly asked her students to write about the dead. In late September, she and her freshmen composition students left the Liberal Arts Center, trekked beyond the Science Center, and passed into Forest Hill Cemetery. After they negotiated the meandering path into and out of Meadow Brook ravine, they gathered on a patch of macadam near the first tombstones. Barbara was short, so she likely stepped up the hill from everyone as she instructed them to each read a different stone, sit beside it, and imagine in a short essay the life of the person buried there. This exercise, which she did every fall in each of three comp classes, had such an impact on how students saw the world that several pitched in to purchase a tombstone for her, which they presented to her on her fiftieth birthday. They placed the stone on the wooded and winding path that she and her students used to cross the ravine.

Established in 1876, Forest Hill invites visitors to linger among the dead. Towering hemlocks, oaks, and maples shade the stones; flowering trees bloom all spring and summer and the fall colors are spectacular. Vaults house some dead; most lie under simple stones; others are buried beneath elaborate art-work: Celtic crosses and marble logs, angels, and lambs. Nondenominational, Forest Hill was laid out to "instill healing truths, of natural death and rebirth, in the cycle of the seasons." With intellectual roots in the transcendentalists' turn to nature, the rural cemetery made the "place of the dead . . . a school for the living."[10]

Modern cemeteries often have no trees, denying shade and shelter to mourners; the markers, flat for the convenience of lawn mowers, don't assert themselves. The grass is too neat, the rows too straight, the horizon too far. One sees a green desert, not a place of rest; a warehouse, not a church. What tales can their dead tell?

Forest Hill and Marywood share the same space. A national arboretum, the college campus offers views of the mountains that form the west side of the valley.[11] Eastern hemlock, white oak, and sugar maple line sidewalks. Kousa dogwood, crabapple, hydrangea, and lilac blooms make the grounds rich in color in spring and early summer. Graceful contours and green spaces invite students to hang out; they read dead poets, sunbathe, play catch. Even neighborhood place names evoke pastoral nostalgia: Green Ridge, Grandview, Richmont, Woodlawn, Fairfield.

From my office windows, I study the heart of campus and know that my reading and my lived experience are too often at odds. I teach *Tintern Abbey* in a classroom that looks out onto a parking lot. I fly to a conference in San Francisco to hear someone in a windowless ballroom read a paper on Thoreau. My office computer brings me, out of nowhere, the Association for the Study of Literature and Environment Listserv, a virtual community that piles up messages about how people define nature, how they frame debates about the environment, how they think through issues of sustainability. I read these messages on a screen fed by electricity from the Berwick nuclear power plant. I hit the delete key, again and again.

You could walk campus and not know the violence that marked the school's early history. When the Sisters, Servants of the Immaculate Heart of Mary (IHM), first purchased property from the Pennsylvania Coal Company, on 1 March 1895, the company sold only surface rights; it kept all mineral rights, a fact that haunts the university to this day. A year after the college's founding, in 1916, a Pennsylvania Coal mining engineer informed the congregation that "the Academy will now experience for about one year, much annoyance and shock from blasting," about which the Sisters "need not have the slightest fear. At no time will your lives or property be in the slightest peril. Apparently, it would seem otherwise, but have no alarm."[12] Cold comfort, it turned out. In the years following, the campus, completely undermined, lived with the effects of mine subsidence and mine fires through the 1920s and '30s, thanks to Pennsylvania Coal.

In 1900, just after the IHM broke ground for Mount Saint Mary's, a school for coal miners' daughters and the forerunner of Marywood, the Lackawanna and Wyoming Valley Railroad "announced a plan to extend its line from Scranton to Carbondale on a proposed route that cut directly across the Green Ridge property and ran almost alongside the site of the new building-in-progress."[13]

The railroad would have interrupted a place devoted to study, a place quiet only because its usefulness to Pennsylvania Coal had ended. With the congregation's plans threatened, the IHM Mother Superior confronted railroad officials, who backed down.

In 2009, the university reminded its employees of this confrontation when it sent us a Christmas card that depicted a bluish rendering of Our Lady of Victory, the campus shrine that marks the conflict. Snowflakes dot the card's gray border, and the gray word "Joy" is written in the lower right corner. The card's close-up frames a crowned Mary sitting next to a standing Jesus, a five- or six-year-old who wears his own crown. Built in 1905, the roofed statue stands at the site where railroad surveyors were seen platting the route, not 150 feet from the school's construction site.[14]

Trains interrupt quiet moments in many American literary texts. Exploring this trope in *The Machine in the Garden*, Leo Marx defines simple and complex pastoral. Moving in one direction, the former embodies a nostalgic yearning for a simpler place, a simpler time, a "naïve, anarchic primitivism"; complex pastoral, however, "has three spatial stages. It begins in a corrupt city, passes through a raw wilderness, and then, finally, leads back toward the city."[15] Each version, simple and complex, distinguishes between here and there; to survive here, we hope to restore ourselves there. The pastoral fantasy creates places where we can go to re-create ourselves, often parks: Fenway, Disney, Yellowstone. As long as we know those places exist, we can go on making malls, mining coal, and clear-cutting timber. What we do here, we tend to think, doesn't matter; those other places are there when we need them. If this is the story we stick to, it's the wrong one, a tragedy. As others have noted, to restore ourselves and the world we need to re-story it. And complex pastoral's irony isn't enough; we need people who can write—and read—with a georgic, an agrarian, sensibility.[16] Our stories, whether taught in school or not, tell us as much about the work we do in the world as they do about our attempts to escape from it.

We tend not to see this work. For example, a 1910 postcard pinned to the bulletin board in my office depicts the Our Lady of Victory shrine in a glade surrounded by second-growth birch. The card remakes Pennsylvania Coal lands into a pastoral idyll; with only the card as evidence, you'd never know that anyone ever turned a shovel here. Describing the first day of classes at Marywood, 8 September 1915, the student newspaper at the time, the *Marywood Chronicle*, "recalled that in the eleven o'clock English lesson, 'instead of the formal, dry rhetoric, the class was invited out for a walk and was told to keep eyes and ears open. It was a beautiful sunshiny day, and we walked all around the grounds, drinking in the beauty of the fair scene.'"[17] The fair scene, though, is not the land's only story. By the time the IHM halted the railroad, the land had long been subdued, stripped of its original forest, farmed, and mined. Surrounded today by sidewalks and buildings, the shrine is as much a memorial to this latter-day "victory" as any other.

In the early years of the Great Depression, just as the college gained its feet, the ground gave way: "Newly paved asphalt roads buckled and began to show deep 'pot holes.' . . . To further complicate matters, a cave hole about forty feet deep broke open . . . revealing a mine fire that had been smoldering for some time. Fumes from the fire were invading the entire region, so there were complaints from the neighborhood and fear of the fire's spreading." The fire in Meadow Brook ravine started in a trash dump whose contributors included Dunmore Borough, community members, and Marywood maintenance crews. Caretakers and good neighbors all. So much for *Sanctitas, Scientia, Sanitas.*[18]

On 16 October 1906, as Bertha Conlogue negotiated her first fall as the teacher at Stone School #7, more than six hundred educators, businessmen, and publishers met in Scranton to celebrate the fifteenth anniversary of the founding of the for-profit International Correspondence Schools (ICS).[19] ICS grew out of a question-and-answer column in the pages of the weekly journal *Colliery Engineer and Metal Miner*; the column mainly answered technical questions from men seeking to pass exams to become certified coal miners. The flood of questions grew so large so quickly that the paper's editor, Thomas Foster, started a "School of Mines, using the correspondence method." Enrolling its first student in its Complete Coal Mining Course on 16 October 1891, the Scranton-based ICS soon evolved into a major distance-education provider.[20] So successful was ICS that by World War II the schools had caught the attention of the U.S. War Department, which granted ICS the "contract to develop the department's training manuals." Aided by Rural Free Delivery and a national rail system, ICS advertised itself as an institution devoted to its students' self-improvement, at an affordable price.[21]

In for-profit education, the student-teacher relationship is straightforward; it's a buyer-seller transfer of information. At ICS's birthday party, for example, Foster announced that he runs a "commercial enterprise," which means that "to get new business, we must satisfy our customers." Customer satisfaction demanded that "courses are all prepared from a utilitarian standpoint . . . [the student] desires to put the knowledge obtained into immediate practical use." The same holds true today. In a 2009 article defending for-profits, Michael Seiden, former president of the for-profit Western International University, makes it clear that "for-profit universities view their students as customers, and to attract and retain those customers, degree programs and curricula must be market-driven."[22]

It's at this point that for-profits and I part company. Not so much concerned with "customer" satisfaction, an education grounded in the liberal arts raises uncomfortable questions about work, questions that markets ignore. For-profits don't bother to—or maybe they refuse to—place work in its wider contexts: How does one's work affect others? The land? To what degree? Does one's work enhance or hinder the flourishing of lives and lands? Even these very general, moral questions about work are rarely raised in workplaces, let alone more specific questions about the impact of individual workplace practices. These hard questions, however, and the choices they imply, must be asked, and answered. To ask the best questions takes guidance and a lot of time spent reading and reflecting. An education solely focused on the student as employee doesn't take the time; an education focused on the student as human being must make the time.

Today's for-profits limit students' access to such questions by paying lip service to their degree programs' "general-education components": philosophy, history, literature. And outright dismissal of these disciplines is not far from the surface. Note how Seiden's sentence construction sells the for-profit model: "Students are motivated to earn their degrees because they aspire to upward mobility in their careers. Therefore, while containing the general-education components that traditional institutions and accrediting agencies view as essential, the curricula at most for-profit colleges and universities consist of courses that students' employers demand." His reference to general education ends up in a dependent clause, a nonessential element of the sentence; if it weren't for "accrediting agencies," I'm pretty sure that these courses would give way completely to "courses that students' employers demand." General education, apparently, has nothing to do with the workplace. The admission Seiden then makes is pretty frightening: the "for-profits' drive for revenue and profitability, and fear of not attracting or losing students, can certainly lead some managers to pressure faculty and staff members to offer a 'user friendly' approach to academics: dumbing down the curriculum, inflating grades, and the like." Welcome to the "nightmare" of the "anti-intellectual university."[23]

ICS also played up the possibility of upward class mobility, in the bootstrap tradition of Horatio Alger stories.[24] And like today's for-profits, ICS advertised its commitment to working people, its business orientation, and its lessons' practicality. In line with later moneymaking models, the "unique but efficient methods [of] this great industrial university has made it easy for parents to realize their hopes concerning the education of their boys and girls." Hopes ran high. By 1906, ICS had mailed lessons to more than nine hundred thousand people, an "army greater than that of the Civil War."[25]

A distance-education provider, ICS "annihilated space," bringing student and teacher, each located no matter where, into close contact via the page. Foster links this erasure of space to the spatial metaphor of class mobility, to the lure of an elusive pot of gold: "An I.C.S. mining student may begin his studies in the coal mines of Pennsylvania, continue them while prospecting in Alaska, and finish them in the gold fields of South Africa." To strike it rich, he argues, just keep digging, here, there, everywhere. Completing a course in mining offers ICS students, apparently, the chance to become forerunners of today's globals, for whom the "world appears comparatively limitless," or, at least, "mobals . . . transnational migrants" who are "drawn by perceptions of opportunity and realities of need" to leave the familiar and prospect where they can.[26] Either way, they're ill-equipped to deal with the moral dimensions of digging all over the place.

Welcoming an audience of ICS celebrants that included muckraker S. S. McClure and United Mineworkers leader John Mitchell, mayor of Scranton J. Benjamin Dimmick argued for the moral and "political necessity of education." In order to "safeguard life, liberty, and the pursuit of happiness," Dimmick claimed, American society "demands not simply strength of purpose, but also clearness of vision—clearness of vision in an atmosphere in which

Fig. 9 ICS Railway School instructors at work, ca. 1902. Courtesy of Penn Foster.

the great orb of truth is not always easily discernible." The mayor identified four areas that "a citizenship with trained intelligence" must think through: (1) "finance"; (2) "the economic merits of the so-called trusts"; (3) "the problem of the negro"; and (4) "the great principle of federal supervision—a supervision which, in my judgment, is destined at no distant date to touch almost every walk of life." This last item alludes, I imagine, to Progressive-era regulation and federal intervention in the 1902 anthracite coal strike. Bottom line: the mayor wants a "trained electorate . . . that can first mentally decide, and then morally determine."[27] He assumes, it seems, that ICS practicality can mold anyone into a moral American.

Not long after, Foster echoed Dimmick, declaring that ICS exerts a "Moral Influence" because its representatives induce men "to give up idleness and spend their spare time in study." Going a step further, Foster asserted that across the world the ICS "plan of teaching . . . can educate and make better men and citizens of working people." Two years later, however, ICS publications asserted that "we are not aiming to train the mind, but to give the student such information regarding the principles, theory, and practice as he can use with the position he is aiming to fill." In short, ICS had no interest in "moral uplift."[28]

Twenty-first-century for-profit institutions, which enroll 11 percent of U.S. college students, are also more interested in making money than exerting a moral influence.[29] For example, John Sperling, founder of the for-profit University of Phoenix, defines his institution strictly as a business. In doing so, he explicitly rejects spatial concepts near and dear to the heart of the liberal arts: "This is a corporation. . . . Coming here is not a rite of passage. We are not trying to develop [students'] values systems or go in for that 'expand their minds' bullshit." But then again, an MTV ad proclaims the Phoenix motto, "An educated world is a better world."[30] Advertising moral uplift is fine, I suppose; practicing it wastes time and money.

Sperling does, however, see the University of Phoenix as a "force for social good," not because it "support[s] his causes" but because it's an "enterprise consistent with his left-of-center worldview." The former history professor once poured money into cloning his dog, something that began as a joke. His attempt to turn a profit from the venture failed; his cloning company, Genetic Savings & Clone, went belly-up, only to be resurrected as BioArts International. Sperling also founded Arcadia Biosciences, which conducts research into sustainable farming practices, and the Kronos Longevity Research Institute, which engages in anti-aging research. Sperling's projects have paid off nicely: the man's personal wealth in 2006 topped $1.3 billion.[31]

A strictly business approach to education has gotten for-profit colleges into trouble with the U.S. government. In 2003, whistleblowers accused the University of Phoenix of "paying recruiters on the basis of how many students they could get to enroll—in violation of federal rules. The charge resulted in a nearly $10-million fine from the U.S. Department of Education." A Government Accountability Office undercover investigation discovered that four out of fifteen for-profit colleges "encouraged fraudulent practices, such as encouraging students to submit false information about their financial status." At all fifteen colleges, recruiters "made some type of deceptive or otherwise questionable statement to undercover applicants, such as misrepresenting the applicant's likely salary after graduation and not providing clear information about the college's graduation rate."[32]

The for-profit crime that often goes unremarked, however, is that about 95 percent of Phoenix instructors work part-time, primarily online, and teach from a common syllabus and texts. Phoenix responds that it hires teacher/practitioners, although it's tough to know whether Phoenix values the practical reading skills of the English professor as much as the practical selling skills of the advertising manager. Unfortunately, Phoenix practitioners graduate in six years only 16 percent of their students, compared with the 55 percent average "across all American universities."[33] So who benefits?

American business likes Phoenix. In a December 2009 report, the Committee for Economic Development (CED), a not-so-nonpartisan gathering of corporate heads and university presidents, praises Phoenix for its teacher training programs, which "familiarize the faculty with Phoenix's culture and practices."[34] Critical of the rest of higher education's failure to adapt to changing times, the report encourages the "application of greater openness through digital technologies," which would include online learning. CED claims that American colleges and universities lag behind other service industries, namely finance and entertainment, in the degree to which they openly disseminate information. Information, by the way, is "open" when few or no restrictions are placed on access to it and when users can "change the information, repurpose, remix, and redistribute it." Would these same folks who advocate ending copyright and intellectual property laws ever propose an end to patent protections? It's unlikely. Phoenix and CED remind me of Foster declaring in 1906 that at ICS "the work of the teacher is made more effective by the invention, by the advertising knowledge, and by the executive and organizing power of the business man."[35] Maybe soon the U.S. Census Bureau won't need to count professors.

Today's teachers are not helping themselves, if the 2008 Modern Language Association (MLA) convention, held in San Francisco, is any indication. At the session "Why Teach Literature Anyway?" a well-known scholar of American literature read a paper titled "Maybe We Shouldn't." In introducing his talk, he mentioned that he didn't enter the profession to teach; he wanted only to write about literature. He certainly wasn't interested, he said, in talking about *The Scarlet Letter* to a bunch of nineteen-year-olds, year in and year out, a remark that brought scattered, and maybe bewildered, laughs from the audience. This scholar pointed out the class divide that higher education promotes: as tuitions rise, only the wealthiest in the nation gain access to higher education, which is required for higher-paying jobs, which perpetuates a vicious cycle. True enough, but he didn't mention his own privileged position within this cycle, one shared by many in the audience, including me. He also didn't acknowledge that his state's taxpayers afford him space and time to write about literature without having to deal with nineteen-year-olds, people he leaves to others to educate, presumably less "productive" colleagues in his department, or poorly paid graduate students and adjuncts, the equivalent of Phoenix practitioners. His remarks' disdain for teaching was amazing, given my wife's testimony about his being a great teacher. In far too many places, or so it seems, good teaching has become a footnote to scholarship.[36] And service? What service?

The 2009 MLA convention, which was held in Philadelphia, offered a session of the same title; big names in the profession attracted an overflow crowd to 201-B, a cavernous, windowless room that was once part of the Reading Railroad terminal. In introducing the speakers, the session chair, John Paul Riquelme (Boston University), joked that as "a poststructuralist . . . [he] doesn't believe in the personal"; he then announced that the father of panelist Jonathan Culler (Cornell University) had ignited his passion for English Romantic literature and that he—Riquelme—had been a grad student with panelist Jean Howard (Columbia University). Small world.[37] About the session, the *Chronicle of Higher Education* noted, "Simple title, tough question—and one that none of the panelists really knew how to answer."[38] If big-name professors cannot answer this question, why should any of us go to an English class?

It's not surprising that Plato would banish poets from his republic: they'd see too many of its details, pay too much attention to its effects on individuals, and warn too readily about its insistence on ignoring the human tendency not to see that things, well, fall apart. In our less-than-perfect world, literature reminds us of our partiality, and brings us face to face with our imperfect nature. Instead of absolutes, abstractions, and ideal forms, literature points us to the concrete, the contextual, the idiosyncratic. Here we live; from here, we dream.

In offering us a place from which to observe how we treat each other and the world, literature encourages us to judge what we see, especially what we'd rather not see. Without its insistence on sharpening our vision, we'd wander in the fog of everyday experience, able only to see the ground at our feet. Making the familiar strange and the strange familiar, a great poem, novel, or play places one with the other.

Like the sign says, stop, look, listen. Otherwise, get run over.

In 2009, Marywood removed teaching and learning from their human contexts. Revising the faculty handbook, a committee redlined the idea that the "responsibility of the teacher as a guide and friend properly extends beyond the walls of the classroom."[39] Their fear—and it was fear—was that the language suggested a relationship that shouldn't happen: teachers and students should not be bedfellows. Of course. But to confine teaching and learning to the classroom—whether real or virtual—is to misunderstand education. Further, the "teacher as a guide and friend" describes how knowledge is passed on, through human connection. If neither the teacher nor the student is in a receptive frame of mind, a friendly frame of mind, nothing happens. Just as one trusts a guide on a walk through unfamiliar woods or a friend through a life crisis, one must trust the teacher for help. Without trust, learning ends, devolving quickly into an exchange of information, a buyer-seller interaction. If learning is merely mining for information, or if teaching is just a transfer of knowledge, then a school can save a lot of people a lot of trouble simply by mailing its stockpile of "knowledge" to students COD.

Teachers can be dangerous. In *Protagoras*, an early Platonic dialogue, young Hippocrates rousts Socrates out of bed to come with him to speak to Protagoras, a famous Sophist, the first to demand a "regular fee" for his services. In no rush, Socrates, who "kept no school, and took no fees," questions Hippocrates about his motives in running to this teacher: "You cannot know to whom you are entrusting your soul,—whether it is to something good or to something evil."[40] Unconcerned, Hippocrates points out that Protagoras is the best at what he, Hippocrates, wants: a practical education in eloquence, which, he hopes, will vault him to the top in politics. If only Socrates would put in a good word for him . . .

After introducing Hippocrates to Protagoras, Socrates sparks a debate with the latter about virtue. Can it be taught? The Sophist is sure that it can be and Socrates doubts it, but by the end of their conversation they have switched positions. The debate convinces Socrates that virtue is knowledge, which makes it teachable. So is virtue knowledge? And if it is, can it be taught?

These are urgent questions at a Catholic university that aims to educate the whole person, body and soul.

On 18 November 2009, Marywood president Sister Anne Munley discussed human trafficking with faculty members in a class titled "Greater Expectations."

She had with her several novels and memoirs, which she encouraged us to assign to get undergraduates to understand systems that buy and sell humans, arm children for combat, and press people into slavery. She stressed teaching in a global context: we should remind students of the links between their communities and others, between here and there, the familiar and the strange.

I then left the library to attend in the Liberal Arts Center a workshop about learning assessment targeted at faculty members in the College of Liberal Arts and Sciences. I arrived five minutes late, in a rush. The room was packed with people, all required to be there, and the only open seat close by was up front. As I sat down, Frank, a new psychology professor, walked back and forth before us, showing us how to measure students' learning. He wrote on the board: "learning objectives," "course objectives," "assessment measures," "=learning." He circled each term and drew lines to connect them.

I thought, I've heard this . . .

"Okay," Frank said. "Give me a learning objective." He scanned the room, smiling. "Anybody."

From the back, Phil, a philosophy professor, said, "To make better people."

I grinned; others laughed.

"What's wrong with that?" he said. "Isn't that what we want?"

Some of us exchanged glances. I thought, yeah. But I wasn't sure others would agree.

"All right," Frank said, writing the phrase on the board. "We can do that."

He turned. "What is a better person? How can we know?"

"They're honest," Phil said.

Frank wrote.

Phil went on, "They don't steal or . . ."

"Okay," Frank broke in, "how can we measure this?"

"That's where I lose it," Phil said. "Every time."

"Watch this," Frank said, and went on to list course objectives and assessment measures.

"See?" he said.

No one did, so he called on Erin, an English professor, to name a course she taught.

"Renaissance literature."

"And what do you want students to learn in that class?"

Erin smiled. "Uh, how to read would be nice."

People laughed.

"I do want them to be better readers," she said. "And I want them to know something about the Renaissance." She paused. "But not everything I want can be measured. Appreciation. Empathy."

Frank pointed at her. "Ah, but we can measure that. Sorta. Indicators are what we need."

I missed the rest, ducking from the room early to gather folders and binders for a Rank and Tenure Committee meeting. We were to evaluate two tenure applications and a promotion file . . .

All education can do is point people toward virtue; it cannot stamp them with it. Education—which is not synonymous with schooling—is about awareness, about paying close attention, which means thinking critically about ourselves and the world in which we find ourselves. The hope of a liberal arts education is that reading—wide and deep—enhances a person's powers to think with empathy, feel with compassion, and respond with appreciation to what's around him.

Would he be more likely to treat the world better? Maybe, maybe.

I don't recall reading books in earnest until I was in junior high, about the time when I was drafted to help milk the cows. What I read then was mainly history, particularly about wars, especially World War II; almost every time my Uncle Jimmy, a World War II vet, drove in from New Jersey, he brought me a grocery bag full of books with titles like *The Longest Day, Iwo Jima, Guadalcanal Diary.* He never mentioned his own service, but years later I found out that he flew missions in the Pacific, off the aircraft carrier *Bonhomme Richard.* At the end of the war, he flew in formation above the *Missouri* as the Japanese signed the surrender papers.

In junior high, I was responsible for carrying pails of milk to the milk house while my father and oldest brother milked our forty or so cows. Between trips, I'd read all I could from a paperback—maybe a page or two—as I sat on the empty pail, tilting the book to the nearest light. Sometimes I'd jump to catch a milker or I'd be told to scrape shit from the barn floor, but I was usually allowed to read as long as the pail was empty. When I entered high school, my father recruited me to milk, and my reading time narrowed to before and after chores.

In summer, when we were putting hay in the barn, I read between loads, which came at irregular intervals, and I often read several pages at a clip while everyone else joked and smoked or drank beer. With a T-shirt matted to my back and perspiration running my face, I sat in the door of the old chicken house, a few feet from the haymow door. My old paperbacks are still marked with sweat and fingerprints. If a book was particularly good, I waited until I heard the elevator clanking or for someone to shout my name before I moved. Every so often, someone had to swipe a book from my hands, tearing me from whatever world I was imagining. Tossing bales onto the elevator, I had time to think about what I'd been reading, and when the load was finished, I wasted no time finding my place again.

If I were sent to the field to rake or ted hay, I'd chafe at the interruption. But I'd bring along a paperback, just in case I had to hang around to roll the outside windrow or to bring a wagonload of hay to the barn. While I drove the tractor, I kept the book stored in the toolbox or under the seat.

One time, while raking the outside windrow in Woodchuck Grove, a hay-field at the Other Place, I tried reading "Song of Myself" while driving the trac-tor. I'd catch a few lines, look up, catch a few more lines, look up, and adjust the tractor's path, unaware of the windrow rolling into a crooked line behind me. Near an apple tree, where two rocks blocked a straight path, I spun the steering wheel, only to have *Leaves of Grass* slip from my grasp. I spent ten minutes tearing apart piles of hay in search of it. Gone. That winter, when I broke open bales to feed the cows, I looked for pages, but never found a word.

My parents noticed me reading, of course, and their reactions seemed a mix of indifference and exasperation. It may have been good that their kid was learning something, but chores couldn't wait. Though the farm stayed in busi-ness, it was never prosperous, and I always had the sense that it was ready to fall apart at any moment. We hired no steady help, so keeping me busy, I later realized, was pretty important. I was skilled labor, after all. Back then, my par-ents never asked about what I read, so I always thought that they didn't really care whether I read, and I had the nagging feeling that they thought reading a waste of time.

But they surprised me on my sixteenth birthday. It was early August, and I was tedding hay when my mother pulled the car off the red-shale road, got out, and stood at the edge of the field. Relieved at the interruption, I stopped the tractor, the tedder still running, jolting, spinning in place. It was hot and sweat ran from under my cap. I looked for a jug of ice water.

"Daddy and I wanted to give you this for your birthday," she said, handing me a copy of *War and Remembrance.* Inside she had penned the date and "Love, Mom and Dad."

Swallows chattered overhead. Around the field hay lay scattered; in the center, though, rows of green reached the far end.

I handed back the book. "Hold onto it," I said. "I don't want to get it dirty."

"You know," she said, against the rumble of the tractor, "we're really proud of you."

"Yeah."

Sweat stung my eyes.

She shielded her own and looked at the field, the tedder, and then the book.

"Daddy wants you in the Twenty-Acre Lot when you're done here."

"Yeah," I said.

I pointed at the novel. "I'll look at that when I get to the house."

The irony escaped me then: a war widow had just given me *War and Remembrance.* My mother's first husband, Bobby Weaver, was declared missing in action in Korea after a Chinese infantry attack overwhelmed his unit not long before the ceasefire. When my mother received the telegram, she was living in Carbondale with two babies under the age of two and a mine fire burning beneath her, a fire that slowly spread, eventually forcing them to flee to Scranton.[41]

While I was growing up, whenever an article appeared in the newspaper about Korean War POWs, she would read it carefully, mention it to me, and sit in silence for a minute or so. On Memorial Days, she stood in the park in Carbondale to hear the names of the war dead.

When the Korean War Memorial was dedicated, on 27 July 1995, my mother and my two half brothers joined a bus trip to Washington, D.C. People thronged the Mall. In his speech on that hot day, President Clinton noted that "thousands of Americans who were lost in Korea to this day have never been accounted for. . . . We have not forgotten our debt to them or to their families and we will never stop working for the day when they can be brought home."[42] Just as the bus was about to pull away from the curb in front of the Lincoln Memorial, my mother happened to glance out the window to see a woman holding a sign that read "Seeking Info about Lt. Price 109th Infantry." My mother forgot to breathe: Price was Bobby Weaver's commanding officer; Weaver was Price's radioman. She made her way outside. My brothers refused to leave the bus.

My father never enjoyed seeing me sitting for long stretches. He wanted me doing something. Scanning the newspaper just before or after chores was okay, but books were a different story. While I was reading, he would sometimes tell me to "shake my ass" or to "get some ambition." I didn't often jump on command. Reading was fun—and its subversive nature made it even more appealing. Offering me glimpses of other places, what I read taught me how other people thought about one another and the world. Staying still, I could unearth some answers.

Reading became more complex when I started noticing connections between what I was reading and what I was doing. For example, when I hunted woodchucks, I took a book. Hunting was a legitimate excuse to be away from the barn, and waiting for woodchucks was an exercise in sitting still. Why not read? On bright, late summer afternoons, I'd sit under a tree on the sidehill above the barn, paging through, say, *A Bridge Too Far*, a rifle beside me, heat waves shimmering against the mountains before me. I had no categories then to know—really know—what I was reading. One moment, all I saw was a book about soldiers killing soldiers; the next, I watched a woodchuck bleed, gasp, go limp.

You never get a good look at your place until you see it through others' eyes. Absorbing *The Unsettling of America* (1977) felt like reading my own mind. Wendell Berry gave form to ideas that I could then only half express. I could hardly believe that someone else's view of the world—at least of farming—could come so close to my own. More than anything else, and what has really stayed with me since, is that Berry introduced me to passionate, solid argumentation. And he connected what he was writing to what he was living.

Reading and writing revealed to me more and more what I was thinking, and they helped me to place myself in context. After Berry's book, I started reading more widely, and realized, of course, that many people have powerful arguments about many issues—some hard to answer. This in itself was unsettling.

Whereas before reading offered a secure vantage point from which to see places beyond the hills around me, now it brought me—more importantly—to opposing perspectives from which I learned to see myself.

While I was in college in the 1980s, I drove over the Moosic Mountains to the University of Scranton, an hour away. I still did chores, but I'm not sure that I was much help to my father. It was always obvious that there was more to do around the farm. And though we didn't usually work together, one labor we did share was pulling leaves from the pasture spring at the Other Place, a name long ago given to an eighty-acre farm my great-grandfather had purchased in 1889.

Surrounded by solid rock, the spring flows from the base of a sidehill. The wet ground slopes toward the line fence—rusting barbed wire and old locust posts set into a fallen stonewall. The spring isn't deep, maybe two feet, but it never stops running, no matter how dry the year. At the bottom is a stainless steel strainer attached to a copper pipe, which runs underground to the wooden trough along the fence. We never brought a shovel with us; we scooped out the leaves by hand.

Once the water cleared, we worked at the trough, dredging up twigs and leaves that had settled there since the springtime before. The water was cold, cold. Everything came up black, and we tossed handfuls of muck over the wall. The trough was six or seven feet long and eighteen inches wide, held together with iron. Older than my father, the planking was green and smelled of nearby hemlocks. My grandfather nailed it together one day after he and his father had buried the pipe to the spring. I imagined the boards new-cut, bright, sharp-edged.

My father and I soon herded heifers and dry cows up over the hill from home, across the road, and into the pasture. They crowded down the lane, swung around the old barn foundation, and took off across the pasture, the heifers raising their tails, breaking free, some heading for the gate into the big pasture, some striking out for the trough. We watched them for a few minutes, my father pointing out which ones were due first. Over the summer, we checked them every week or ten days, more often when one was near to calving.

One July day, my father said to me, "Go check on them at the Other Place."

He was replacing a knife in a cutter-bar.

"One due?" I said.

I picked up a rivet.

"I checked them yesterday," he said, tightening the vise. "Counted only nineteen."

"A cow due?"

He grabbed a ball peen hammer. "Second one from the south door. Lower side."

I tried to picture her.

"Here," he said. "Hold that end while I get this goddamn rivet in."

I held the cutter-bar.

"Bring salt," he said, pounding the rivet, sparks flying. "And don't forget to count them."

"Yeah, yeah."

Before heading up the hill, I found loops of baler twine, poured some salt into a plastic pail, and stuffed a book in my back pocket.

Searching the shade in the Big Pasture's upper back corner, under the old maples there, I hoped to see a newborn slumbering, its mother standing contentedly nearby. No such luck. The cow was calving.

After putting out salt for the others, I strolled over to her, upended the pail, dropped the book on top, and started lacing together the baler twine.

With the cow down, I tied the twine to the calf's legs and started pulling. The calf came hard. I sat in last fall's leaves and dug in my heels. The cow arched her back, groaned, and swung her head. I pulled, the strings burning my palms. A nose appeared. As she pushed again, I pulled. The calf's head came free, the tongue lolling. An eye blinked. The cow rested a minute, pushed, and the calf slipped out. A heifer. I wiped her mouth and nose and dragged her before her mother. The cow immediately began licking her, the calf rocking with each swipe. Pretty soon, other cows arrived, stood, stared. One or two bawled. The mother struggled to her feet, afterbirth plopping behind her. It wasn't long before she had the calf licked to a bright black and white. Not quite dry, but not wet.

After reading Henry James for a while, I grabbed the calf, picked her up, and started for the gate. The cow followed, bawling. When her calf answered, she only bellowed louder. Pretty soon the whole herd was with us.

A new calf can kick, so I had to stop a few times to get a grip on her and the pail. Every time I stood with the calf at my feet, all the dry cows, and the mother, sniffed and licked at the new one. Their instincts were touching, I thought, but then it dawned on me that the licking was deliberate. Readjusting the book in my back pocket, I wondered, are there states of consciousness we cannot imagine? Inevitably, the calf stirred, and once across the road, I gathered the cows for evening milking and brought mother and daughter home.

Forces war on this moment, hoping to sweep it from human memory. Acknowledging that animals—and the rest of creation—may be looking back at us would make it more difficult for people to accept, say, confined animal feeding operations or wholesale, closed-door slaughter. We need, as Michael Pollan points out, glass-walled slaughterhouses.[43] As it is, few people see the way most cattle die; the majority of us encounter cows as pictures on milk cartons or as meat on grills. How the milk and meat get there, we have no clue, and would rather not know. If we knew, we might treat what we eat differently. We've been so successful learning how to relieve ourselves of growing our own food that too few of us could grow enough food to last the year, year in and year out. We've pretty much lost the art of gardening, canning, even cooking. Most farmers I know don't bother to plant a garden; my mother buys milk at a grocery store ten miles from home, despite living on a dairy farm. But farmers, particularly small family farmers, are the last best hope of helping us to see others looking back at us. These farmers, at least, must face the faces they kill.

I sometimes teach Charles Frazier's *Cold Mountain*, a novel that starkly represents two competing visions of the world, one of war and erasure, the other of work and survival. The book's chapters alternate between two lovers, Inman and Ada. A veteran of Lee's army, a wounded Inman turns his back on the Civil War to journey home to his twin loves, Ada Monroe and his home, Cold Mountain, North Carolina. Daughter of a minister whose investments include crops worked by slaves, Ada moves from the comfort of Charleston high society to learning to work for her living on a small farm.

Inman's education moves in another direction. As a student in an ungraded rural schoolhouse, he flings his hat outside while his teacher chatters on about "grand wars fought in ancient England"; ordered to retrieve the hat, the boy Inman "stepped out the door . . . and walked away, never to return" (5). Twenty years later, he finds himself at Fredericksburg, where the "land lay bleak as nightmare and seemed to have been recast to fit a new and horrible model, all littered with bodies and churned up by artillery. Hell's newground." A boy soldier next to Inman says, as they sit behind the stone wall beside the sunken road, "Right there's what mostly comes of knowledge" (117). Having confronted the "metal face of the age," Inman returns home, seeking the "healing realm" near Cold Mountain (4, 23).

Ada's chapters offer an agrarian sensibility that serves as an alternative to the bloodletting of Inman's chapters; instead of describing the trials of a lone journeyman, Ada's chapters develop an egalitarian relationship between Ada and her new friend, Ruby. Born at Cold Mountain, Ruby teaches Ada how to labor within the rhythms of the natural world. Ruby's insistence on planting in "strict accordance with the signs" suggests to Ada an "expression of stewardship, a means of taking care, a discipline. They [the signs] provided a ritual of concern for the patterns and tendencies of the material world where it might be seen to intersect with some other world" (134). Eventually, Ada learns a new language, one "composed mainly of verbs, all of them tiring. Plow, plant, hoe, cut, can, feed, kill" (104). Ada's education moves her from embracing the abstract "formulas" of social convention to enjoying the concrete satisfactions of "liv[ing] fully in a place all your life . . . aiming smaller and smaller in attention to detail" (373, 388). She discovers an answer to the question, "Where am I?" (330).

Moving back and forth between perspectives, the novel searches for balance between technology and craft, reading and experience. Inman has learned too well the technologies of war; Ruby introduces Ada to the constellation of crafts that are small farming. Separated, Inman and Ada communicate through letters, and they read books, books that allude to the other's life. As he travels, Inman takes comfort in Bartram's *Travels*, which describes Inman's homeland. Ruby may teach Ada about farming, but Ada teaches Ruby the pleasures of storytelling by reading to her *The Odyssey* (140). In struggling to come up with the right words to write to Inman, Ada "had to admit that, at least now and again, just saying what your heart felt, straight and simple and unguarded, could be more useful than four thousand lines of John Keats" (344). Amen.

At the May 2005 rededication of the Civil War monument in Montrose, Bridget and I listened to fifteen- and sixteen-year-old boys read letters from Civil War soldiers. We stood among the crowd on the green behind the Susquehanna County Courthouse, beneath old maples and oaks that offered a shifting shade. In full sun and standing beneath the granite, the boys—dressed in white shirts, black pants, and Union blue kepis—read descriptions of camp life and battle, their voices rising and falling on a warm breeze. We saw them as the former selves of the dead whose letters they spoke, voices aged with war. When the boys went silent, an honor guard, men in their fifties and sixties, older than the veterans at the first dedication, marched to the edge of the shade. Three volleys. "Taps." Silence.

Before 1889, the Other Place had been the farm of Gregory O'Neill, whose brothers and cousins had adjoining farms. The story of the O'Neills lay all around me—house and barn foundations, fieldstone walls, apple trees, traces of a road, the spring. All abandoned. Growing up, I didn't know what it meant. All I knew was that the barn had burned the year I was born. I didn't know, for example, that the fields were small because they had been laid out for scythes and pitchforks, not haybines and balers. I often stood in the ruins and looked around. Who lived here? Why here?

My questions rested on the premise that change didn't touch my world. Reading overturned that assumption, and the more I read, the more meaningful the Other Place became, especially after I came across in a British Romantics class Wordsworth's "Michael," which, I remember, touched me in ways I couldn't articulate as an undergraduate. The anthology we used in that class now stands in the bookcase behind the desk in my office. In the margins I had written, "This world is disappearing . . . dying breed of people trampled on by industrialism . . . what is hoped for doesn't always come true." After line 95, the margins are untouched. The poem taught me that in fact the Other Place was never abandoned; it teemed with traces of lives lived there, remnants akin to the oak and the sheepfold in Wordsworth's work.

Poems are other places. One place I visit regularly is Robert Frost's "The Pasture."[44] I return to the poem again and again because it invites me to clarify my thinking about the connections that I see—and feel—between literature and farming, language and experience. Recalling my own ties to springs and calves, the poem challenges me to express how I cope with the tensions those connections create. A ground for understanding work and human relationships, "The Pasture" also reveals to me that many people see farming only through poetry.

The Pasture
I'm going out to clean the pasture spring;
I'll only stop to rake the leaves away
(And wait to watch the water clear, I may):
I shan't be gone long.—You come too.

I'm going out to fetch the little calf
That's standing by the mother. It's so young
It totters when she licks it with her tongue.
I shan't be gone long.—You come too.

As an undergraduate, I was puzzled by the first critical readings I came across. After studying literature for a few years, I knew that the pastoral mode was important in literary criticism, and that in the pastoral a character retreats into a rural world to escape the pressures of "civilization." After interacting with a more natural world, the character is restored and can then return to his life better able to cope with city stresses. Driving an hour to Scranton every day, I thought I had been living this, only in reverse: college was my retreat. In class on a snowy day, I didn't have to worry about spreading manure in subzero weather or about frozen pipes in the barn or about whether the driveway would fill with snow before the milk truck arrived. Back then I cut my life neatly in two: farm work and schoolwork, worlds away from each other.

Literary critics read "The Pasture" as a simple pastoral. This interpretation would not be so irksome if it were not used as the Rosetta stone of Frost's collected works. Frank Lentricchia asserts that the poem offers "an invitation to the pastoral experience evoked in [Frost's] poetry" and that, further, the poem reveals "some of his basic poetic strategies and intentions." Leo Marx even uses the poem to show how the pastoral mode's pattern of retreat and return governs not only the content of Frost's poetry but also the poet's understanding of the "creative process" and poetry itself.[45]

Impressive, I think, but I'm still irritated.

Glancing at the poem's surface—its rural setting, some spring water, a calf—critics see only "an ideal pasture,"[46] a place embodying the "simplicity and innocence of pristine reality." They see what they seek. To see "the beauty in such natural, everyday things," the "average person," one critic declares, must "abandon knowledge as the great world understands it . . . for only within the humble, out-of-the-way rural world is this special mode of perception possible." The poem's rural world is "remote from ordinary life" and every reader knows that this farm scene is "a plane of existence inferior in many respects to that on which he lives."[47] How is this interpretation not a dismissal of rural life?

Following John Lynen's lead, Lentricchia claims that "The Pasture" defines the pastoral experience as "that particular moment when 'mature,' self-conscious, and complex awareness is suppressed, and when single, naïve vision—a return to the Edenic innocence of unself-consciousness within a psychically soothing pastoral scene—is encouraged."[48] This reading suggests that anyone versed in country things—someone who really does clean a spring or carry a calf to the barn—is naïve and immature, someone with no complex awareness. But, I want to say, Frost was a farmer—even if not a good one—and a poet who knows how to make the complex seem simple.

When I first read "The Pasture," I thought that it envisioned an interdependent relationship between human work and the natural world. It was obvious to me that the poem is less about returning to Eden than it is about sustaining a human foothold in an indifferent nature; it's about farming for a living rather than living for lingering. It's about acts of creation—poetry. By definition a pasture, like a poem, is a bound place, a human-made landscape that contains and restrains the wild. I want to say to critics: I've kept the bounds. I've re-piled stonewalls, repaired barbed-wire fences, and ripped out thistles and thornbushes. Work shapes and clarifies one's physical and mental landscapes.

But then again, words define experience. My dictionary tells me that in Latin pasture is *pastura*, from *pastus*, the past participle of *pascere*, to feed. Like we all must, the speaker-farmer in "The Pasture" works at ordinary tasks—work that keeps the farm that keeps him—because he knows that to survive physically and spiritually humans must keep defining and redefining the world. Good work preserves the possibility of working again. Like poems, his farm tasks are works of knowing. Like poems, these tasks are, as Frost might put it, "momentary stay[s] against confusion."[49] Is not all the best work? And does not the best work keep the world we make from ruin?

The pasture may not be wild, but the wild is present, ready to throw the place into the confusion that threatens in each stanza. In the first, dead leaves choke the spring's life-giving flow. Sweeping away the leaves, the speaker channels the water, creating the clarity that gives birth to the calf. No longer a wet spot in the woods, the spring makes the pasture that sustains the cattle. Only by disciplining the wild can people create a responsible place within the world, a place conducive to the arts—culinary, literary, and the rest. The poem's invitation acknowledges that we all do this work; we are invited to make and maintain a clearing.

In the second stanza, the farmer-speaker takes care: the tottering calf is most likely less than an hour old. He fetches the calf because the cow will soon hide it; left alone, the calf will run wild. Without a respect for limits, the domestic is not possible. From the barn, the calf will make its home in the herd, and the cycle of life in this clearing will continue. Working to protect her calf, the cow licks it, drying it and stripping away any afterbirth. Clean, the calf is brilliantly new. The mother's tasks are as life giving and poetic as those of the speaker-farmer.

Now teaching in the city where I first attended college, I offer "The Pasture" to students in my world literature classes as an invitation to journey through the semester's readings. After going over the syllabus on the first day, I hand out the poem, and a volunteer reads it aloud. I ask for initial reactions, and then we discuss the poem's parts and how they work to create the whole. Seeking ever more clarity in our reading, we explore our insights together and tie the poem to our own experiences. We teach; we learn.

This is what I tell students: Frost reminds us that the human world is daily made. Cast in the present tense, the poem conjoins past and future in its title and its contents: the dead leaves, the unsteady calf. Clearing one makes way for the other. The human relation to the natural world—the farming—depicted in the poem is not dominating or damaging; with help, the spring flows clear and the calf is looked after. The poem illustrates that work makes and maintains order in local and particular ways. Inviting readers to help make moments of clarity that forestall confusion and ruin, the poem affirms that meaning is a community act. All human connection, like farming and writing, like reading and learning, is a necessary and daily activity that is at once individual and communal. Through work we come to know a place. Just as individual agricultural acts sustain our collective physical lives, poetic acts sustain our imaginative lives. Frost poses a basic question: Confronted with an indifferent nature, what do we do? An answer: We make a difference; we make meaning. We farm; we write.

My brother Danny took over the farm in the 1990s, a few years after he graduated from high school, because my father was unable to work day in and day out. His heart simply refused to accept any more heavy labor and long hours.

Danny gave the farm what it never had before, a public name—Con-Acres—which made sense, more sense than he knew. By this time I was in graduate school in Maryland. One day, leafing through a history of Ireland, I was surprised to learn that *conacre* was a significant word in the nineteenth-century Irish land system, designating a patch of prepared ground that a tenant family might let by the season.[50] Tying our place back to our Donegal ancestors, the word underscored the precarious nature of making a living by farming. The word also dovetailed with my childhood understanding of our surname; as a kid, I always thought that Conlogue meant "with discourses." The farm and family names pointed directly at me, I thought, but by then I had left the place—going from sticks to stacks, I suppose—though the place didn't leave me. I ended up writing about connections between farming and American literature. Working in a rental along Route 1 just north of Washington, D.C., a few miles from the National Agriculture Library, I was more aware than ever of where I was not.

Living near the farm now, I help hay in summer, and sometimes Danny asks me to help fix fence. I walk the sidehill, or stand in the pasture, heifers coming to me for salt, while dry cows near to calving hang back, chewing their cud, content. Remembering the foundations at the Other Place, now long gone on pallets, I picture traces of the trough, and hear the spring, which, I know, never runs dry.

6

Rendering the Mounds of Home

It gives such divine materials to men, and
accepts such leavings from them at last.
—Walt Whitman, "This Compost"

But waste was of the essence of the scheme.
—Robert Frost, "Pod of the Milkweed"

how can we intercede and not / interfere
—A. R. Ammons, *Garbage*

In the fall of 2004, a Lackawanna County judge complained to courthouse custodians that he couldn't stand the smell in his office. Following up on the complaint, a maintenance man opened a drop ceiling in the small bathroom attached to the judge's workspace. For his trouble, the worker got a face full of pigeon shit. Further investigation revealed that pigeons had been roosting for decades in a courthouse turret, their dung piling to a depth of two feet, amounting to about twenty tons.[1] A few days later, workers searching for more waste discovered another mound of droppings above the bathroom of a second judge. County commissioners used the crap to argue for a multimillion-dollar courthouse renovation: "The feces . . . is an indication of the condition of the entire building."[2]

The Lackawanna County courthouse stands on waste from the city's first industries. An 1854 map of Scranton shows a marsh, Lily Pond, covering the area where the courthouse, federal building, and post office now sit.[3] To fill the marsh, workers hauled from the Iron Furnaces slag and ash, courtesy of Lackawanna Iron and Coal. Despite the fill, in 1881 construction crews coped with unstable ground in raising the courthouse; workers had to dig down an average of thirty feet before hitting solid rock. Recalling the "transformation of this swamp to the center of the city's life," nineteenth-century historian Frederick Hitchcock noted that "they built better than they knew." Until, that is, the 2005 courthouse restoration revealed that the building had settled several inches; at the same time, removing the pigeon dung unearthed the corruption of two county commissioners.[4]

If how we work is how we tend the world, my neighbors and I haven't paid much attention to what we do. Up and down these valleys, evidence of violence reveals our blindness: polluted streams, stripped land, moonscape mountains of culm. To tend is to care, if not love, and proper care attends to details, but the record of our work within this watershed uncovers an attention deficit disorder that casually sacrifices people, places, plants, and animals. As we rip and tear at the earth, refusing to sense its rhythms, we invite disaster. Farmers and miners know this. A farmer who cannot read the sky soon sells out; a miner who cannot hear the earth work quickly gets crushed.

I'm not the first to accuse people in the region of poor vision. In 1928, local artist John Willard Raught diagnoses area residents of astigmatism: "We become hardened and indifferent to the conditions around us and to the ugliness of our hamlets and towns." Lamenting the loss of the "virgin land of a few centuries ago," Raught points to stumps of "giant white pines . . . sad reminders of our waste and extravagance." The artist also notes that although visitors to Scranton wonder at the "meaning of this pessimistic cloud that has fallen over the face of Nature . . . as if some blight had passed and only left desolation in its wake," natives of the city only "give an indifferent glance at the busy scene." In 1894, visitor Stephen Crane, Raught recalls, "at once grasped the sombre reality of it all."[5] But Raught and Crane aren't the only artists who have tried to get us to face the waste in our work. Sometimes seeing more than the rest of us, several artists—some living here, others visiting—have called us to account.

The Lackawanna Valley

Artists ask us to pay attention, because they know that how we look at land affects how we use it. What we see determines what we do. When we write, paint, or film land, we frame it, turning it into a landscape, a human construction that we too often mistake for land itself.

Confusing land and landscape has a long history in the United States. Early American geologists combined in their writings scientific investigation and nature tourism. For example, pointing out "views," "scenery," and "tints" in his report of the First Geological Survey of Pennsylvania, Henry Rogers sounds more like a traveler who paints than Pennsylvania's first head geologist. The particulars of "complex structure," the rock strata he named after parts of a single day, disappear when he describes the "mountain-zone of the State": "The valleys and plains . . . are full of landscapes, blending the bold and the beautiful." As if relating his own experience, he tells us how to get the best looks: "Let the tourist place himself a little way off from one of these rivers . . . he will usually see spread before him a truly noble picture." Geologist I. C. White uses the same rhetorical strategies to record what he saw during the Second Survey. He moves from studying rock as a record of time to rhapsodizing about extensive views. For example, from Prospect Rock on the South Knob of Elk Mountain, he records that the "eye takes in at one sweep . . . the curling smoke from the hundreds of mines along the Lackawanna, as far south as Scranton, while beyond this still, in a long line of billowy crests, rise the blue outlines of the Moosic mountain range." He nods to his own shift in stance—from scientist to tourist—when he concludes this paragraph by noting that a "carriage road extends to within a short distance of the 'view' and it is frequently visited by pleasure parties."[6]

Hudson River School artists inspired the rhetorical moves of Rogers and White. This is not surprising. Hudson School painters avidly followed and incorporated into their work developments in geology, then a new science. Shaping American attitudes toward nature, artists Thomas Cole and Frederic Church extolled America's "wilderness heritage." Cole, however, believed that "man's optimum environment is a blend of wildness and civilization," an idea he explored in his 1836 series "The Course of Empire."[7] Another Hudson River School artist, George Inness, who accepted similar ideas, painted in 1855 *The Lackawanna Valley*, a "striking representation of the idea that machine technology is a proper part of the landscape."[8]

When the machine becomes a dominant part of the landscape, the land suffers. Inness completed the painting on the cusp of an explosion in anthracite mining, which accelerated the rapid expansion of regional railroads. Commissioned as an advertisement for the Delaware, Lackawanna, and Western Railroad (D. L. & W.), the painting announced the company's arrival in the valley coal-and-railroad market. Formed in 1853, the D. L. & W. thrust itself between the domains of the Delaware and Hudson Canal Company to the north and the Pennsylvania Coal Company to the south, two businesses that had a lock on mining and shipping anthracite to New York City. To assert itself, the upstart railroad offered the "first competing outlet from the Lackawanna Valley." Up against older, established companies, the D. L. & W. gained a foothold not only by laying a line to the Delaware River to access New York City, but also by building a line from Scranton to Great Bend, where it connected with the Erie Railroad, opening upstate New York and western markets to anthracite.[9]

The painting may have advertised the D. L. & W., but it also promoted Scranton, a city then in infancy. The Scranton family, owners of the next-door Lackawanna Iron and Coal Company, backed the creation of the D. L. & W. to "launch a city-building venture"; the railroad not only "became a market for Scranton iron, it provided an outlet for Scranton coal, and it promoted trade for Scranton city."[10] In effect, railroad and painting encouraged investors, entrepreneurs, and skilled workers to bring their money and talent to the valley. For these groups, the D. L. & W. roundhouse, located in the heart of town and near the center of the painting, symbolized the city's industrial vibrancy and its economic possibilities.

Inness places the roundhouse, representing a new era of industry and technology, opposite the era's passing faith, a church, the First Presbyterian, located at Washington and Lackawanna, where today stands, of all things, an upscale hair salon. In the center of the painting sits the Lackawanna Iron and Coal works, from which the city grew. To right of center, the roundhouse, its tin roof bright, dominates the middle ground, railroad tracks radiating from it; the dark First Presbyterian spire, rising to the left, stands shadowy, less well-defined. Columns of clouds pair roundhouse and meetinghouse, but the smoke rising behind the steeple likely comes from a factory and the steam cloud coming from the roundhouse rises from locomotive boilers. The steeple's verticality links it to the lone tree in the left foreground and the single tree in center-left; horizontal rail tracks threaten them all. The trees recall the woods newly missing in the foreground, which is dotted with stumps and through which the train moves, heading north, pulling several loads of anthracite, the railroad's main source of income and its reason for being. That the train rolls north over the Lackawanna River would signal to the D & H and Pennsylvania Coal that the D. L. & W. had arrived: unlike the other companies' outlet, this second route from the valley refused to rely on the D & H Canal.

Stumps also call attention to the missing forest on the valley floor. Wood fuels the trains and supports the tracks, but the trees could have as easily fed the demand for cleared fields, building lumber, and mine props. Beneath the surface of the built landscape runs a maze of anthracite mines, the first, the Diamond, opened in 1852 or 1853, just before Inness arrived.[11] The stumps knit together the middle landscape of the farm not only to the wilderness but also to the new industrial landscape represented by the train.[12] Signaling things to come, however, the industrial landscape occupies center stage.

Apparently, *The Lackawanna Valley* did not meet company expectations. Never displayed, the painting may have been sold with a collection of office furniture, so little did D. L. & W. executives appreciate Inness's effort. In a quirk of fate, thirty-five years later Inness bought the painting for a song at a junk shop.[13] What was once trash is now a masterpiece.

The D. L. & W. yard depicted in the painting is today the Steamtown National Historic Site, home of a rebuilt roundhouse (see map 2, in the front matter of this volume). A few years ago, a Steamtown park ranger found where one would stand if one were observing the painting's scene from within the world of the painting: the fourth-floor deck of an apartment building on St. Frances Cabrini Street in West Side.[14] Using photographs taken roughly from the same spot in 1859, 1883, 1900, and today, the ranger created a Photoshop image that overlays the Inness painting with the subsequent images of the valley's evolution. The effect: the machine has crowded from the frame all vestiges of the garden.

Culm Banks

These days, though, the machine is disappearing. Between 1970 and 2000, the region lost 48 percent of its manufacturing jobs; in the same period, Pennsylvania lost 38 percent; the United States, 3 percent. In Lackawanna County, between 1998 and 2007, the "Health Care and Social Assistance industry" led the local economy in number of employees; in 2001 retail trade bumped manufacturing as runner-up. And coal mining? In 2007, the business employed fewer than one hundred people in the county.[15] Nothing symbolizes more the latter statistic than the almost complete disappearance of the once-ubiquitous coal breaker. A single relic remains: the Huber breaker in Ashley. Scores of others, dismantled and sold as scrap, survive only in paint and print.

Breakers sized coal and separated out waste. Size mattered: a fire kindled in anthracite demands same-sized pieces to stay alight, because "individual pieces of anthracite only burn on the surface." A fire started with large and small pieces, a load, say, directly from mine to furnace, soon snuffs out because smaller pieces fill gaps between larger ones. Before the coal breaker, workers wielded sledgehammers to shatter anthracite; they pounded it against iron sheets, tossed aside slate, and shoved chunks of coal onto perforated iron screens that sized pieces before they fell into bins below.[16] Eliminating much of the heavy hand labor in this process, the coal breaker made possible massive mining.

First appearing in the 1840s, the coal breaker took advantage of gravity: coal was hauled to the top of the structure, dumped across iron bars that caught the largest lumps of rock and coal; the rest rumbled down chutes and over a series of spiked rollers that crushed smaller chunks into finer pieces, which fell onto a sizing screen before cascading into assorted storage bins. As the material navigated the chutes, slate pickers, or breaker boys, as young as eight, "sat astride the moving mass of coal, controlling the flow with their feet," and tossing rock into chutes that fed a waste pile outside. The coal breaker was so distinctive that by 1909 a mine with no breaker was no colliery.[17]

Although breakers were hard to miss, people hardly noticed them. In 1915, when John Willard Raught, who made his name painting coal breakers, exhibited his work at the Scranton Century Club, admirers didn't pay much attention to his breaker paintings.[18] Curators hung them on a stairway wall, suggesting that they were scenes that gave way to more important work. Reporting on the exhibit, a Scranton newspaper gave short shrift to the breakers, despite noting that their "technique is complete, original, and modern. These breaker pictures are entirely new in art." Instead, the paper devoted ink to works titled "Campbell's Ledge," "Autumn at Dunmore Reservoir," and "Hill from South Scranton," which "express[ed] on canvas the beautiful character of our own valley and mountains, its clear streams and crystalline air."[19]

Everywhere a company built a coal breaker, it piled culm, inferior coal and slate. The culm bank, remains of a reordered geology, represents what happens when humans reshape the earth. Black and virtually treeless, often conical, culm banks crowded homes, polluted streams, and altered the region's geography. As if acknowledging culm banks as natural formations, topographic maps noted their height, a practice that continued through the 1980s.

Many culm banks are still valley landmarks. For example, a massive culm bank in Simpson dominates the ground where the valley narrows; several hundred feet high, its crown dotted with stunted trees, the mound overshadows the spire of St. Michael's Roman Catholic Church, which itself towers above the former homes of mine workers, a medieval arrangement emblematic of the region's historical hierarchy. Contemporary poet Sherry Fairchok catches this felt dominance in "Stoning the Breaker," which describes the Moffat breaker in her native Taylor, a town bordering Scranton, as "That coal-crushing tower, half factory, / half machine . . . the tallest thing in town, / rising between culm banks like a feudal castle" (13–15).[20]

Culm banks can burn. In "Culm Bank in Taylor, Pennsylvania," a companion poem to "Stoning the Breaker," Fairchok points to Taylor culm fires, which fogged and fouled the air there for years.[21] Fairchok compares the bank to a momentarily quiet sea creature, a "surfaced whale in one of those sea tales, / which basks long enough for trees / to sprout from its shoulders" (13–15). Unlike those unfamiliar with the town, who are likely drawn to the culm bank's vistas, "Only we who have seen it grow / higher than actual hillsides know it isn't a mountain" (9–10). Roving land developers, the sailors in this analogy, who "light a beach fire to dry their trouser legs," buy the site, intending to raise condominiums (19). In response, ex-miners, who suffer black lung and a blacker irony, "old men who gutted this ground / and call it home," know better than to buy there, telling us to *Look at them ritzy ass houses / they're putting up / on top of Moffat's collum dump / I wouldn't live there / if you paid me a buck t'ree-eighty*" (28–29, 37–41). Their lungs awash in black phlegm, the miners understand that the "strange heat / from the beach fire" will soon light this "mile-high culm bank / overlooking Taylor"; the whale, then "Aroused and restless . . . heaves and rolls / down toward its dark home / and drowns them all" (7–8, 42–43, 44–46). Imagined plans for condos may have fallen through, but a Wal-Mart opened there in 2010.

Taylor, like many mining communities, grew as culm banks rose, a circumstance that later caused serious headaches, especially when the Moffat mounds began burning. In a 1954 case that paved the way for tougher environmental laws, the Waschaks, a brother and sister in Taylor, sued Moffat Coal Company, claiming that hydrogen sulfide emitted from Moffat's culm dump had discolored the white paint on their house. In response, the company pointed to *Pennsylvania Coal Company v. Sanderson*: an industry's benefits to the community outweighed any "trifling inconveniences to particular persons." The Pennsylvania Supreme Court agreed, declaring that as long as the company continued in "'the normal and customary use of their land' . . . it would be immune from liability for resulting harms." Apparently, dumping mine waste in the middle of residential areas amounted to customary land use. In support of its reasoning, the majority quoted a ruling in a county court case about Pittsburgh's notorious smog: "One's bread is more important than landscape or clear skies."[22]

Dissent in the case, however, suggested that the law would eventually take into account environmental damage done by private landowners.[23] Disagreeing with the majority, Judge Musmanno, who first authored the line about Pittsburgh, asserted that smelly and poisonous gases amounted to a major nuisance, not a "trifling inconvenience." What could be more of a nuisance than the constant smell of rotten eggs? The gases caused headaches, insomnia, and nausea, so much so that local residents launched organized protests. Anticipating Fairchock's sea analogy, Musmanno compared the culm banks to a massive ship, "loaded stem to stern with rotten eggs." In addition, Musmanno declared, the defendants offered no evidence that they needed to locate "culm banks in the

Fig. 10 Marvine culm banks burning, 1968. Courtesy of the Lackawanna Historical Society.

very midst of the residential areas of Taylor." The judge went on to note that a Moffat partner lived outside the borough and "never found it profitable to spend a single night" in town.[24] Following Musmanno's lead, later judges would rule that private landowners who inflicted significant damage on others ran afoul of the public interest.

Landfills

Aldo Leopold exhorts me to think like a mountain: "Only the mountain has lived long enough to listen objectively to the howl of a wolf." If I'm hearing him right, to think like a mountain is to see the connectedness of all life, to think long-term, to let the world unfold in its own time, on its own terms. To do so, Leopold claims, is to realize "Thoreau's dictum: In wildness is the salvation of the world."[25] But what happens, I wonder, when we confuse mountains and culm banks? Or when we assume that we live on a mountain, only to discover it's really a landfill. These days, too many mountains stand as monuments of our own making, and they all think like us.

We think like a landfill. A confused intermingling of items tossed from their contexts, a landfill jumbles the natural and the human-made in layer upon layer. We create these sealed-off waste spaces, bury them, and then plant there parks and housing developments. After we build on a built environment made up of what we've made to toss away, we refuse to remember that we ever dumped on the place. Our thinking shuttles between extremes. Sometimes we think like the ideal landfill, which, according to garbologists, is "dry, quiet, and relatively inert," much like a culm bank. At other times, our thoughts spew like the worst landfill, volcano-like: "A landfill that is wet, teeming with roisterous activity, and spilling its insides into the outside world, is the situation that one wants to avoid. That way lies Fresh Kills, which pours at least a million gallons of leachate into New York Harbor every day." The ultimate dark field, a landfill, like too much of our thinking, creates heat but little light, despite flares of genius.[26]

A case study of ironies in the circulation of waste, northeastern Pennsylvania once exported fuel to heat and light New York, Boston, and Philadelphia. Today, the region imports the same cities' garbage, creating artificial mountains among culm piles. Once marked by the export of natural resources, parts of the area are now layers of imported waste, much of it from New York.

Two landfills bookend Scranton: Alliance to the west and Keystone to the east. On 16 June 2011, I visited Alliance, and talked with John Hambrose, Community Relations Coordinator there for Waste Management, the landfill's owner. A seven-hundred-acre swath in the shadow of Bald Mountain, Alliance overlooks the town of Taylor.[27] From the opposite side of the valley, the place is hard to miss. Alliance looks like, well, a landfill trying not to look like a landfill: its green gets higher the more forest-green trucks rumble to its top. Acutely aware of the site's visibility, Alliance works hard to manage its image. For example, the landfill originally included an on-site diner, now closed, to encourage long-distance truckers not to stop and eat in nearby towns.

Long before Waste Management built this "dry tomb" landfill, people had been mauling Bald Mountain.[28] In the nineteenth century, coal companies cleared the forest there to make way for deep mining, which lasted into the first quarter of the twentieth century. During the 1930s through the 1960s, strip miners moved in, ripped up the surface, and tore out the coal, leaving large gashes across the mountain face, gashes that became dumping grounds in the late 1960s for Scranton municipal waste.[29]

Waste Management advertises Alliance as a mine reclamation project. When another private company first built the site in 1986, it dug a pit, lifted out tons of coal, and backfilled spots to insure that no mine fire would later light its rubbish. With a double-lined sac and wastewater collection system in place, workers then removed trash from strip mines to the landfill liner. Waste Management defines its "continuing reclamation project," which the state has approved for expansion, as an antidote to acid mine drainage.[30]

Aware of complaints from local residents about its visibility, Alliance carefully arranges its environment. On Earth Day 2004, for example, workers planted on the landfill cap small stands of white pine, black locust, and birch. Those who monitor the stands have discovered that, instead of penetrating the cap's "geo-synthetic blanket," tree roots have woven themselves into its top mesh layer. Not only have the plantings created "habitat for a growing number of wildlife species," but also "the trees and shrubs have improved the appearance of the landfill."[31] To keep up appearances, landscape contractors make the site's slopes "as green as possible."[32]

Birds often mark a landfill, so I was surprised during my visit to see none flying at the waste face, and only one or two flitted here and there along the landfill's edges. With the help of an airport expert, Hambrose explained, birds have been "trained to stay away," which I took to mean that they're too frightened to stay. But it's hard to imagine that the ninety bird species that have been identified at Alliance won't ultimately find the courage to defeat the landfill's no-fly zone of simulated shotgun blasts, kestrels, and spiked roosts. The tension between attracting birds with stands of trees and training them to keep their distance from active slopes finds further expression in Waste Management's affiliation with the Wildlife Habitat Council, whose membership rolls include some of the biggest polluters in the world, Exxon and BP among them.

As Hambrose drove me around the perimeter of the property in a company SUV, I couldn't help but notice more ironies. Constructed atop coal mines, the landfill boasts three hundred wells that siphon off landfill gas, which is 50 percent methane, to an on-site processing facility; piped nineteen miles to a power generation plant in Archbald, the gas produces enough electricity to power twenty thousand homes, reducing, at least a little, our dependence on coal and natural gas. When I asked what would happen to the place after the final face is full, Hambrose pointed out that some landfills become parks and golf courses, but then he remarked that they might all soon be mined for what they contain. The irony was too much: a strip mine becomes a landfill that gets strip-mined for recyclables.

Before Alliance and Keystone, New York City garbage fed the largest landfill in the world, Fresh Kills in Staten Island, originally a "vast marshland, a tidal swamp," now the "highest geographic feature along a fifteen-hundred-mile stretch of the Atlantic seaboard" from Maine to Florida.[33] With the landfill's closure in 2001, city planners began work to convert the site to a multi-use park "almost three times the size of Central Park, comprising four vast waste mounds set within an estuarine landscape of creeks, tidal wetlands, low-lying meadows, and upland forested areas." Titled "lifescape," the winning design proposal "called for a combination of soil strategies: amendment of existing soils, purchase or manufacture of new soils." As at Alliance, landfill methane will be "cleaned and converted to pipeline quality gas for domestzic [sic] use." A successful project, planners believe, requires that the "human-made environment and natural systems, human and nonhuman habitats, be understood as a single living, experiential continuum." But success here, as at Alliance, is a double-edged sword: a park may be better than a landfill, but the conversion rests on the assumption that we can destroy a place and then "heal" it, which only licenses us to destroy the next place, even if we know, as we do at Fresh Kills, that "we have senselessly and severely damaged a previously vital and beautiful ecosystem."[34]

It's easy to read a landfill as a large compost pile, but most landfill waste stays waste; newspapers, for example, which constitute 13 percent of landfill space, often remain readable for decades. With little biodegradation happening within them, landfills "are not vast composters; rather, they are vast mummifiers," which is a good thing. A biodegrading landfill threatens to leak its contents, potentially poisoning the land around it. One of the few times that a Garbage Project crew—University of Arizona archaeologists who excavate landfills— has come across biodegradation was at Fresh Kills when, as they watched the hoisting of garbage from the 1940s and '50s, a wind blew into their faces a "gray slime, redolent of putrefaction."[35]

What to do with what our creativity leaves us has long been a problem. Ancient Trojans didn't dispose of household garbage beyond burying it underfoot; after a while, homeowners had to raise roofs and redo doorways. This remodeling elevated Troy 4.7 feet every hundred years. In the United States, many parts of New York and New Jersey, for example, rose on rubbish, which was often dumped as fill to extend city limits across wetlands.[36] Today, we usually truck our refuse away and bury it deep, putting it out of sight, out of mind, but "even when it's *in* sight garbage somehow manages to remain out of mind."[37] Unfortunately, we're now creating so much waste that it threatens to overwhelm us.

Garbage

To appreciate garbage, I guess I need to take a longer view. If matter can be neither created nor destroyed, our makings simply circulate in the world. All is energy, at least potentially, although things cycle at different times, at different rates, sometimes in abundance, sometimes in short supply. Whereas Aldo Leopold wants me to think like a mountain, A. R. Ammons wants me to think like the universe, which, he admits, is cold comfort.[38]

A book-length poem, Ammons's *Garbage* takes the long view, spinning out a "spindle of energy," a continuum of constant change (25). When energy takes material form, the speaker observes, it "resembles the gross, and when / fine it mists away into mystical refinements," which, for him, means that garbage is "the poem of our time because / garbage is spiritual" (18, 25). Emblematic of this transfiguration, fire turns matter into spirit—energy, motion—so it makes sense that Ammons often points to the pillar of fire that one often sees at landfills. The purifying flames, signaled by a "priestly plume," represent "incinerations of sin, / corruption, misconstruction" (30). But the exalted fire finds its source, methane, in a more lowly transformation: biodegradation.

Pausing in his work of spreading garbage, a bulldozer operator stands before the fire and has a revelation akin to Wordsworth's at Tintern Abbey. This spindle of energy, he realizes, represents a motion that runs through all things, a motion and a spirit that he addresses as, "O eternal / flame, principle of the universe, without which / mere heaviness and gray rust prevail" (31). Transfixed by the "terrifying transformations" of the burning, the garbage spreader "stares into it as into / eternity, the burning edge of beginning and / ending, the catalyst of going and becoming" (31, 32). He sees that "everything is marvelous" because "all is one, one all" (33, 34).

Garbage may be about recycling, but, taking inspiration from a Florida land-fill, Ammons doesn't ignore waste. Garbage isn't just a metaphor for renewal; it piles up, "stinking, turning brooks brownish and / creamy white" (18). Although the universe recycles its own extravagance, human recycling systems can't keep up with putting our things back into play. Chicken feed, for example, may be "ground fine / in gizzards" and be "transmuted into the filigree / of ant feelers' energy vaporizations," but a plastic lid only "finds hidden security in the legit / museums of our desecrations—the mounds, the / heights of discard" (85). What to do with the lid is a problem for us.

As I write, mounds of paper surround me. Books and articles, clippings and Post-its pile up, these pieces of other piles, from libraries, presses, and publishers: "a waste of words" (74). What am I wasting, exactly? Space? Time? Energy? But what's the matter with a little waste anyway, I wonder, until I'm reminded that "since words were / introduced here things have gone poorly for the / planet: it's between words and rivers, / surface-mining words and hilltops" (74). All around him the speaker in *Garbage* sees "poetry to no purpose! all this garbage! all / these words: we may replace our mountains with / trash: leachments may be our creeks flowing / from the distilling bottoms of corruption" (75). I glance around; paper everywhere, on the desk, the floor, the shelves. What am I doing? Is it right? I mean, I could be milking a cow or pounding a post or spreading manure, but here I sit, picking over words, sorting sounds, collecting phrases, writing, writing . . .

Then again, Ammons dedicates *Garbage* "to the bacteria, tumblebugs, scavengers, wordsmiths—the transfigurers, restorers." The list reorders the world. Bacteria break down bodies, and scavengers return pieces of trash to their contexts, or remake them in new ones. Scavenging words and images, poets enliven worn meanings; recycling stories, they help us to see the world with fresh eyes. Creativity is a kind of biodegradation: "there is a mound, / too, in the poet's mind dead language is hauled / off to and burned down on, the energy held and / shaped into new turns and clusters" (20). Good work. I mean, who would not want to do this, to be a tumblebug, rolling crap into balls, burying it, and planting it with eggs? A symbol of resurrection, the tumblebug reminded ancient Egyptians of the sun rolling across the sky. Imagine . . .

Composting

Two centuries of strip-mining the world's creative capacity has punctured any easy faith that the earth renews itself. In building landfills, we apply the latest technologies to contain the extravagance of our latest technologies. We take pieces of the world, remake them, and lock them away so they cannot return. Not creative enough to do more with our creativity, we waste our waste. One result: these days, cool drinks from the well don't taste so good, and the winds really are infectious. With the earth threatening to become our last landfill, I need, instead of mining and landfilling, a new guiding metaphor, one about return: composting, maybe.

Nature, after all, may be extravagant, but it wastes nothing.

Walt Whitman wonders at this fact in "This Compost" (1867).[39] The poem opens with the speaker discovering that "Something startles me where I thought I was safest" (1). His world turned upside down, he shrinks from the thought of "every continent work'd over and over with sour dead" (10). Although he initially wants to isolate himself from "distemper'd corpses"—he won't walk in the woods or swim in the sea—he feels compelled to run a "furrow with [his] plough" to "expose some of the foul meat" (9, 14, 15). He finds, however, that the earth is not a toxic supersite, but a giant compost pile that resurrects the dead as the living. In a burst of joy and relief, he sings "That all is clean forever and forever, / That the cool drink from the well tastes so good" (37–38). His initial fright transformed into awe, he marvels at forces beyond him: "Now I am terrified at the earth! it is that calm and patient, / It grows such sweet things out of such corruptions" (43–44).

About a backyard compost pile, Maxine Kumin's "The Brown Mountain" explores how we can interfere without interceding. The pile gathers assorted leftovers: "sunflower heads . . . picked clean," "eggshells, moldy potatoes," "rotten squash, burst berries" (6–7, 10, 31). This mountain of matter grows as an alternative to lifeless culm banks, mummifying modern landfills, and toxic superfund sites. Unlike W. S. Merwin's burning black mountain, which vents deadly carbon monoxide, Kumin's "turgid brown mountain / steams, releasing / the devil's own methane vapor," itself an equivocal miasma, at once a sign of organic transformation and an accelerator of climate change (25–27). Whereas culm banks stand as tokens of the powerful enriched and gone, and landfills function as collective reminders of how the powerful dump on the rest, compost piles level hierarchies. The brown mountain cooks "our castoffs," creating a "rapture of blackest humus. / Dirt to top-dress, dig in. Dirt fit / for the gardens of commoner and king" (28, 34–36). Compost, our common ground, equally feeds us and receives us; from compost we live, to compost we go. In all ways, "Compost is our future" (24).

I learned from an English professor the difference between shit and manure. While offering feedback about my early attempts at fiction, he leaned forward, puzzled, and pointed.

"You say shit here," he said. "You mean manure."

I shrugged. He smirked.

"Shit is shit," he explained. "Manure is shit and piss and hay . . . a mix."

I thought, you're right. I knew that, or should have known that.

Spreading manure puts waste to use. Nutrients get back into the ground. Grass grows. Cows eat; milk flows. Shit piles up, though, when a farm confines too many animals in too small a space. A single factory farm can create more waste than a small city. Though a city's waste disposal system may be tightly regulated, a farm's often isn't. And large systems can create big problems: in 1999, for example, when a hurricane hit North Carolina, floods inundated several hog farms, whose waste lagoons overflowed, polluting rivers and water supplies.[40]

Some winters, with snow too deep in the fields, we'd pile manure between the gates. In spring and summer, the pile would crust and sink, eventually becoming dry and black, a rich fertilizer. Someone would toss seeds there, squash, pumpkins, or zucchini, and a riot of green would soon hide bright-colored vegetables. A fall or two later, we'd cart the leavings to meadow and pasture.

But we had another pile, not so temporary, which we mentioned less, one that raised only itself. What we couldn't burn, we dumped at the Other Place, on the stone foundation of a long-gone farmhouse. For years, we tossed there tin cans, bedsprings, glass bottles. What else could we do? Recycling came later.

As a consolation, locusts grew there, nicely shading what we wasted, and once in a while we'd cut one into a pile of fence posts.

In "The Wood-Pile" (1914), Robert Frost imagines another kind of composite waste, one that also opens out to renew the world: poetry. Like the stone wall in "Mending Wall," this pile is a poem, a "measured" bit of "handiwork" that the hewer had forgotten in "turning to fresh tasks" (24, 35, 36). Like any good poem, the pile "warm[s] the frozen swamp as best it could / With the slow smokeless burning of decay" (39–40). As if to remind readers that poems bridge exterior and interior worlds, the woodpile stands between a "tree / Still growing, and . . . a stake and prop" (32–33). The line break underscores the aliveness of the tree; the next break points up the provisional quality of the human-made stake and prop, which are "about to fall" (34). Coming upon the pile gives the speaker not only a sense of kinship with a worker who has gone before him, much like in "The Tuft of Flowers" (1913), but it also orders the woods, offering him a location, much like the jar in Wallace Stevens's "Anecdote of the Jar" (1919). Despite the frozen swamp, the speaker has hope of home: he may not be warmed enough for comfort, but he's comforted enough by the thought that someone here was warmed with work.

As does Whitman's poem, "The Wood-Pile" begins in uncertainty; unlike "This Compost," however, Frost's poem ends with a-less-than-sure affirmation. The speaker, "Out walking in the frozen swamp one gray day," finds himself in a cold, fallen world, where he is as unsure of his footing as of his location (1). Disoriented and lost—all he knows is that he's "just far from home"—he comes upon a cord of wood, an artifact that connects him to another (9). What had made him lose his way, a confusion of tall trees, "lines / Straight up and down," has been shaped into something he recognizes: short, horizontal sticks of stove wood (5–6). Although the trees look "Too much alike to mark or name a place by," he finds someone else's mark on the world "piled—and measured, four by four by eight" (7, 24). The finite nature of the human-made, its eventual "decay," demands that this work go on; to make it, to orient ourselves, we must pile more wood, more poems (40). To fight the cold and the darkness, to fire our imaginations, we must work where we are, in the woods, to transform in a "useful fireplace" matter into energy, life into spirit (38). If we don't, we'll stay lost, chasing connections we can't quite make, imagining that the others of the world imagine us as we do.

Some of our markings, though, so blast the world that its renewal is more hope than fact, making our own renewal even less likely, circumstances explored in a film and a play set in northeastern Pennsylvania. Each represents characteristic—and opposing—responses to environmental damage. The film portrays passivity; the play, active forgetting. Together, they represent the main ways that most people in the region have responded to environmental catastrophe: apathy and amnesia.

To depict wasted lives, the film and the play create parallels between hollowed-out people and hollowed-out places. The film, *Wanda* (1970), for example, uses shots of mine waste to frame the passive title character's interactions with the men who undermine her sense of self-worth. The main characters in the play, *That Championship Season* (1972), residents of a trashed land, have wasted their lives in self-damaging attempts to keep up appearances, which the play constantly undercuts. I end the chapter by exploring a local problem that serves as a metaphor for the damage suffered by all these characters: mine subsidence, which opens gaps in surfaces, revealing raw wounds.

Wanda

Pairing person and place, the film *Wanda* and the play *That Championship Season* portray lives masking deep emotional damage. *Wanda* follows a passive, working-class woman who is unable, until the film's final moment, to see herself as herself. The play reunites middle-class men who rely on bygone glory to make their lives meaningful. Whereas in the movie Wanda travels the length of the Lackawanna Valley to get nowhere, the men in the play remain confined to a single house.[41] The play ends with the men reaffirming a collective nostalgia; the film, however, ends with Wanda, facing an uncertain future, alone in a crowd. Despite the differences, characters in each confront a postindustrial landscape that has laid them waste. Director Barbara Loden, who had little prior knowledge of the region, and playwright Jason Miller, who had much, understood environmental contexts as critical elements of our humanity.

Play and film helped me to see this place anew. They re-presented to me what I thought I knew well; they made strange the familiar, the familiar strange. Watching *Wanda*, for example, I experienced shocks of recognition; places I had grown up seeing, I understood from new angles. In an opening scene, Wanda, a distant figure, walks among culm banks, a ground that I had come to look beyond. Now in the foreground, the piles suddenly loomed larger. I thought, how barren, ugly, lifeless . . . Eventually, I noticed the irony: as Loden filmed herself navigating this waste space, men were planting a flag on the moon.[42]

Filming in Forest City, Carbondale, and Scranton, Loden spent ten weeks in the Lackawanna Valley. She chose the region, in part, because she couldn't afford to travel further into Appalachia. To keep costs down, she shot the film in documentary style using a handheld 16mm camera. Her entire crew consisted of a cameraman, a soundman, and an assistant; Loden's husband, filmmaker Elia Kazan, sometimes "helped out with the street scenes." A first-time director, Loden also starred in the movie, but, aside from a few professional actors, "most of the other characters in the film were just ordinary people living in the area." For example, a few minutes before shooting one scene, Loden knocked on doors to discover a woman doing laundry; agreeing to participate, the old woman "just happened to bring a rosary," which added to the pathos of the filmed moment.[43]

Although *Wanda* has been virtually erased from movie history, critics call it a cinema verité classic. In its production and feminist themes, *Wanda* "worked against the grain of its time"; the film was no slick, big-budget Hollywood movie that cast women as sirens or saints.[44] As a "pioneer female filmmaker . . . working without a net, without role models, without a network of female collaborators," Loden sought "to make the antithesis of a movie where everyone is beautiful and wears beautiful costumes."[45] Although the original screenplay emphasized a Pygmalion relationship between Wanda and Mr. Dennis, Loden abandoned this theme during shooting because she found it "phony." She also realized that she couldn't stick to her script because she was working with non-professional actors and had to film where and when she could. She had "to wing it every day." Work on most scenes began with Loden saying, "Well, let's shoot and see what happens": there were no rehearsals.[46] Uncertainty fostered improvisation; *Wanda*'s "strongest moments came from chance encounters."[47]

Wanda connects person and place. To create a *"similarity between the exterior landscapes in the film and Wanda's inner landscape of decimation,"* Loden looked for a "locale that was outside of the big cities, underdeveloped and typically American . . . and finally selected the Anthracite Region in Pennsylvania." In the same interview, the filmmaker asserts that much of the United States is an "ugly sight—particularly the cities, the architecture and the highways. The bleakness of the environment is bound to have an effect on the art and on the emotional life of the people. It has to affect you, it makes you feel ugly."[48]

Nodding to this aesthetic, the film opens on a bank-mining operation: all we see are a huge culm pile, a pay loader, a truck, and a bulldozer.[49] No vegetation; nothing green. Hemmed between the culm bank and a colliery powerhouse stands the unpainted home of Wanda's sister, where Wanda wakes up on a couch. She then wends her way across the culm to reach a bus so that she can make it to divorce court. Dressed in light-colored clothing, which stands out against the gray background, Wanda is at once lost in this landscape, a part of it, and separate from it. The stripped place points to the stripped lives lived there.

Wanda responds with apathy to this "environment that is so overwhelmingly ugly and destructive." When her husband accuses her in court of desertion, she simply tells the judge to grant him the divorce he seeks. When her boss tells her that he won't hire her again, she simply thanks him. Loden, who understood Wanda as an expression of herself, explains that "everything has been knocked out of Wanda. She has been numbed by her experiences, and she protects herself by behaving passively and wandering through life hiding her emotions. This apathy is her defense, her way of surviving." Her surface passivity, however, conceals an "inner hidden turmoil." In a few scenes, Wanda strikes back.[50]

Made as the Vietnam War raged, the film shows how mining sacrifices people and places. Early on, an old woman telling her rosary sits before a window, staring at the mining operation outside. Behind her rocker stands a dresser topped by a crucifix, a votive candle, and a photo of a Marine, presumably dead. A side shot shows the woman through a French door as she helps a little boy into her lap; a U.S. flag decal obscures her head. Caught between love of country and loss of country, all this woman can do is pray. Similarly, before entering divorce court to face her mine-worker husband Wanda stands, as if lost, in front of the Carbondale war memorial, on which is inscribed, among others, the name of my mother's first husband, Robert, a casualty of the war in Korea.

Wanda depicts a working-class woman's struggle to survive on her own. In conceiving the film, Loden was "influenced by certain literature . . . Dostoevsky and Zola—about the problems of the poor working class and the horrible lives that people led."[51] To underscore this, exchanges of money dominate Wanda's life. As she walks among the culm banks, for example, she comes upon a coal picker who is, ironically, dropping anthracite into a two-gallon oilcan. After he tells her that the coal is all but picked over, which confirms for us his own poverty, she asks him for money, and he hands her a dollar or two, all he can spare. When she complains to the dress factory boss that she received a nine-dollar check for twelve-dollar-a-day wages, he points out that part of her gross went to taxes, an explanation that suggests that this was her first job. In a shopping mall, a clean and well-lighted place, she studies the latest fashions on expressionless, blonde mannequins that look much like her, a moment that reminded me of Carrie Meeber window-shopping in Chicago. Not long later, after Wanda falls asleep in a movie theater, someone steals the money from her purse, leaving her almost destitute.

After the theater scene, Wanda meets three men in three different bars. Shots of mine-scarred land comment on the first and third encounters. In the first bar, a traveling salesman, who speaks only to the male bartender, buys her a drink, and the two end up in a motel bed. When he tries to leave her there, she jumps into his station wagon, but he soon abandons her at the Tastee-Freez in Forest City. As she silently watches his car speed through town, she stands framed by the Hillside Coal and Iron culm bank, a landmark of my youth, one that local boosters leveled to build the Vision2000 industrial park, a still-empty space. While Loden was shooting this scene, on 9 August 1969, preparations were underway at Max Yasgur's dairy farm, thirty miles east of Forest City, to accommodate music fans at Woodstock, which kicked off on 15 August.[52] The contrast between grimness and gaiety, "free sex" and free love, could not be more striking.

Meeting Mr. Dennis in the bar he's robbing is nothing like her encounters with the salesman. With Dennis, she asserts herself. She forces her way inside to use the bathroom, sits at the bar eating potato chips, and asks for a drink. Anxious about discovery, Dennis complies with her demands; he pours her a beer, gives up his comb, and hears her chitchat about losing her money. After they leave, Dennis buys her a meal, and they talk more like a long-married couple than like strangers.[53] Alternately abusive and kind, Dennis quickly introduces Wanda to a world of petty crime. They become partners.

Robbing a bank is their ultimate assertion of self in a culture that dictates that one must have things in order to be. As Loden points out about Mr. Dennis, "He thinks that if he gets enough money he will have dignity." To represent this desire, Loden improvised with a model airplane that one day disrupted filming. A "Don Quixote image," the toy flies away from Dennis, who shouts for it to return; he even jumps on the roof of a car to call it back, a doomed effort to get closer to the plane, which symbolizes his "flailing at imaginary things against him or reaching for something unattainable."[54] When in the same scene Wanda confesses that she has nothing and that she never will have anything, Dennis tells her that if you don't have anything, you're nothing, not even a "citizen of the United States."

To acquire the means to get things, to become U.S. citizens, the couple tries to rob Scranton's Third National Bank, which had long piled money made from mining. Although Wanda complains that she cannot go through with it, she helps Mr. Dennis to kidnap a bank official; she strikes their hostage, holds him at bay with a gun, and orders the man's wife to sit, which she does. Afterward, Dennis tells Wanda—in his last words to her—that she did a good job, the first positive reinforcement she's received. Due to his own impatience to get the money, however, Dennis dies in the holdup. Wanda, unaware of this, arrives late with the getaway car because she lost her way to the bank, got stopped for making a U-turn, and had to ask the cop for directions. Wracked with guilt after Dennis's death, she finds herself in the third bar, where she falls into the arms of an army sergeant.

The bar scene with the sergeant reminds us of the scene with the salesman. The sergeant buys Wanda several beers and berates her about her refusal to talk. She doesn't speak because she's listening to news reports of Dennis's death. He then drives her to a landscape reminiscent of the opening scene: lifeless dirt frames shots of his red convertible. When he tries to have sex with her, Wanda at first passively succumbs, but then she fights him off, escapes through a green wood, and ends up outside a roadhouse.

The roadhouse at the film's end offers Wanda the shelter of community. As she stands alone, in the dark, outside the inn, she meets a woman who asks whether she's waiting for someone; the camera then cuts inside to a happy crowd listening to bluegrass. Men and women feed Wanda a hot dog, offer her cigarettes, and pour her beer. No one tries to pick her up. The film closes with a freeze-frame of her that suggests the "terror of self-realisation. . . . The distant figure in a landscape of grey slag is now a fully formed person, sitting alone in a crowd, in silence and pain, thinking."[55] Here, Wanda meets herself.

That Championship Season

New York theater critic John Simon ties *Wanda* to *That Championship Season* in describing Scranton as an "unprepossessing milieu, this small, cultureless, coal-mining town, and treated without close knowledge (as in Barbara Loden's film, *Wanda*), it can strike us as completely dehumanized." Unlike Loden, Jason Miller explores his native Scranton with "intimate knowledge and understanding of the people portrayed," offering his criticisms of the region "regretfully, without rancor, almost with love." In a 2001 interview, Miller himself says that the play "speaks to universal experiences—that of betrayal and that of forgiveness . . . it is in a sense more of a love play than a hate play." Noting that Miller undermines the urbanite's nostalgia for small-town life, Simon points out that the play exposes the "good and simple folk back in the small towns . . . to be weak, cowardly, prejudiced, corrupt and sustained, if at all, by self-delusion."[56] These human failings may be universal, but the substance of self-delusion in *That Championship Season* is nostalgia, both personal and regional, for long-gone—and violent—glory days.[57]

The play recounts the twentieth annual reunion of the 1952 Pennsylvania state champion high school basketball team. One team member, Martin, has never attended a get-together. Another, Tom Daley, a writer, is at his first gathering in three years. Still directed by the tyrannical Coach, the other three have met every year since the winning season; for the last four years, they have also teamed up in town politics. Taking the championship, however, has remained the high point in each man's life, despite one becoming mayor (George), another serving as junior high school principal (James), and a third running a successful strip-mining business (Phil). Adrift since their moment in the sun, the men remember their perfect season as a way to give meaning to their now "desperate" lives.[58]

In the analogy that structures the play, the basketball team represents the people of the Lackawanna Valley; both limp along in the aftermath of better times. To underscore that he speaks to the region, Miller locates the setting, Coach's house, "somewhere in the Lackawanna Valley," likely in Taylor, and not Scranton, as many assume.[59] Although he charges his once-and-future neighbors with racism, cronyism, and religious bigotry, Miller wants them most to understand that though they yearn for aspects of their coal-mining history (e.g., its culture and relative prosperity), they pay scant attention to the violence those days did to people and the land.

Despite good reasons to leave the region as mining ended in the 1950s and '60s, people found it tough to go, or to stay away when they did leave. Some laid-off miners who found other jobs elsewhere felt nostalgia for their former work, even though they urged their sons never to be miners. Hoping to return, many who migrated from the region maintained the homes they left, and others commuted long distances to new employment, sometimes returning only on weekends. A number of migrants who moved away did return, many to retire in their hometowns. People forced to migrate due to the Carbondale mine fire not only recalled the "horror of living in 'the zone,'" but also the "close family and neighborhood ties they had there."[60]

The year before the play's premier, in 1971, Pennsylvania established the Anthracite Museum Complex to collect and preserve anthracite history. The complex encompassed several sites: the Scranton Iron Furnaces and the Anthracite Heritage Museum, in Lackawanna County; Eckley Miners' Village, in Luzerne County; and the Museum of Anthracite Mining, in Schuylkill County.[61] Although the Anthracite Museum, for example, devotes much space to machinery, tools, and the insides of representative homes, textile mills, and churches, it houses few visual representations of the human and environmental costs of coal mining. The Iron Furnaces, shorn of their sprawling rolling mills, offer little to suggest that they polluted Roaring Brook. Kept clean for tourists, Eckley, a site for filming the 1970 movie *The Molly Maguires*, cannot quite return the visitor to the sights, sounds, and smells of the patch town; although Eckley's mid-nineteenth-century miners' homes are original, filmmakers built its coal breaker, and the manicured village lawns invite picnicking, not coal picking.

To expose the region's selective memory, Miller creates in *That Championship Season* players who reunite not only to recall their triumph, but also to forget the damage they inflicted on others. For example, George at first denies remembering that the team raped a mentally challenged woman, but, when pressed, tells Tom, "Don't ever breathe a word" (8). Forced into retirement from his job as a teacher for hitting a student, Coach refuses to dwell on the fact that he broke the student's jaw (42). The team participates in a collective amnesia about its greatest sin, the championship game, which it won because—following Coach's orders—Martin, the absent player, broke the ribs of an opponent (45).

The play links this buried violence to nostalgia. Opening stage directions describe two racks of loaded, hair-trigger shotguns hanging in a room whose "dominant mood . . . is nostalgia" (5). Act 1 starts with Tom brandishing a shotgun; it ends with George threatening to shoot Phil (5, 22). Beside the gun racks hang "overlarge" photos of John Kennedy and Joe McCarthy, which recall Kennedy's assassination and McCarthy's witch hunt for communists, along with a photo of Teddy Roosevelt, whom Coach approvingly misquotes, "Walk softly and carry a big stick" (5, 10). Twenty years ago, Coach practiced this threat of violence by running his team until their "blisters busted . . . bloody socks and all" (47). Winning, he declares, demands pain: "You endure pain to win, a law of life. . . . It's good to hurt" (27).[62]

Allusions in the play to local history remind audiences of violence done to the land. Up for reelection, George faces Sharmen, who is running on a progressive platform of economic and environmental renewal. Sharmen's name recalls a major post-mining regional employer, the Charmin Paper Products Company, a subsidiary of Procter and Gamble. Built in the mid-1960s, the plant employed in 1971 approximately two thousand people and consumed hardwoods trucked from within a seventy-five-mile radius. Wood suppliers, who were "concerned largely with production of mine props in the past," now turned to Charmin, whose foresters worked with "owners of woodlands and other suppliers to promote good improvement of forest lands," which included "harvest cutting"—that is, clear-cutting woodlots of a thousand or more acres.[63] After mining's collapse, Lackawanna Valley residents, left with a collection of "dress factories . . . car lots, bars and empty mines" (35), found employment beyond the valley in plants such as Charmin's, trading ties to one set of environmental injuries for ties to another.

Miller uses strip mining, which after the 1920s put more and more miners out of work and accounted for more and more anthracite extracted, to call attention to the valley's environmental damage.[64] In exchange for financing George's first mayoral campaign, Phil received "all the strip land he's leased from the city." In the latest campaign, however, Sharmen, whom George calls an "ecology nut," has vowed to "break that lease" (8). Later, when Phil unsuccessfully tries to cut a deal to elect Sharmen, he identifies himself as "the number one threat to the environment . . . the friendly pollutionist" (30). Emblematic of strip mining's power to damage the land is the "shovel working for [Phil] now, looks like a dinosaur." With this huge dragline destroying mountains, Phil becomes an object of ridicule in his alma mater's newspaper, which uses his name as the caption for a photo of a pig. Angry, Phil declares that "the stupid bastards don't realize you can't kill a mountain. Mountains grow back" (14). It's hard to hear him today and not picture mountaintop removal, a current coal company practice that kills mountains in West Virginia.

Strip mining also buries the elephant in the room, quite literally: the shame of winning. After George's single accomplishment as mayor, opening a zoo, becomes a costly embarrassment with the death of an elephant, the zoo's main attraction, he orders the body buried in an abandoned mine shaft (16). Appropriately, in a play much about selective memory, George at first wanted to stuff the carcass and display it in a museum (20). For residents of the Lackawanna Valley, however, the elephant's death recalls the real-life Tillie, a beloved elephant euthanized in 1966 at Scranton's Nay Aug Park zoo.[65] Although Tillie's grave was kept secret, the "42-year old pachyderm [was] placed in an abandoned strip mine pit . . . a map sketching the burial plot [was] made and filed with the city engineer's office to avoid any confusion if and when Tillie's remains are uncovered in the future." Miller may have been drawn to this incident because the zoo's next elephant died, "ill with extensive bloating," in 1971, the year before the play's production.[66] In any case, burying the elephant, an animal famous for its memory, is a metaphor for the men burying the memory that they had to wound an opposing player to win the championship. Similarly, in terms of the region, burying the elephant symbolizes a collective forgetting of the environmental costs of industrial prosperity.

Strip-mining, which visibly scars land, serves as a metaphor for the men "savagely turn[ing] on each other," an outward expression of inner loathing at using violence to steal the championship (41). Told that Phil has had an affair with his wife, George threatens to kill his friend, who he claims "prey[s] on people" (22). A self-professed "talented man being swallowed up by anonymity," James, who campaigns for George because he wants a "share of the spoils," has no problem offering to replace George as candidate (20, 21). "All cheap cynicism and booze," Tom, James's alcoholic brother, cannot help offering sarcastic comments at his friends' expense (33). In an effort to advance his protégé's career and to maintain his own illusion that he made his players into "winners," Coach convinces an unwilling George to institutionalize his newborn baby, who was born with Down's syndrome (32, 37, 47). All but Tom turn on Martin, a "perfect ballplayer" until they recall his insistence that they cheated to win; he then becomes a "real sonofabitch" (12, 35, 46).

Coach physically defends his team's preferred story of the championship game. After Tom challenges him to remember what really happened—"we stole that trophy, championship season is a lie"—Coach slaps him and forces him to leave the house.[67] After ostracizing this unbeliever, Coach reminds the faithful that the glory is still theirs, "it's history now. In the books" (45, 46). No accident, the phrase "history now" emphasizes how the past overrides the present: once recorded, the story cannot be revised, ever. Committed to the narrative he and his team annually relive, Coach refuses to acknowledge any other version of the past. As if to underscore the violent claustrophobia implied in this doctrine, Miller sets the play wholly indoors, in the house Coach inherited from his parents, a home in the "Gothic-Victorian tradition," an allusion to the late nineteenth century, when mining spread up and down the valley (5).

To ensure that the team's sanitized version of history will not be forgotten, Coach exaggerates it to national significance. Although Phil frankly acknowledges that "nobody but us remembers that game," Coach insists that the championship gives "this defeated town something to be proud of . . . a victory!" (30). Without irony, he equates team, town, and nation: "We are the country, boys, never forget that, never. Thousands of cities like ours; we fire the furnace, keep it all going round, indispensable!" (18). The present tense here reveals his inability to see what local audiences would know: by 1972, deep mining had ended in the valley. Grounded in an "Old Testament temperament," Coach, a "man of immense and powerful contradictions," rallies the others against Tom's story by boasting, "I chose my country, God forgive me. I made the supreme sacrifice and went to work in the mines for my country," a job he defended by breaking the legs of a communist union organizer (9, 28, 46–47). To work in the mines is to die for the nation, the team writ large, which is now "fighting for her life[,] and we are the heart and we play always to win!" (47). In Coach's mind, uniting to defeat Sharmen, the "communist," the environmentalist, takes on national urgency (21).[68]

Although meant to counter Tom's truth telling, Coach's nostalgic reminiscence, the only allusion to green space in the play, points to violence inherent within the region's interwoven cultural, environmental, and economic histories. Right after exiling Tom, Coach recalls a time when the "whole town would come together. We'd have these huge picnics, great feasts of picnics. . . . Gone now, all gone, vanished. Lake, picnic grounds, gone now. All concrete and wires and glass now. Used car lots now. Phil's trucks came and took it away." Strip mining may have destroyed Eden, but paradise can be regained, George claims, telling Coach, ironically, "We can bring it back, Coach, urban renewal, preserve the environment" (46). Ignoring George, Coach caps his drunken reverie by playing a recording of the team's win, during which the "*men sit, transfixed by the memory*" (47). After the record ends, the itinerant Tom returns, the men forgive one another, and all agree to work together to defeat Sharmen, the mayoral candidate who seeks to end political corruption and environmental violence (47, 48). The play concludes with the team, gathered round the trophy, shooting commemorative photos of this twentieth reunion (48).

Mine Subsidence

At first glance, the Lackawanna Valley appears solid, a collection of streets, homes, and businesses; traffic, strip malls, and parks; forests and fields. But appearances deceive. This land has been turned upside down. Forests are third and fourth growth; fields, often mine-reclamation sites. Hills are mounds of mine waste; their trees, usually cherry or birch, apparently the only vegetation that grows in mine rock; and the dirt often isn't soil, but simply more waste.[69] For that matter, one can never be sure of one's ground; every once in a while it gives way, exposing space. The past here eats at the earth, threatening at any moment to plunge one into darkness. To keep history at bay, people prop up surfaces with mine tailings.

The valley is a palimpsest of unstable ground: crisscrossing mines that brought untold wealth to few now menace many. Subsidence, caused by the collapse of mine pillars, has long plagued the place. Although infrequent, holes open in yards, buildings tip, sidewalks crack. Sometimes parking lots and roads crumble. Not only is subsidence a metaphor for the valley's present economic instability—as I write, unemployment hovers near 10 percent—but also for the instability of all things; subsidence hurts people, damages property, and shakes one's confidence in certainties.[70]

In 2003, the Office of Surface Mining reported that between 1984 and 2003 the northern field averaged about 60 mine cave-ins each year; in the same period subsidence annually damaged more than 159 structures. Two kinds of subsidence haunt Scranton: sinkholes and troughs. The former, and most common, happens when a mine roof caves, creating an "abrupt depression"; the latter happens when "overburden sags downward due to the failure of remnant pillars," creating a "shallow, yet broad depression."[71]

Mine subsidence has not escaped the notice of the region's writers, who see it as a metaphor for exposure, a revelation of fragility. In "Three Towns," Sherry Fairchok describes a woman surrendering to the moment when the surface gives way, opening up what had been hidden: "Under a jittery ceiling light, / her dust cloth balled in her fist, she waited, / resigned, and watched next door's / place open up / like a dollhouse, all its peony-patterned / wallpaper revealed, / its staircase steady / through a mist of plaster dust" (17–22). In "Carbondale Cave-In," Karen Blomain, describing a "night the earth shrugged, cracked / like a hollow egg," follows a family from their destroyed home as they negotiate a "funhouse stair, cross a makeshift / gangplank and fall / into the eager crowd" (1–2, 24–26). Gawkers drive by, "each window / full of greedy refusing eyes," to catch sight of the house: "Pink blossoms and grey / doves cling to wallpaper trees / against the stare of floodlights" (29–30, 31–33).

Tragedies pockmark the history of mine subsidence in the Anthracite Region. In 1869, most members of two Hazleton-area families died when their homes disappeared into the earth. In 1944, the ground under a Pittston sidewalk swallowed a two-year-old girl who stood a few feet from her aunt. In 1982, in downtown Scranton, a caving swallowed a heavy equipment operator and his machine; the man had been "working under a federal contract to fill an abandoned mine shaft." In no way tragic, but still unsettling, in 1994 subsidence opened the lawn in front of the Marywood Science Center; ten years later, a ten-by-eight-foot hole appeared in a nearby parking lot.[72] To keep their places, miners throughout the Lackawanna Valley undermined their own communities, a fit metaphor for any extraction industry.

Anxiety about cavings has subsided since the end of mining, probably due to their rarity, some people's ignorance of the possibility, and others' dismissal of the odds of it happening to them. One of my neighbors, for example, insists that since we live so close to where many mine owners once lived, there could be no mines beneath us. My answer: we may live in the mine owners' neighborhood, but we live just as close to the site of the former Marvine colliery, once the largest operation in the northern field.[73] When I recall that mine owners permitted mining under their homes, I don't mind paying subsidence insurance.

In its original sales agreement with Jordan, Hannah, and Jordan, Pennsylvania Coal retained all mineral rights to our lot; we own only surface rights. And our deed stipulates in bold that we cannot stop the company or its descendants from driving tunnels under our home: "**THE OWNER OR OWNERS OF SUCH COAL MAY HAVE THE COMPLETE LEGAL RIGHT TO REMOVE ALL OF SUCH COAL AND, IN THAT CONNECTION, DAMAGE MAY RESULT TO THE SURFACE OF THE LAND AND ANY HOUSE . . .**" Admitting that it has already mined beneath Richmont Park, Pennsylvania Coal tells us that neither the company nor its descendants can be held liable for injuries or damages as a result of mining, ever. This exemption from responsibility is named, appropriately, a cutthroat waiver.[74]

When mining was in its infancy, the cutthroat waiver seemed like a good idea: companies could get coal, workers could get a place to live, and a growing city could benefit from both. People assumed that miners could never remove all the coal, and in those early days the miners couldn't. By the 1890s, however, mining engineers had perfected the art of robbing pillars—that is, removing coal left to support the surface—which meant that miners would, from then on, hollow out more thoroughly the veins beneath their own homes. This second mining made real the abstract space created by separating surface and subsurface rights; a mine cave-in reminded everyone how unreal was the separation.

In the decades to follow, mine subsidence, particularly on Scranton's West Side, grew to become a constant concern. On 29 August 1909, for example, pillars failed under General Lafayette School, dropping the building six to eight feet. Although it denied responsibility, Peoples Coal Company had last mined beneath the property. Occurring in a "hive of buildings," the subsidence, declared the *Scranton Times*, was the "worst the city has encountered."[75] The same day that General Lafayette School dropped, a backyard mine cave nearly swallowed three children in nearby Dunmore.[76]

Once you know that the ground under you is hollow, a reported cave-in makes you wonder whether it might happen to you. West Siders especially were scared, and the controversy over the cave at General Lafayette led to the

Fig. 11 Mine subsidence, 1923. Courtesy of the Lackawanna Historical Society.

formation of the Scranton Surface Protective Association, a citizens' group that lobbied the state to force anthracite coal companies to compensate people for property damaged by subsidence. In response, Pennsylvania appointed in 1911 a commission to study the problem; debate about what to do, predictably, dragged on for years.[77]

The entire city may not have been disappearing into the earth, but high-profile problems kept people on edge. For example, on 11 August 1911, ten months after Peoples Coal declared St. Ann's monastery safe from subsidence, a mine shaft shifted, damaging the building. Two years later, St. Ann's suffered another "'squeeze' . . . whereby the underground caverns stabilized," a subsidence that, ironically, assured that the monastery could be rebuilt; people attributed the new stability to St. Ann, patron saint of miners. To guarantee that the monastery stood on solid ground, the community raised $37,000 to buy the coal—and the voids—beneath the church.[78]

Taking a lead in the fight for surface protection, Scranton attorney Philip Mattes devised in 1915–1916 a legal strategy he called the Third Estate, the right to support or cave property.[79] His reasoning: if a cutthroat waiver separates surface and subsurface rights, the surface owner must possess a third right, the right of surface support, which he can transfer to someone else. In effect, the owner has the right to destroy or protect the surface. After the Third Estate concept received legal force in *Penman v. Jones* (1917), many of the "most prominent coal company officials" purchased the right to protect their homes.[80] With the Third Estate, a landowner held the legal right to undermine his place. With a cutthroat waiver, a company sold someone land that it retained the right to wreck. Both concepts, the cutthroat waiver and the Third Estate, rested on the same assumption: that we have the right to do what we will with the earth; keep it, cave it, lay it waste.

A grandson of Charles Mattes, who helped the Scranton family found Lackawanna Iron and Coal, Philip Mattes had firsthand experience of surface and subsurface issues. He served as counsel for the Scranton Surface Protective Association, backed a successful Scranton mayoral candidate's "platform of mine-cave relief," and, as the new mayor's city solicitor, fought for surface protection all the way to the U.S. Supreme Court. According to the 1921 *Scranton Directory*, Mattes lived on Fisk Street, under which ran the Pennsylvania Tunnel, which drained the mines that had polluted Meadow Brook in the 1870s, fouling the Sandersons' fishpond and water supply.[81] About the time that Mattes lived on Fisk, Scranton Coal Company "caved in and wrecked" Boulevard Avenue, an important thoroughfare and a Fisk cross street.[82]

When Lackawanna Iron and Coal sold surface rights to developers in 1873, Mattes found, it retained mineral rights and the right of support, but when the company transferred its mineral rights to its subsidiary, Lackawanna Iron and Steel, it forgot to transfer the right of support. The latter company then passed its mineral rights to the Scranton Coal Company. When Lackawanna Iron and Coal went bankrupt, a Scranton bank ended up with its assets, which, according to Mattes's theory, included the right of support to land that Scranton Coal was then mining, which was much of downtown. After *Penman v. Jones*, the bank transferred to surface owners—for a small fee—the right of support.[83] For other Scranton property owners, however, cutthroat waivers limited them to surface rights.

Subsidence in West Side continued, escalating tensions. Irresponsible mining at the Oxford mine, operated by Peoples Coal, a lessee of D. L. & W., collapsed buildings on 3 February 1919; despite orders to stop, Peoples Coal continued mining, sparking the Battle of the Oxford, in which a Peoples employee assaulted the Scranton mayor as he led police into the mine to discover evidence of the company's defiance.[84] A small incident, the Battle of the Oxford illustrates just how at odds industry and community had become over the issue of mine subsidence. The state felt pressure to intervene.

In 1917, the year of *Penman v. Jones* and the peak year of anthracite production, the major coal operators responded to pending state mine-cave legislation by announcing that they would repair all mine-cave damages up to $5,000.[85] Companies saw the assumption of responsibility for damage to a surface property, even when they were not at fault, as good public relations and as a means to retain their workforce, given that most of those affected by subsidence worked for the coal industry, whether directly or indirectly. Increasing incidents of subsidence coincided—maybe not accidently—with the advent of subcontracting, in which coal companies leased subsurface rights to smaller companies, which, in turn, enabled the larger companies to escape the costs and liabilities of actually mining coal.[86] In these years, too, an anti-monopoly case forced railroads to divest themselves of their coal lands. D. L. & W. began to separate its coal and railroad operations in 1921, a process completed in 1926 when the D. L. & W. Coal Company merged with the Glen Alden Company. The coal department of the Delaware and Hudson became the Hudson Coal Company, which operated the Marvine colliery.[87]

In 1920, in answer to a proposed state tax on anthracite to fund relief for mine subsidence, W. H. Williams, Senior Vice President for Hudson Coal, claimed—a little counterintuitively—that continued mining would solve the mine-cave problem. And besides, he argued, subsidence was not a big issue; it mainly affected Scranton, after all, and not even the whole city. The problem could easily be solved, Williams noted, in either of two ways: (1) people could purchase the pillars beneath them or add artificial support; or (2) the people affected could simply move. The latter, he pointed out, was accomplished out west when a "large built-up community" was relocated so that an "extensive and valuable deposit of iron ore" could be mined. Just in case no one bought these ideas, Williams ended his response with a third option. Instead of taxing the companies that undermined the city in the first place, the residents of Scranton should tax themselves in order to raise funds to purchase surface support.[88] Hudson Coal, of course, bore no responsibility for tearing the surface.

Echoing Justice Clark in *Pennsylvania Coal Company v. Sanderson*, W. H. Williams wanted people to believe that the inconvenience of a few must not stop an industry that benefits all. Williams claimed that nothing "prevents full protection to life and limb if the proper safeguards are taken [e.g., purchasing pillars or moving]. This protection may involve some inconvenience to property holders in a very small portion of the anthracite territory."[89] This would work as an argument but for the fact that inconveniences to a few, which he would isolate, accumulate and add up to major inconveniences, not only to people, but to the health of the watershed, a fact made visible in the history of the Lackawanna River.

Despite the arguments of Williams, the Surface Protective Association kept pushing the state to help. To convince legislators that mine subsidence was a serious problem, the association distributed to them photographs of mine caves. The booklet led with a photo of a casket opened by a mine cave in Cathedral Cemetery and a shot of a damaged school.[90] Association lobbying paid off in 1921, when the Pennsylvania legislature passed on the same day the Kohler and Fowler acts. Kohler prohibited anthracite mining in developed areas; Fowler created an optional tax on coal companies that was meant to fund repair of subsidence damage. A company that refused to pay the Fowler tax would be subject to Kohler; if a company paid the tax, however, it could mine under built-up areas. An attempt to circumvent the cutthroat waiver, the Kohler Act was designed to transfer the Third Estate from mine owners to surface owners.[91] These attempts to protect Scranton's surface laid the grounds for one of the most important Supreme Court cases of the twentieth century, one that echoes still today.

The Pennsylvania Coal Company wasted no time responding to the acts. Four days after their passage, the company notified H. J. Mahon that it would soon rob the pillars beneath his home, which he had purchased from his father-in-law, a Pennsylvania Coal executive. Fearing a subsidence that would damage his house, or so he claimed, Mahon obligingly sued the company, using the Kohler Act as leverage. Filing an "amicable action," Mahon, an attorney who lived in Pittston, a Pennsylvania Coal company town, sued in Luzerne County court, which kept the case out of Scranton.[92] Philip Mattes, then Scranton city solicitor, contributed briefs to the case, and claimed that "Mahon had brought the suit at the behest of the company to have the trial located in a favorable jurisdiction," a circumstance that "complicated the city's [Scranton's] legal strategy." According to Mattes, Luzerne County Judge Henry A. Fuller "brusquely informed counsel that he did not care for any oral arguments and promptly declared the act unconstitutional." So much for weighing facts. Despite the ruling, the plaintiffs appealed.[93]

Eventually, the case made its way to the U.S. Supreme Court. In *Pennsylvania Coal Company v. Mahon* (1922), the court ruled that Pennsylvania Coal had every right to remove anthracite from beneath Mahon's home because Mahon's deed expressly gave the company subsurface mineral rights. In claiming that the Kohler Act had violated the company's property rights, the court, in effect, upheld the validity of the cutthroat waiver.[94]

The ruling has become a major moment in U.S. legal history because the decision asserted that "land-use regulation could amount to an unlawful taking of property." Prior to the ruling, "compensation for takings had applied only to physical confiscations of private lands, not to regulations." The case posed a problem no one has solved: where is the line between seizure of property and regulation of it?[95] When the court ruled that the coal company's property rights had been violated, the justices established a "frustratingly vague 'goes too far' limit on government's police power." The court's thinking in *Mahon* mirrored that of the Pennsylvania Supreme Court in *Pennsylvania Coal Company v. Sanderson*: "Trifling inconveniences to particular persons must sometimes give way to the necessities of a great community."[96]

Although several much-publicized mine cave-ins happened in West Side, the problem was not confined to that neighborhood. For example, subsidence threatened the establishment of Marywood, which was founded in 1915 on land that the Sisters had purchased from Pennsylvania Coal. Seeking to ensure solid ground, in May 1914 the congregation asked to buy from the company the coal pillars beneath their main building; two years later Pennsylvania Coal obliged, selling the pillars in the Pittston vein for $8,310, with the understanding, of course, that the "coal in the other veins will have to be purchased in the future." The sale included coal within ninety feet of the seminary building; beyond this boundary the company could mine away. A 1917 blueprint shows a honeycomb of mines surrounding the seminary building; miners drove two chambers part-way beneath the structure. In 1919, the company let the nuns know that mining might collapse the IHM cemetery.[97]

Following *Mahon*, tensions about subsidence eased, but not because of the ruling, which made little difference in resolving the controversy. Instead, public pressure and economic interdependence forced cooperation between Scranton and the coal companies, which rededicated themselves to repairing subsidence damage.[98] In flush times, most companies fixed damages and refilled mines, but after mining ended in the early 1960s, the burden of fixing and refilling fell to the city.

In 1912, mining engineer Eli Conner, in an evaluation of several methods to support the surface, concluded that "flushing with culm, crushed rock, or sand is practically the only proper and available method for the support of overburden, and the ultimate recovery of the pillar-coal." Flushing not only protected the surface, he noted, but also, by 1911, was a "generally-accepted method of disposal of refuse."[99] In removing layer after layer of anthracite, miners may have hollowed time and space, but in flushing mines they refilled the space with other times, other places. A kind of reverse mining, flushing combined culm and water in a mixture meant to shore up surfaces.

Unfortunately, Conner's recommendations fell on deaf ears; major flushing projects got underway in Scranton only in 1960, immediately after the president of Hudson Coal Company warned that water from the 1959 Knox disaster could spill into city mines. In response, throughout the '60s and into the '70s, workers trucked crushed culm to hoppers across town, added water, and piped the mess underground, where other workers sprayed it into worked-out veins.[100] Hardened, the mix made a mine pillar.

Mountains of culm disappeared into the earth. For example, running sixteen trucks for sixteen hours a day, a city contractor flushed Marvine silt under the University of Scranton in 1961. By decade's end, one Green Ridge culm bank, the Von Storch, was shoring up ground beneath the Lackawanna County courthouse and much of western downtown.[101] Workers flushed the Von Storch pile, which took thirty or more years to accumulate, in five years.

Unfortunately, as culm settled, gaps appeared, so, despite all the flushing, mine subsidence still happens. Most recently, in June 2011, the "earth opened" a ten-by-ten-foot hole in a Scranton street that "partially swallowed an 8-ton dump truck." Ironically, the truck hauled fill for a site where a blighted building had just been torn down. The city director of public works blamed the collapse, to no one's surprise, on an "underground vault or shaft," one of a "series of such incidents around the city in recent months."[102]

On the same day, across the street from the Lackawanna County Courthouse, two former county commissioners stood trial in federal court, accused of pay-to-play corruption. After a day's deliberation, a jury convicted them of bribery, extortion, and tax fraud, ending "perhaps the most sensational corruption trial in county history." Prosecutors brought the charges following testimony in a 2008 corruption trial that had accused a lifelong friend of one commissioner of an alleged "shakedown scheme involving a no-bid contract to remove tons of pigeon dung from the top of the county courthouse." In defending themselves at their trial, the commissioners touted their record of good works, which, they pointed out, included renovating the courthouse. Commenting on the guilty verdicts, a local reporter noted that the "façade of innocence" that the defendants "had worked so tirelessly to build came crashing down around them." In an editorial, the local paper asked a good question that implies a great hope: "When will business as usual be viewed as a vestige of the past, like anthracite coal?"[103]

If our history and literature are indications, neither coal nor corruption can be completely cut from the county's geology.

Coda: Watersheds in Play

Is this memory or promise?

—Wendell Berry, "The River Bridged and Forgot"

In 1972, the Commonwealth of Pennsylvania officially committed itself to conceiving of the natural world as more than a commercial and industrial resource. As a result of increased national awareness of environmental issues, which led to the first Earth Day in 1970, Pennsylvania amended its constitution to include respect for the nonhuman environment. Article 1, section 27, of the Pennsylvania Constitution states, "The people have a right to clean air, pure water, and to the preservation of the natural, scenic, historic and esthetic values of the environment. Pennsylvania's public natural resources are the common property of all the people, including generations yet to come. As trustee of these resources, the Commonwealth shall conserve and maintain them for the benefit of all the people." It's hard to understate how significant—at least theoretically—this amendment was in a state that had devoted much of its existence to promoting mineral extraction industries. In practice, however, the state—the machinery of government and the people—has since the 1970s compiled a mixed record of success in adhering to this constitutional principle.

Scranton and Con-Acres may each be a "diminished thing," no matter the standard one uses, but my response to this fact cannot be all "grief and rage."[1] The world finds a way: some places heal, and some people work hard to right wrongs. Although not pristine, the Lackawanna and Lackawaxen rivers run cleaner now than a hundred years ago; of course acid mine drainage still kills the last three miles of the Lackawanna, but even this may soon change. Here and there, examples of renewable energy, although scattered, have taken root. Visible from each watershed, for instance, forty-three windmills atop the Moosic Mountains generate enough electrical power for twenty-two thousand households.[2]

For a while, I helped to pollute Chesapeake Bay. When our home was built in 1907, the contractor diverted roof runoff into underground cast iron pipes that led directly to the Lackawanna River, a tributary of the Susquehanna, which feeds the bay. In 1970, the city tied the pipes to its sewer network, but heavy rains often overflowed the waste treatment facility, flushing raw sewage into the river. In response to federal mandates to restore the Chesapeake, in 2006 Scranton made it illegal to link downspouts to the sewer system.[3] Neighborhood by neighborhood, the Scranton Sewer Authority disconnected storm runoff from sewage disposal.

Marywood has put some of its coal legacy to positive use. In 2010, for example, the school drilled into mines to cool its architecture building; subterranean pumps push mine water at 58–60 degrees through ceiling-mounted chilled beams before returning it underground. The chilled beams—cooling coils—eliminate machine air conditioning, rely on natural convection, and require no electricity.[4]

In 2008, the Pennsylvania Bureau of Abandoned Mine Reclamation reclaimed forty acres of campus, a third of the institution's footprint, "old mine workings, including one pit 250 feet long and 40 feet deep." After "using excavators and bulldozers to recontour the former no-man's land," workers trucked in topsoil and planted grasses, creating a "gently sloping, terraced hillside." A lacrosse field tops the site, and plans are in the works to build additional athletic fields. About the project, a state spokesperson said, "When you think about it, it's really dramatic. . . . It's gone from gray and black to green."[5]

Extending this project, Mary's Garden will restore land. An alternative to single-minded reclamation (e.g., planting grass, building athletic fields), the proposed garden will evoke the site's promise and memory in interweaving the "healing power of nature" and "vestiges of the mining era." Planned to encompass five acres, the garden will link the Paleozoic to more recent times in using sculpted flowers to refashion this once-blasted space. A "filter feeder in ancient swamps," a crinoid will stand at the "center" of a Madonna Lily; another flower, Mary's Rose, will unfold the geology of the Lackawanna Valley in its "circles of 'petals.'" Former culm piles, "rusted pipes," and "'breathing holes' for the mines below" will remind visitors that beneath them lie "seven levels of subterranean passages and chambers." Across the garden will cut a ravine, a "miniaturization of the Lackawanna Valley with a tiny river running at its base." Above the ravine, a crown of thorns, made of roses and blackberries, will line the edges of Mary's Rose, and include "hematite nodules . . . which rust and drip like blood." Emblematic of Marywood's mission, the projected garden "frames the world and makes The Word visible."[6]

Such resurrections have not spread to all parts of each local watershed. In Mount Pleasant Township, on 3 April 2009 someone reported to state police five men dumping an "oily substance" across dirt roads near Johnson Creek. The five emptied three fifty-five-gallon drums of material, either ignorant of the damage it could do to a "wild trout stream" or knowing and not caring. A Department of Environmental Protection spokesperson explained that "The substance did get into Johnson Creek, but it was raining so hard the substance flushed out." Despite this assurance, local residents and an investigating conservation officer felt "frustrated . . . because it was deliberate."[7]

The Johnson Creek pollution may have been small, but it was different only in degree from similar incidents in the Lackawanna and Susquehanna watersheds. In 1984, for instance, a court convicted a Scranton homeowner of pouring over three million gallons of wastes into a borehole accessible through a garage drain. Two feet in diameter and one hundred ten feet deep, the borehole funneled into a mine pool liquids from "food processors, solvent recyclers, and pharmaceutical manufacturers." Federal officials feared that the wastes would migrate through mines, spill into the Lackawanna, and flow on to the Susquehanna, endangering fish.[8]

In Pittston in the 1970s, an oil company dumped tanker loads of "liquid industrial wastes, including oily wastes, into underground mine areas via a mine ventilation borehole" located at an auto service station. By 1979, the wastes had made their way through a mine tunnel and into the Susquehanna, staining a thirty-five-mile stretch. Added to the EPA's superfund list in 1987, the mine pool now primarily poses the threat of a "flushout of oil into the Susquehanna River," which last occurred in 1985, when heavy rains brought "100,000 gallons of waste oil" into the waterway.[9]

Natural gas drilling challenges the commonwealth's constitution like no other issue. In size and scope, drilling in Marcellus shale has overwhelmed the ability of state machinery to keep track of what's going on, let alone prepare for its environmental repercussions. More than eighty companies have been given a green light to punch holes here, which means billions in investments.[10] An example of interest in shale gas: between 2005 and 2010, the Pennsylvania Department of Environmental Protection has approved just over 8,100 Marcellus well-drilling permits; however, DEP issued 2,123 of them in the first eight months of 2011 alone. In the period 2005 to 2010, workers drilled 3,806 Marcellus wells; in the first eight months of 2011, they bored 1,222.[11] Meanwhile, crews scrambled to lay pipe and construct compressor stations, creating an infrastructure that further binds rural Pennsylvania to East Coast cities.

Marcellus money has flowed into the region, enabling hard-up farmers to pay debts and bringing small towns back from the edge of erasure. New businesses have sprung up, increased revenues have buoyed local economies, and many unemployed have found good-paying jobs. Late-signing landowners have really hit it big; in September 2009, for example, when one drilling company paid Susquehanna County "property owners $5,500 per acre and 20 percent royalties," another went further, to "$5,750 per acre with the same 20 percent royalty."[12] In one of the poorest counties in the state, it would be tough not to sign a lease.

Like any industrial boom, however, this one has had its share of costs: "Wells have blown out, and explosions from methane contamination have destroyed homes." Workers have gotten hurt, and spills have polluted streams and damaged woods. Even as they study what's happening, scientists admit that they know little about how the boom might affect the "land, streams, and available water supplies in the Appalachian Basin."[13]

Penn's woods may be at risk. Marcellus shale lies under 71 percent of the state's forests and game lands. With just over two million acres of woodlands,

Pennsylvania is home to "one of the top four [forest] systems in the nation." Of these 2.2 million acres, the state owns no subsurface rights to at least 290,000 acres, or 13 percent of the total, which makes each acre open to drilling. By 2010, almost a third of the state's forests had been leased, approximately 675,000 acres of state and private lands; the Commonwealth itself has leased to natural gas drillers 385,400 acres of timberland. The Nature Conservancy estimates that by 2030 Marcellus activity will eat up 34,000 to 82,000 forest acres, mainly in regions of the state where the "largest and most intact forest patches could be fragmented into smaller patches."[14]

What has kept most people on edge, however, is not lost woods but the prospect of poisoned water. Hydraulic fracturing uses three million gallons of water, and injects into the earth "more than 80 chemicals," which pass through aquifers via heavily encased piping. Much of this water resurfaces, so companies either recycle it to frack other wells, or truck it to municipal waste treatment facilities, which are "often incapable of screening all drilling-waste contaminants."[15] A bad casing job could kill an aquifer.

In 2011, Duke University researchers found methane, the key component of natural gas, in 85 percent of the sixty drinking water wells they tested. The billion-dollar question: did the contamination come from near-surface biodegradation, or from Marcellus shale, thousands of feet below? The data showed that water wells near drilling sites had higher levels of methane than did wells in non-active zones; significantly, the chemical signature of this methane suggested that it arose from deep underground, and not from shallow sources. The study asserted that "leaky gas-well casings" likely allowed methane to migrate upward from shale to drinking water aquifers, although researchers did not rule out the possibility that hydraulic fracturing created new or wider fissures through which gas migrated upward through the existing "fracture system."[16] Methane in water wells can ignite, as it did when it shattered a concrete well cover in Dimock, Susquehanna County, on New Year's Day 2009.[17]

Today's natural gas frenzy echoes the western Pennsylvania oil boom of the 1860s, the world's first, which began along Oil Creek, in Venango County. Within days of Edwin Drake's success, early boomers convinced farmers, unaware of "their own land's skyrocketing value," to sign leases at "bargain rates." Money and people soon flowed into Oil Creek Valley, and, in what may be an early form of fracking, drillers used nitroglycerin "torpedoes" to increase well flows. The most important similarity, however, is just now happening in northeastern Pennsylvania: the Oil Creek boom radically reordered the land. As leases quickly traded, a farming-and-lumbering community transformed overnight into the site of "an industrial undertaking that had neither understanding nor appreciation of the local culture and ecology." Photographs from the period show a land stripped of trees and crowded with well derricks. Due to boat leakages and accidents, Oil Creek, a setting for "horrifying fires," absorbed upward of two-thirds of all oil it floated to market. Into the creek seeped so much oil that skimmers, sometimes collecting it in tin cups, turned a profit. Although a few wells still pump what oil remains, the boom that enriched some and employed many died within fifteen years, leaving behind a "sacrificial region," a place destroyed and forgotten.[18] With projections putting a drill pad on every eighty acres, land alteration in the Marcellus will be no less brutal, no less complete, and, in the end, no less forgotten.[19]

If advertising is any indication, natural gas companies want us to believe that they look out for their neighbors, work alongside us as fellow patriots, and stay in business solely to protect the environment. A December 2009 Chesapeake Energy ad in the *Forest City News* explains hydraulic fracturing, and then notes that—as "America's Champion of Natural Gas—Chesapeake is committed to being a good neighbor and responsible corporate citizen." Endless Mountain Energy, headquartered in Olyphant, ran ads in the same weekly to appeal to local loyalties: "Pennsylvania Land, Pennsylvania Gas, Pennsylvania Families, Let's Keep It: Pennsylvania Jobs, Pennsylvania Profits, Local and Pennsylvania Proud!" For a number of weeks, the *Forest City News* also carried a Chesapeake ad titled "A Champion of Natural Beauty"; the accompanying photo depicted not drilling rigs but clusters of flowers set against distant, wooded hillsides.[20]

As concerns about water came to dominate the news, Chesapeake reassured the public that it shared people's concerns. In a September 2010 ad in the Scranton *Sunday Times* Chesapeake explained that "natural gas is the most water-efficient energy source"; the ad appeared beneath an article about the 2010 BP Gulf oil spill. A June 2011 advertisement in the *Forest City News* quotes a Chesapeake employee, a "landowner relations coordinator," saying about her hometown, "I'm happy with Troy as it is. I'm also excited for Troy as it can be"; about her employer she reassures readers that "we work very closely with DEP

(Department of Environmental Protection) and other state agencies to ensure the water in this area is protected."[21] Although multinational corporations may contribute much to the community—jobs, taxes, bottled water—Troy should beware of behemoths bearing gifts.

That a company works closely with state agencies is no recommendation. In September 2010, the *Harrisburg Patriot-News* reported that the Pennsylvania Homeland Security office had been "tracking anti–gas drilling groups and their meetings—including a public screening of the film 'Gasland,'" a documentary critical of fracking. The office shared its intelligence with law enforcement agencies and gas drilling companies. When the information found its way to a pro-drilling website—where it was discovered by anti-drilling folks—the Homeland Security head "sent an e-mail of reprimand to the woman who e-mailed it," telling her that "we want to continue providing this support to the Marcellus Shale Formation natural gas stakeholders, while not feeding those groups fomenting dissent against those same companies." Part of this state tracking of citizens for the sake of free enterprise was to make cops and companies aware of public meetings that had been "singled out for attendance by anti–Marcellus Shale Formation natural gas drilling activists," including "township ordinance and zoning meetings in Butler, Wayne and Alleghany counties." When asked whether "planned activities of pro-drilling groups" had been followed, the state homeland security official was, in response, "at a loss."[22]

Natural gas companies have jealously guarded their self-image. When *Gasland* was nominated for a 2011 Academy Award, the Independent Petroleum Association of America (IPAA) wrote to the Motion Picture Academy to argue that the film should not win. IPAA also compiled "Debunking *Gasland*," a report that challenged assertions made by the Milanville (Wayne County) resident and New York filmmaker Josh Fox, creator of the documentary. Fox responded with his own report, "Affirming *Gasland*." As IPAA deflected questions, qualifications, and cautions, its membership drilled on.[23]

Demanding that we confront hard questions about what we value, poets remind us to pay attention now, or pay later. In "The River Bridged and Forgot," Wendell Berry, for example, mourns "our false prosperity" (e.g., big bank accounts) as he watches a river in "unwearying descent" carry the "soil / of ravaged uplands, waste / and acid from the strip mines" (2, 3–5, 6–7). These "poisons" constitute "everything / that we have given up, / the materials of Creation /

wrecked," all for a few dollars more (6, 10–13). Rolling across a bridge, built at cross-purposes to the river, people speed over the stream without accounting for what lies beneath. Because our technologies make the river neither barrier nor boon, we can simply forget it; no longer confronting it as a force of nature, or a source of life, we don't see that it carries what comes of our inattention and amnesia, evidence of land abused, ruined.

Refusing to be apocalyptic, however, Berry switches perspective, beginning the next stanza with "But" (15). Ravages observed in the first section give way to "still afternoons / of summer, [when] the water's face / recovers clouds, the shapes / of leaves" (15–18). In contrast to the "slow / cortege" of the destroyed in the opening stanza, this set of lines brims with life: "Maple, willow, / sycamore stand light / and easy . . . yellow / warbler, swallow, oriole stroke their deft flight" (9–10, 18–20, 22–24). The once-roiling river calms to mirror trees and sky. Although this reflection is a copy of the scene—much like the poem is a copy, a corruption, of life—"it shows the incorrupt"; in other words, the reflection, and the poem, glimpses the wild (27). At this point, the speaker does not know what to make of what he sees: "Is this memory or promise?" (28).

The next stanza, which is almost as long as the first two combined, turns our attention to the human observer, whose "grief" and "anger" amount to little beside the "unfinished" river (29, 30, 31). Unable to satisfy his "desire / for clarity," the individual may succumb to "despair" knowing that he "must by nature fail" (34–35, 46, 51). Instead, he takes solace in his work, which is the "lifework / of many lives that has / no end . . . [and] takes for pattern the heavenly / and earthly song"; his work, "Beside / this dark passage of water," which, for Berry himself, includes writing and small farming, "has turned away / the priced infinity / of mechanical desire," represented in the poem by the bridge (37–39, 43–44; 35–36, 52–54).

The final stanza places farming and writing in an even larger context. Although this human work "teaches the mind / resemblance to the earth / in seasonal fashioning," it is destined, like all things human, to "fail at their season's / end" (56–58, 64–65). Meanwhile, the "seasonless river," which "lays hand and handiwork / upon the world," flows on, "obedient / to a greater Mind, whole / past holding or beholding" (65, 66–67, 67–69). Humans can never comprehend fully this Mind, but we can see that its "flexing signature"—the river— heals by gathering the dead, "all the dooms," which, resurrected, "become the lives of things" (70, 71, 72). The best we can do: mimic translation and trust our lease on life.

In 2009, I attended the annual meeting of the Wayne County Extension Service, which took place in the cafeteria of the former Honesdale elementary school. The invocation, the poem "Out in the Fields with God," told me that I should toss my "foolish fears of what might happen . . . Among the new-mown hay." So simple; so certain. As I listened, I noticed on the evening's program a circle of green fields, trees, and partly cloudy skies: the logo of the Wayne County Chamber of Commerce.

I came to the meeting to hear Terry Engelder, the geologist who made the initial case for the presence of extractable natural gas in Marcellus shale. Baking a layer cake was the governing metaphor of his talk, "The Marcellus Gas Shale: Nature's Kitchen Under Wayne County."[24] The chemical processes that produced the gas, he explained, are akin to the processes of baking a Lord Baltimore cake.

Engelder made a point of telling us that this was his 113th public talk about Marcellus; by the time I heard him, he had spoken to 6,276 people, and Wayne was the twelfth county in which he'd offered a public presentation. He then asked us all to sign a register, which he passed around, that asked us to identify the high school or college we had attended. I couldn't tell whether he was recruiting for Penn State, starting a file on each of us, or trying to determine the level of education among people in the region. But he quickly engaged me with his cake baking, and offered clear talk about a complex topic.

Where you live in Wayne County determines whether you'll see from your kitchen window a natural gas well. According to Engelder, northern Wayne County falls within the Marcellus play; southern Wayne doesn't. Of course the farm straddles the line, in west-central Wayne County, making it a tough call to say whether it's in play. To make it even less clear, Engelder mentioned that in October 2009 Matoushek #1, a Stone Energy well a few miles south of our place, showed discouraging numbers. Despite the report, Stone Energy kept its options open, getting approval in 2010 to withdraw water from the West Branch of the Lackawaxen, just in case, I assume, it decided to frack the well. In 2009 and into 2012, however, the Delaware River Basin Commission kept drillers idle in the Delaware watershed as it rewrote its regulations.[25] So a well nearer to us hasn't been sunk, so far.

The right amount of heat in shale determines whether natural gas is present in sufficient and extractable quantities. The term %Ro (r naught) measures thermal maturity; a 3.0 on the %Ro scale is optimal for drilling. Matoushek #1 measures 4.0, which is less than optimal. Where to draw the line between the right and the not-quite-right temperature is difficult to determine because the exact orientation of subterranean isothermals—areas of constant temperature—is virtually impossible to discover.[26] The same guesswork would help in baking a cake over an open fire.

After Engelder ended his talk, I went for a piece of chocolate cake, a sheet cake, and there near the baked goods I first met Dave Messersmith, a Wayne County Extension educator, formerly assigned to crops and soils, who now spends upward of 80 percent of his time engaged in research and discussions about Marcellus Shale. Two years later, in his office, Messersmith explained that many fracking chemicals are friction reducers, which are meant to magnify pumped water's power to fracture rock. When I asked him what will likely be the largest impact of the drilling boom, he paused for several seconds before saying "Change." New people, new money, and new ways of thinking will rupture, rapidly, settled lives and places.[27]

Natural gas drilling will likely happen at the headwaters of the Lackawanna watershed—the Tennessee gas line crosses the Moosic Mountains there—but will likely not happen in the Lackawanna Valley, where any gas was probably burned away ages ago.[28] Drilling remains on hold in the Lackawaxen watershed, for now, courtesy of the Delaware River Basin Commission, mainly because New York and Philadelphia hesitate to risk their drinking water.

Although drilling isn't happening in Lackawanna Valley, gas companies truck drilling waste here. On 31 May 2011, Keystone Landfill, already the "second-busiest garbage dump" in the state, applied to the Pennsylvania Department of Environmental Protection for permission to absorb 1,500 more tons of trash per day. The increased tonnage would consist mainly of "rock waste from Marcellus Shale natural gas drilling," which Keystone has been accepting for three years. In 2010, Keystone buried 1.26 million tons of trash, half of it from New York, all of it covered with drilling waste.[29] If DEP approves the application, the landfill will bury even more rock waste, enabling Marcellus gas to power New York, even as New York, which ships its garbage here, blocks

Fig. 12 Natural gas drilling site in northeastern Pennsylvania. Used with the permission of the Scranton *Times-Tribune*.

drilling in its own watershed, circumstances that confirm rural northeastern Pennsylvania's colonial status in relationship to the city.

Although in the short run the gas boom may economically benefit north-eastern Pennsylvania, in the long run drilling will damage the land in ways I cannot foresee. Drilling is mining, after all, so I suspect that there will be only degrees of difference in the coming decades between gas rigs and coal breakers, between wastewater pits and culm banks, between boomtowns and company towns. As things stand now, the Marcellus region looks to become a much larger version of sacrificial places that the shale underlies: Oil Creek and Lackawanna Valley.

With so many watersheds in play, there can be no here and there, now and then; there's just here, now . . .

Notes

INTRODUCTION

1. De Blij, *Power of Place,* xi.
2. Buell, *Endangered World,* 7.
3. Vobejda, "Agriculture," A1.
4. Hess, "Imagining," 90.
5. Cronon, "Trouble," 85; Welling, "Ecoporn," 57; Hess, "Imagining," 90, 91.
6. *American Heritage Dictionary,* 2nd college ed. (1985), s.v. "working," defs. 4, 6b.
7. Conforti, *New England,* 5; Wilson, introduction to *New Regionalism,* xiii.
8. Miller and Sharpless, *Kingdom of Coal,* 3, 5.
9. Lackawanna Heritage Valley Authority, *Anthracite Coal,* 3, 5. Anthracite is 86 percent carbon (Miller and Sharpless, *Kingdom of Coal,* 5).
10. Kumpas, "Timbering," 4.
11. Berry, "Is Life," 185.
12. My assumption about G. F. Vasey Company is based on Vasey's prior work history (Hitchcock, *History of Scranton,* 594).
13. McPhee, *Former World,* 147–48. Braun counts three glaciers crossing the Scranton region and ten alternations between "cold, glacial-periglacial conditions and warm, humid temperate interglacial conditions" ("Surficial Geology").
14. Lesley, "J. P. Lesley," 335; see also G. Martin, *Soil Survey,* 2. Although geologists concluded that the county had no valuable minerals, including coal, anthracite was eventually mined in and around Browndale (Lesley, "Letter," vi; White, *Geological Survey,* 178). Part of the Appalachian Highlands, Wayne County divides geologically into two provinces, the Appalachian Plateau and the Ridge and Valley, which runs along the county's western border (G. Martin, *Soil Survey,* 2).
15. In his 1881 report of his survey of Mount Pleasant Township, state geologist I. C. White notes that, "as for shells, I have not noticed a single specimen of a *molluscan fossil* in the *Catskill* rocks anywhere within this district: if any exist they must be exceedingly rare" (*Geological Survey,* 63).
16. G. Martin, *Soil Survey,* 2, 14.
17. White, *Geological Survey,* 39. See also McGurl, *Lackawanna River,* 2.
18. White, *Geological Survey,* 177.
19. Hoskins, "Celebrating," 5. For the report, see Rogers, *Geology.*
20. Healey, *Coal Industry,* 62; Hoskins, "Celebrating," 5.
21. Rogers, *Geology,* 2:382.
22. Engelder and Lash, "Draft," 9, 15; Engelder and Lash, "Marcellus Shale" (quote).
23. "Super giant gas fields": Engelder, "Marcellus 2008," 18; "four state area": Engelder and Lash, "Marcellus Shale."
24. Engelder, "Marcellus 2008," 22. He acknowledges that this works only "if the gas could be produced fast enough, which, of course, it can't."
25. Engelder and Lash, "Draft," 15.

26. Smith, "Presidential Theme."

27. "Encounter the world": Marshall, *Story Line*, 7; nineteen ecocritics: "Narrative Scholarship." For examples of narrative scholarship, see Ian Marshall, *Story Line: Exploring the Literature of the Appalachian Trail* (1998) and *Peak Experiences: Walking Meditations on Literature, Nature, and Need* (2003); Diane Freedman, *Autobiographical Writing across the Disciplines: A Critical Reader* (2004); Corey Lee Lewis, *Reading the Trail: Exploring the Literature and Natural History of the California Crest* (2005); Laird Christensen and Hal Crimmel, *Teaching about Place: Learning from the Land* (2008); and Scott Slovic, *Going Away to Think: Engagement, Retreat, and Ecocritical Responsibility* (2008), which includes the published version of his WLA paper, "Ecocriticism: Storytelling, Values, Communication, Contact," pp. 27–30.

28. "How ecocritics write": Cohen, "Blues," 21; "American nature writing": Gifford, *John Muir*, 108; "significant academic reputations": J. Williams, "Belletrism," 415–16.

29. Cohen, "Blues," 21–22; Ball, "Literary Criticism," 237; Gifford, *John Muir*, 108–9.

30. Recent books that point to this multidisciplinary tension are Ruth Behar, *Translated Woman: Crossing the Border with Esperanza's Story* (1993); Barbara Laslett, Mary Jo Maynes, and Jennifer L. Pierce's *Telling Stories: The Use of Personal Narratives in the Social Sciences and History* (2008); and, more generally, *Academic Lives* (2009), in which Cynthia Franklin explores within the humanities the intersections among, as her subtitle notes, "Memoir, Cultural Theory, and the University Today."

31. Howard, "MLA Convention."

32. See Dublin and Licht, *Face of Decline*, 25.

33. Miller and Sharpless, *Kingdom of Coal*, 323; Woods, Omernik, and Brown, *Level III and IV*, 29.

34. Conzen, "Landownership Map," 11.

CHAPTER 1

1. MCF is one thousand cubic feet of gas. MER means most efficient recovery. PIG stands for pipeline inspection gadget.

2. VanBriesen, "Water Quantity."

3. "Gold rush," "second chance," and "both ways": Kanjorksi, address; "right way" and "mistakes": Casey, "Government's Role"; "long-term play": Klaber, "Economics"; major setback: Quigley, "Mineral Rights"; look to Texas: Kelsey, "Community Impacts."

4. A. Munley, "Welcoming Remarks"; Casey, "Government's Role." Attendees received a folder with an insert that read, "Northeast Pennsylvania's coal mining history offers a unique perspective on the issues surrounding natural gas drilling. While the coal boom of the 20th century led to prosperity for many, it also left an indelible mark on the region's environment and caused long-term economic disarray from dependence on a single industry. Many former coal-mining towns in Pennsylvania are still struggling to recover from the outcomes of unchecked industrial development" ("Overview").

5. Falchek, "State Loses Out," 5. See also Quigley, "Mineral Rights."

6. "First Wayne County."

7. Hoffman, "Managing and Protecting"; VanBriesen, "Water Quantity."

8. "Examples of spills," "middle of a state forest," and "geyser of gas": Legere, "Dangers," 1, 6; "allowing methane": Legere, "State," 1; "hydrofracturing lubricant": "Lubricant Spills"; "forested area": McConnell, "Activist," A1.

9. Hoffman, "Managing and Protecting."

10. Legere, "What Effect," A11. See also VanBriesen, "Water Quantity"; Engelder, "Marcellus Gas."

11. Esch, "Senate OKs Moratorium"; "Basin Hydrology," 16; Delaware River Basin Commission, *Natural Gas.*

12. McConnell, "Philly." See also Delaware River Basin Commission, "DRBC Approves."

13. Austin, *Land of Little Rain*, xxxvi, 3. Austin would have understood Gary Snyder when he says, "Our relation to the natural world takes place in a *place*, and it must be grounded in information and experience" (*Practice*, 42).

14. Lewis, *Reading*, 51.

15. Corey Lewis points out that "the quest for water, in Austin country, underlies everything that one does and sees" (ibid., 52).

16. Ibid., 48.

17. For the politics of the California water wars, which continue today, see Kahrl, "Politics."

18. Lowenthal, *From the Coalfields*, 154. Before the aqueduct, a dam across the Delaware enabled canal boats to cross the river (LeRoy, *Delaware and Hudson*, 51).

19. Lowenthal, *From the Coalfields*, 71, 176.

20. Ibid., 66–67; see also D. Torrey, *Memoir*, 102. Wurts purchased one hundred acres for $1,000; he sold the parcel to the company for $4,000 (Lowenthal, *From the Coalfields*, 67, 282n81).

21. Lowenthal, *From the Coalfields*, 238; quotes on 64.

22. Mathews, *History of Wayne*, 637–38; Sanderson, *Canalway*, 118, 120. Average annual rainfall in northeastern Pennsylvania is forty-seven inches (McGurl, *Lackawanna River*, 2).

23. Lowenthal, *From the Coalfields*, 239.

24. M. V. Newton, "The Tanneries of Wayne County," 4, Tannery Industry file, Wayne County Historical Society, Honesdale, Pa.; Ammerman, "Mount Pleasant," 219; "Berlin Township," 260; LeRoy, *Delaware and Hudson*, 77.

25. In 1841, the company "complained to the owners of a leather factory at Beatysburg [New York] that their bark (used in tanning) was clogging the channel" (Lowenthal, *From the Coalfields*, 222).

26. Newton, "Tanneries of Wayne County," 3, 5.

27. Lowenthal, *From the Coalfields*, 248.

28. Ibid., 263, 275. See also Sanderson, *Canalway*, 66, 68.

29. For a photo of an underground electric pump in use in 1921, see Percival and Kulesa, *Anthracite Era*, 64.

30. Wolensky, Wolensky, and Wolensky, *Knox Mine Disaster*, 14, 35, 52, 77, 61n4; quote on 72. Despite the company mining too close to the river bottom, a violation of law, engineering, and common sense, "the legal system never actually found any individuals or organizations guilty for causing the events of January 22, 1959" (101). Knox leased its mines from Pennsylvania Coal Company (71).

31. Lackawanna River Corridor Association, *Conservation Plan.*

32. McGurl, *Lackawanna River*, 19. As early as 1954, at least one coal company executive knew that ending pumping in the valley would create an underground pool ten miles long, 250 feet deep, and one to one and half miles wide ("City Pushes," 8).

33. McGurl, *Lackawanna River*, 6.

34. "God Is Good"; see also "City Prides." The Scranton Gas and Water Company was the "largest privately-owned water company in the United States and one of the few water systems operated solely by gravity" ("Early Development").

35. McGurl, *Lackawanna River*, 9 (quote); "Early Development"; "City Prides."

36. McGurl, *Lackawanna River*, 9, 10. This may be changing. A river-walk project is creating walking trails along the river, from Taylor to Forest City.

37. Ibid., 5, 15; quotes on 2–3.

38. Klein, "Gulf Oil Spill."

39. Hitchcock, *History of Scranton,* 133; Norma Reese, personal interview, 30 July 2010.

40. Sloane, *Great Necessity,* 80, 77, 72.

41. Reese, personal interview.

42. Sloane, *Great Necessity,* 80; quote on 77.

43. Reese, personal interview. See also Hitchcock, *History of Scranton,* 133; *Atlas.*

44. McPhee, *Former World,* 161.

45. Pennsylvania Coal Company v. Sanderson, 113 Pa. 126, Supreme Court of Pennsylvania, 1886, available at http://academic.lexisnexis.com/ (accessed 5 September 2011).

46. See *Atlas.* Independent coal operator John Jermyn sank the Centennial shaft in 1875; his construction crew completed the breaker in May 1876 (Healey, *Coal Industry,* 377; for a photo of the breaker, see plate 11).

47. For the case, see *Pennsylvania Coal Company v. Sanderson.*

48. Ibid. J. Gardner Sanderson testified that in August, often a "dry time," mine water would more than double the flow in Meadow Brook.

49. Ibid.

50. Ibid.

51. Ibid.

52. Freyfogle, *Land We Share,* 73.

53. See *Atlas.*

54. Hitchcock, *History of Scranton,* 133. See also B. Folsom, *Urban Capitalists,* 40.

55. B. Folsom, *Urban Capitalists,* 73; quote on 41.

56. A friend who later betrays Tayo, Harley, tells him that beer can cure: "Get this man to the cold Coors hospital!" (158).

57. Quote from Allen, *Sacred Hoop,* 119.

58. See ibid. Paula Gunn Allen describes Ts'eh as the "creative and life-restoring power . . . those who cooperate with her designs serve her and, through her, serve life" (118). Robert Nelson describes Spider Woman/Ts'eh as the "'spirit of place,' a more-than-human being who represents the land's own life" (*Place and Vision,* 15).

59. Its counterpart being a cave where snakes "restore life to themselves," the mine shaft is unlike the worlds below this world: "Down below / Three worlds below this one / everything is / green / all the plants are growing / the flowers are blooming" (35, 54; see 82).

60. Robert Nelson notes that Ts'eh, Thought Woman, Night Swan, and the woman Tayo encounters on Tse-pi'na are all manifestations of the same "energy" (*Place and Vision,* 15). See Allen, *Sacred Hoop,* 119.

61. Allen, *Sacred Hoop,* 126.

62. Shields, *Centennial History,* 140; G. Martin, *Soil Survey,* 37–38.

CHAPTER 2

1. Marshall, *Story Line,* 147. Marshall notes that "literary critics in general have neglected fieldwork." Interest in field-based instruction is on the rise. See Crimmel, *Teaching*; Christensen and Crimmel, *Teaching About Place*; and Lewis, "Beyond."

2. Lewis, *Reading,* 43, 42.

3. "Smothered and silent": Merwin, "Burning Mountain," 19; "at last cannot": Merwin, "The Miner," 25–26; "inexcusable / Unavoidable": Merwin, "Luzerne Street," 38–39.

4. Francaviglia, *Hard Places,* 214–15.

5. "Lunar landscape": Marsh, "Continuity," 337; "sacrificial zones": Goin and Raymond, "Living in Anthracite," 29; "grievously scarred": Dublin and Licht, *Face of Decline,* 171.

6. E. Folsom, "Long Time," 226. See also Merwin, *Summer Doorways,* 3; St. John, "Last Troubadour," 201.

7. Due to the decline in the anthracite industry, the Washburn Street Presbyterian Church stopped paying Merwin's father, which "affected [his] father's moods and behavior at home. For months at a time [his] mother managed the household on almost no money" (Merwin, *Summer Doorways,* 25–26).

8. Dublin and Licht, *Face of Decline,* 7; Miller and Sharpless, *Kingdom of Coal,* 323.

9. "So objective" and "poetic voice": Davis, *W. S. Merwin,* 73; "master-poem" and "radically recasts": Brunner, *Poetry as Labor,* 18; "focussing on one place": MacShane, "Portrait," 7.

10. C. Nelson, "Resources of Failure," 88. See also MacShane, "Portrait," 6.

11. Perry, *"Substantial Piece,"* 39.

12. B. Folsom, *Urban Capitalists,* 35–38. Historian Burton Folsom notes that "America's industrial revolution in coal and iron began in Pennsylvania—at Scranton, in the Lackawanna Valley. There American ingenuity combined the available coal and iron to challenge England's world dominance in manufacturing" (13).

13. Perry, *"Substantial Piece,"* 37.

14. An early draft of "The Drunk in the Furnace" is reproduced in Folsom and Nelson, introduction to *W. S. Merwin,* 7.

15. "Invent a figure": MacShane, "Portrait," 12–13; lame god of fire: Hamilton, *Mythology,* 34–35; "harmonious relation" and "myth based on ego": Elliott, "Interview," 3.

16. MacShane, "Portrait," 6.

17. St. John, "Last Troubadour," 202.

18. Dublin and Licht, *Face of Decline,* 185.

19. Merwin and his father had a stormy relationship; in fact, Merwin rejected his father's faith.

20. Merwin, interview by Bill Moyers.

21. Brunner, *Poetry as Labor,* 71.

22. Merwin, "Flight Home," 136.

23. Ibid., 136, 135.

24. Dublin, *Mines Closed,* 34–36.

25. Marsh, "Continuity," 347. Marsh also notes, "Feelings of the uniqueness of the anthracite landscape are supported by an exaggerated belief in the beauty of parts of the local country."

26. Dublin and Licht, *Face of Decline,* 171. At the 2009 Anthracite Heritage Conference, only one presentation touched on the land's destruction, and this was through photographs of the Carbondale mine fire. The presentation itself was primarily about the people's struggle with the fire.

27. Goin and Raymond, "Living in Anthracite," 42–44.

28. "Face of nature": [L. Miner], *Valley of Wyoming,* 16–17; "unresisting hills": Hollister, *Lackawanna Valley,* 463. The 1970 film *Wanda* sees the Anthracite Region as a bleak landscape. See chapter 6.

29. Marsh, "Continuity," 341. According to historians Dublin and Licht, "The Delaware & Hudson Canal Company and the Delaware, Lackawanna, & Western Railroad cornered ownership of coal lands in the Lackawanna Valley of the northern field by the 1860s" (*Face of Decline,* 18). Dublin and Licht also note that "seven major railroad companies controlled fully 91 percent of all coal produced in the anthracite region" (20).

30. Goin and Raymond, "Living in Anthracite," 29. Lackawanna, Luzerne, and Schuylkill, the three main counties in the Anthracite Region, lost 15 percent of their "working-age population" in the 1950s (Dublin and Licht, *Face of Decline,* 137). In the same decade, 29 percent of residents between the ages of fifteen and twenty-four left Lackawanna County (157).

31. Erikson, *Everything*, 255; Erikson, *New Species*, 22.

32. Dublin and Licht, *Face of Decline*, 27–28; quotes on 25, 49.

33. Ibid., 49. See also Derickson, *Black Lung*, 137.

34. Brunner, *Poetry as Labor*, 84; Kim, Justin, and Miller, "Mine Fire Diagnostics," 3.

35. "Nauseated or knocked out": "Fire Under"; "silt-bearing water": "Fire Under" and "Fire Area." See also K. Munley, *West Side*, 78, 117.

36. K. Munley, "Carbondale Mine Fire"; K. Munley, *West Side*, 51.

37. "Fire Under"; K. Munley, *West Side*, 77, 104.

38. "Fire Area"; Lee, "Hot Seat," 71, 74; K. Munley, *West Side*, 69–71.

39. "Living context": Merrill, "Vibrancy," 44; "different in kind" and "wrong way": J. Frazier, *From Origin*, 45–46.

40. Merwin, interview by Bill Moyers; Bryson, *West Side*, 109.

41. See *Insurance Maps*.

42. The bears' knowledge of trees echoes people's lack of the same knowledge in "Native Trees," which appeared in *The Rain in the Trees* (1988), a poem that points to our "lack of attention to and awareness of the more-than-human world around us" (Bryson, *West Side*, 103).

43. The breaker was owned by the Delaware, Lackawanna, and Western Railroad (*Insurance Maps*). The Glen Alden Company, which was spun off from DLWRR, closed the Hyde Park colliery in 1931 (Dublin and Licht, *Face of Decline*, 72).

44. Merwin, interview by Bill Moyers.

45. Parini, "Second Pulitzer Prize."

46. McGurl, *Lackawanna River*, 6.

CHAPTER 3

1. *Oxford English Dictionary*, 2nd ed. (1989), s.v. "fix," defs. 1a, 5c.

2. "Middle British Colonies."

3. Pownall, *Topographical Description*, 129, 129n1; see also Wallace, *Indians*, 135. Wallace dates the purchase to 1749 (154). These lands also show up as a blank in C. J. Sauthier's 1777 *Map of the Provinces of New York and New Jersey, with a Part of Pennsylvania and the Province of Quebec*.

4. Wilkinson, "Philadelphia Fever," 41 (quote); Goodrich, *Wayne County*, 100. Wilkinson claims that in 1792 the state offered its vacant land for 13.5 cents per acre, plus fees (42).

5. Wilkinson, "Philadelphia Fever," 42–44. Securing title to vacant land in the 1790s was a multistep process. With a small fee and a simple slip of paper that often didn't even bear the applicant's signature, a potential buyer purchased from the state land office a warrant to authorize a land survey. Although "generally vague in describing the tract it covered," the warrant initiated title to the property and established the grounds for legal settlement, but it didn't convey all property rights (46). The survey, which determined boundaries and acreage, was returned to the land office with a drawing and a narrative description of the lands the buyer sought. The drawing noted watercourses and the ownership of bordering lands; if the bordering land was unclaimed, it was called vacant. As a verbal description of boundaries, the returned survey resembled a patent, the official document that conveyed all ownership rights. The law limited each person to one warrant, but nothing stopped one from buying warrants from others, including one's spouse, children, and "friends."

6. Ibid., 54. See also Goodrich, *Wayne County*, 101.

7. Recorded in record group 17, Northampton County, vol. P, no. 32, p. 657, bk. C114, pp. 48–49, Survey Maps, Land Office Records, Pennsylvania State Archives, Harrisburg, Pa. (hereafter abbreviated as Survey Maps).

8. Whitman, "Song of Myself," 48.

9. Torrey earned a footnote in the history of mapmaking when he drew the earliest U.S. county property map that shows landownership. "Exhibiting the situation and form of the original or warrantee tracts," his 1814 map made county property lines official and stable. J. Torrey, "Proposals by Jason Torrey of Bethany, in Wayne County, for Publishing a Map of Wayne and Pike Counties in Pennsylvania," 6 April 1814, Jason Torrey Papers, Luzerne County Historical Society, Wilkes-Barre, Pa. (hereafter abbreviated as Jason Torrey Papers); see also Conzen, "Landownership Map," 11.

10. D. Torrey, *Memoir*, 22–23, 53–54.

11. Grun, *Timetables*, 244; *Oxford English Dictionary*, 2nd ed. (1989), s.v. "survey," def. 2.

12. D. Torrey, *Memoir*, 23. See also Jason Torrey, *Diary of Jason Torrey: 25 December 1791–6 June 1801*, transcribed by Augustus P. Thompson, 1938 (printed by Donald G. Thompson, 2000), 2, Wayne County Historical Society, Honesdale, Pa.

13. J. Torrey, *Diary*, 1. See also D. Torrey, *Memoir*, 19.

14. D. Torrey, *Memoir*, 24; J. Torrey, *Diary*, 2; J. Torrey, "Purdon Survey," 16 July 1793, Jason Torrey Papers.

15. D. Torrey, *Memoir*, 26; quotes on 119 and 27.

16. "List of Forty-Three Tracts of Land Supposed Vacant," 30 May 1795, Jason Torrey Papers. See also D. Torrey, *Memoir*, 28.

17. D. Torrey, *Memoir*, 29; quotes on 30. In December 1795, Torrey was back in Philadelphia, again working in the "private offices" of land speculators (32). This work offered him more and more information about lands in northeastern Pennsylvania.

18. J. Torrey, *Diary*, 54; D. Torrey, *Memoir*, 34–35; Kimble v. Torrey, "Summons in Ejectment in the Common Pleas of Wayne County," Dec. term, 1809, Jason Torrey Papers. The Jason Torrey papers have not been organized. I found scattered documents related to three court cases. The first is *Kimble v. Torrey* (1809). Documents related to this case are also dated 1811. Two other cases, which cover the same ground as the first, are *Torrey v. Kimball* (n.d.) and *Torrey v. Kimble and Beardsley* (1817). I analyzed the cases' internal evidence and the documents' handwriting to determine which undated documents referred to which case. See Torrey v. Kimball, n.d., and Torrey v. Kimble and Beardsley, "Summons in Ejectment," Common Pleas of Wayne County, Nov. term, 1817; both in Jason Torrey Papers.

19. D. Torrey, *Memoir*, 35–36; quote on 37. His trip likely included a stop at the home of Henry Drinker, who was trying to create a sugar maple industry in the Beech Lands, his fifty thousand acre holding in northeastern Pennsylvania. A Quaker, Drinker hoped that maple sugar would replace the "'polluted & wicked' Caribbean cane" used in rum (Doerflinger, *Vigorous Spirit*, 323). Torrey was one of Drinker's land agents (Maxey, "Of Castles," 420).

20. D. Torrey, *Memoir*, 37–38; quote on 29.

21. D. Torrey, *Memoir*, 52, 121. See also Goodrich, *Wayne County*, 103.

22. *Merriam Webster's Collegiate Dictionary*, 11th ed. (1998), s.v. "topography."

23. "West Indies, Mexico, Central America, and Northern South America," Portolan Atlas, 1547, Huntington Library, Art Collections and Botanical Gardens, San Marino, Calif. (reproduction).

24. Wordsworth, *Tintern Abbey*, 28.

25. W. Walsh, *Curiosities*, 143; Hole, *English Custom*, 57.

26. Herbert, *Country Parson*, 284. The Romans celebrated Terminus, the guardian of boundaries and "god of landmarks. His statue was a rude stone or post, set in the ground to mark the boundaries of fields" (Bulfinch, *Golden Age*, 12). This custom may have given rise to beating the bounds in England (Hole, *English Custom*, 57; W. Walsh, *Curiosities*, 141).

27. Rodriguez, *Brown*, 197; *Oxford English Dictionary*, 2nd ed. (1989), s.v. "discrete," def. 1d.

28. Wallace, *Indians*, 111, 121–22; Merritt, *Crossroads*, 33 (quote).

29. Stefon, "Wyoming Valley," 143, 148; Williamson and Fossler, *Susquehanna Frontier*, 33.

30. Stefon, "Wyoming Valley," 136, 145–46, 235–36n2; quote on 139.

31. C. Miner, *History of Wyoming*, 490; Wallace, *Indians*, 155.

32. Of course, the Iroquois may have knowingly sold the same land twice.

33. "No confidence": *Torrey v. Kimble and Beardsley*; "burnt in effigy": Goodrich, *Wayne County*, 28; "end to settler opposition": Moyer, *Wild Yankees*, 151.

34. *Kimble v. Torrey*. According to his neighbors, Torrey was not above engaging in "sharp practice" (Maxey, "Of Castles," 420n23); others asserted that he was a "rogue" ([?] Morgan, "I Certify . . . , " deposition, 23 July 1811, Jason Torrey Papers). For a positive description of Torrey, see "W. K. Has Not Only . . . , " Kimble v. Torrey, Apr. term, 1811, Jason Torrey Papers. Local historians tend to see him in a wholly positive light.

35. Benjamin Kimble tells this story in *Torrey v. Kimble*. Not long after buying the warrants, Torrey fell ill for about four weeks (J. Torrey, *Diary*, 55; D. Torrey, *Memoir*, 35).

36. *Torrey v. Kimball*, 2–4; Goodrich, *Wayne County*, 100. See also Survey Maps. According to Torrey's land patent, the Kimbles received deeds on 13 August 1796 (Patent Book #61, Land Office Records, Pennsylvania State Archives).

37. Wilkinson, "Philadelphia Fever," 44; quote on 45.

38. C. Miner, *History of Wyoming*, 474.

39. See Moses Killam's testimony (*Torrey v. Kimble*). Jacob Kimble told the same story: "About the close of the year 1796, I [Jacob Kimble] was in the woods, hunting on the waters of Dyberry, in company with Walter Kimble and Moses Killam Esq. Esquire Killam told him it was a pity he had sold his warrants, for he might have got other lands on them, if the lands he meant them for was gone by other warrants. Walter Kimble said he had sold them and got his money for them and was glad of it—that if he could not have the particular lands they called for, he would not have any—that if he should take other lands, it would be at the North Pole or the Devil's Arse" (*Torrey v. Kimble and Beardsley*).

40. "Singularly interesting specimen": C. Miner, *History of Wyoming*, 473; "said hard things": *Torrey v. Kimble and Beardsley*.

41. "[Kimble] was shown": *Torrey v. Kimball*, 4; "400 acres": *Kimble v. Torrey*; "situate[d] on the waters": record group 17, Northampton County, vol. P, no. 61, bk. C103, p. 48, Survey Maps.

42. Patent Book #61. See also White, *Geological Survey*, 20.

43. *Kimble v. Torrey*.

44. *Torrey v. Kimball*, 8.

45. Record group 17, Northampton County, vol. P, no. 61, bk. C103, pp. 37–38, Survey Maps.

46. Patent Books #61. In December 1801, Torrey relocated to Bethany, the village he had platted (D. Torrey, *Memoir*, 63).

47. D. Torrey, *Memoir*, 82; quote on 61. See also Sanderson, *Canalway*, 25.

48. Whitman, "Song of Myself," 73.

CHAPTER 4

1. Michael Pollan points out how Whole Foods, one example of the "industrialization of the organic food industry," has created a "Supermarket Pastoral" to hide the fact that "some (certainly not all) organic milk comes from factory farms" (*Omnivore's Dilemma*, 138–39).

2. A. Martin, "Largest Recall." The average food item travels about 1,500 miles before it reaches the local Giant supermarket (Pollan, *Omnivore's Dilemma*, 239).

3. See A. Martin, "Largest Recall"; Austen, "Canada."

4. Helleiner, *Travellers*, 31.

5. Jason Torrey to Thomas Cronon, deed, 12 April 1834, Wayne County (Pa.) Courthouse; Tax Assessment, Mount Pleasant Township, Wayne County, 1850, entry #55, Pennsylvania State Archives, Harrisburg, Pa.; Diamond State Data Services, *Pennsylvania*.

6. Hugh Cronon and Michael Cronon to Peter and Matilda Conlogue, deed, 20 April 1878, Wayne County (Pa.) Courthouse.

7. Noble and Cleek, "Sorting Out," 49–50.

8. McMurry, *Transforming*, 182.

9. For photos and a discussion of basement barns, see Glassie, "Variation."

10. Rhoads and Block, *Trees*, 137–38; see also Hupkens, Boxma, and Dokter, "Tannic Acid," 57. In 1850, the township boasted two tanneries; ten sawmills cut annually two million feet of lumber. Most of Wayne County's leather was sole leather. See Whaley, *History*, 57; M. V. Newton, "The Tanneries of Wayne County," 5, Tannery Industry file, Wayne County Historical Society, Honesdale, Pa.

11. DuPuis, *Perfect Food*, 78, 154; quotes on 160 and 104.

12. Ibid., 19; quotes on 18, 76.

13. Ibid., 153.

14. Haggerty, "Farmers," A7; Haggerty, "Pricing Imbalance."

15. Haggerty, "Feds," A1, A7.

16. Norris, *Octopus*, 62, 65–66, 259–60. As E. Melanie DuPuis points out, "The milkmaid, overseeing the purity of milk, therefore symbolized this nostalgia for the nurturing countryside, this idea of perfection as the antidote of the downfallen city." *Perfect Food*, 97; for images of milkmaids in nineteenth-century advertising, see 92–93, 96.

17. McMurry, *Transforming*, 201–2; quote on 203.

18. "Masculinization of milking": ibid., 202; "widely accepted": "Liberation," 52.

19. Glasgow, *Barren Ground*, 269, 427, 468.

20. "DeLaval Announces."

21. The industrialization of dairying in the mid to late nineteenth century marked an "unmistakable trend in dairy work for men: it was getting longer, harder, more anxiety-ridden, and less independent" (McMurry, *Transforming*, 198). Increased industrialization has done nothing but accelerate this trend.

22. Ritchie, *Loss*, 8.

23. Vobejda, "Agriculture," A1.

24. DuPuis, *Perfect Food*, 144.

25. Thoreau, *Walden*, 108–9.

26. Wordsworth, "Two-Part Prelude," Part One, 1.288, 293, 320–22.

27. Burton, "Memory."

28. Brox, *Five Thousand*, 149.

CHAPTER 5

1. Cy McKenna to Rita Wenders and William Conlogue, 5 November 1991, author possession. Four octagon schools operated in the county; one still stands in South Canaan ("Octagon"). For photographs of Stone School #7, see O'Hara, *People*, 155, 160, 161, 169.

2. Ammerman, "Mount Pleasant," 222; McKenna to Wenders and Conlogue. For the class photo, see O'Hara, *People*, 160.

3. "Records of the Department."

4. Galpin, *Rural Life*, 125–26; quotes on 146, 126, 35.

5. Ibid., 126.

6. Ammerman, "Mount Pleasant," 222–23. Two recent consolidations—of post offices and of Catholic churches—are modern-day analogues to the early twentieth-century consolidation of schools: neighborhoods and places lose their identity. Numbers tell the township's diminishing significance as a proportion of the county's population. In 1850, township residents numbered 1,737 (Whaley, *History*, 56), or 8 percent of Wayne County's total population of 21,890 (U.S. Census Bureau, *1850*). The 1870 census recorded 33,188 people in the county ("County-Level Results"), with 1,952 in the township, about 6 percent of the total (U.S. Census Bureau, *1870*). The 2000 U.S. Census found a total county population of 47,722; Mount Pleasant Township was home to 1,345, about 3 percent of the total (U.S. Census Bureau, *2000*).

7. "Records of the Department" (quotes); Ammerman, "Mount Pleasant," 223; Hall, "Plan."

8. Maclean, "Life," 339; "Looking Back." Maclean claims that the people of Forest City drank 1,000 barrels of beer each year; according to her, the town had the reputation of drinking "more than any town in the Lackawanna valley" (340). In 1970, the population of Forest City stood at 2,322; in 1980, 1,924 (U.S. Census Bureau, *1980*, 24). The 2010 U.S. Census counted 1,911 people in Forest City (U.S. Census Bureau, *2010*).

9. Cather, "Neighbour Rosicky," 1514.

10. Wills, *Lincoln*, 65.

11. The arboretum "has 42 species of trees that contain 103 varieties, and a comparable number and variety of shrubs, as well as ornamental grasses, perennial, biennial and annual blooms." See the Marywood University Arboretum website at http://www.marywood.edu/arboretum/ (accessed 3 January 2010).

12. Edward F. Blewitt to M. Germaine O'Neill, 11 December 1916, Land Records file, Sisters, Servants of the Immaculate Heart of Mary, Scranton, Pa. See also Keenan, *Sisters*, 79.

13. Yarina, *Marywood*, 10.

14. Ibid.

15. Marx, *Machine*, 11, 71.

16. Major, *Grounded*, 44; Freyfogle, "Introduction," xvii–xviii.

17. Yarina, *Marywood*, 21.

18. Keenan, *Sisters*, 104. Adopted in 1915, "Holiness, Knowledge, Health" is Marywood's motto.

19. Watkinson describes ICS as "by far the largest single educational institution in America's history" ("Education," 348).

20. Knies, "Correspondence Schools"; *Business of Building*, 4; *Fifteenth Anniversary*, 63. In May 1870, after hearing about the Avondale disaster, Foster started the weekly *Shenandoah Herald*, in which he advocated improved mine safety. He moved his printing office to Scranton on 1 February 1889. See "ICS Story," 7, International Correspondence Schools Collection, folder 333, University of Scranton, Scranton, Pa.; Keary, "Foundation," 3.

21. Watkinson, "Education," 349–50.

22. "Commercial enterprise" and "new business": *Fifteenth Anniversary*, 67, 69; "utilitarian standpoint": Watkinson, "Education," 350; "for-profit universities": Seiden, "For-Profit."

23. Seiden, "For-Profit." For the "nightmare" of the "anti-intellectual university," see Donoghue, "Prestige," 156.

24. Knies, "Correspondence Schools." In 1910, ICS started an Encouragement Department, which sent personal letters to students falling behind in completing their lessons; the department published a periodical, *Ambition* ("ICS Story," 17).

25. *Fifteenth Anniversary*, 47. During the Great Depression, when unemployment was high and breadlines long, ICS advertising claimed that "the student does not have to give up

his present work and income in order to get ready for a bigger job. Nor is he required to do his studying at a specified place and time. In the *spare moments that usually go to waste* he can prepare himself and make his I.C.S. study a clear profit" (*Business of Building*, 16).

26. "Annihilated space" and "mining student": *Fifteenth Anniversary*, 51, 68–69; "limitless," "mobals," and "perceptions": De Blij, *Power of Place*, 5–6.

27. *Fifteenth Anniversary*, 50.

28. "Moral Influence," "idleness," and "plan of teaching": ibid., 71–72; "train the mind": Watkinson, "Education," 350; "moral uplift": Knies, "Correspondence Schools."

29. Lewin, "Scrutiny." For-profits spend about 30 percent of their budgets on marketing and advertising; their students account for 43 percent of all student-loan defaults (ibid.).

30. "This is a corporation": "Haven from Prejudice"; "better world": "University of Phoenix."

31. Bartlett, "Phoenix," A11–A12 (quotes on A1, A10); see also Rosin, "Red, Blue." BioArts ended its dog-cloning services in September 2009 (Carlson, "BioArts"). The Phoenix founder is Kronos's "only real patient" (Bartlett, "Phoenix," A12).

32. "Paying recruiters": Bartlett, "Phoenix," A13; "fraudulent practices" and "questionable statement": Kutz, "For-Profit," 7.

33. Dillon, "Troubles." At ICS, "very few who began long courses, such as engineering, finished them—less than five percent in fact" (Watkinson, "Education," 364).

34. Digital Connections Council, *Openness*, 67. CED's Digital Connections Council, a group of "information technology experts," wrote the report (ix). CED's motto is "The Best of Business Thinking."

35. "Application" and "change the information": Digital Connections Council, *Openness*, ix, 1; "work of the teacher": *Fifteenth Anniversary*, 72.

36. A 2001 survey of English department faculty search committee chairs found that 32 percent of respondents at doctoral institutions rated teaching a class during the interview process as *"extremely unimportant"* (Broughton and Conlogue, "Search Committees," 47). Another 28 percent of respondents in doctoral departments thought that observing a candidate's teaching performance was extremely important. At baccalaureate institutions, however, 60 percent of respondents thought that teaching a class was extremely important.

37. I suspect that such personal ties are not rare, because "only a small percentage of the research universities produce the English PhDs likely to be hired by other research universities" (Shapiro, "Survival," 19). Six programs train many faculty members at twenty top English departments: "Columbia, Cornell, Duke, Harvard, Berkeley, and Yale" (20). The speakers at this session were Jean Howard (Yale); Jonathan Culler (Oxford); and Wai Chee Dimock (Yale), who teaches at Yale. Where you learn matters.

38. Howard, "MLA Convention."

39. "Evaluation of Faculty," 25.

40. "Regular fee" and "cannot know": Plato, *Protagoras*, 349a, 312c; "kept no school": Lamb, "Introduction," xi.

41. In Scranton, the family lived in a row home built in 1870 for workers at the Lackawanna Iron and Coal Company furnaces ("Then and Now").

42. U.S. Office of the Press Secretary, remarks by President Clinton and President Kim.

43. Pollan, *Omnivore's Dilemma*, 235.

44. The poem served as the prologue to Frost's second collection, *North of Boston* (1914); the introductory poem to the *Complete Poems of Robert Frost* (1949); and the origin of the title of his final work, *In the Clearing* (1962).

45. Lentricchia, *Robert Frost*, 23; Marx, "Pastoral Ideals," 253, 259.

46. Marx, "Pastoral Ideals," 258.

47. Lynen, *Pastoral Art,* 22–23.

48. Lentricchia, *Robert Frost,* 25.

49. Pasture is *pastura: Oxford English Dictionary,* 2nd ed. (1989), s.v. "pasture"; works of knowing: Poirier, *Robert Frost,* 293; "momentary stay[s]": Frost, "Figure," 394.

50. *Oxford English Dictionary,* 1933 ed., s.v. "conacre"; Salaman, *History,* 247.

CHAPTER 6

1. McNarney, "Decades," A1, A5; Nissley and Singleton, "Reporters' Notebook."

2. McNarney, "Courthouse," B1. See also McNarney, "Pigeon."

3. See *Map of City of Scranton,* 1854, Lackawanna Historical Society, Scranton, Pa.

4. Kashuba, *Brief History,* 58 (quotes); Dupuis, "Renovation," A1; McDonald, "Seeds."

5. Raught, "Tragedy."

6. Rogers, *Geology,* 1:31, 32, vii; White, *Geological Survey,* 137.

7. Nash, *Wilderness,* 82, 81; see also Bedell, *Anatomy,* 13. Philip Hone, namesake of Honesdale and a mayor of New York, was a Cole patron (Bedell, *Anatomy,* 24).

8. Marx, *Machine,* 220. Although Nicolai Cikovsky claims that Inness completed it in 1856 or 1857, the painting is usually dated 1855 ("*Lackawanna Valley,*" 75).

9. Lowenthal, *From the Coalfields,* 231 (quote); Miller and Sharpless, *Kingdom of Coal,* 63. D. L. & W. also wanted to "make a special appeal" to get customers to purchase its coal; part of this appeal was to prepare anthracite in breakers before shipping it in sizes (Murphy, "Transportation," 102).

10. B. Folsom, *Urban Capitalists,* 38.

11. Murphy, "Transportation," 102. For a photo of the Diamond breaker, see Healey, *Coal Industry,* plate 8.

12. In 1840, second-growth oaks and pines covered much of what is today Scranton; the D. L. & W. ground was then a farm (Throop, *Historical Notes,* 5).

13. Cikovsky, "*Lackawanna Valley,*" 73, 75, 83. Inness says that the junk shop was in Mexico. Nicolai Cikovsky points out that many places in the United States are named Mexico, including a town near Harrisburg (90n6).

14. This section of Scranton is the location of the Oxford mine, which Stephen Crane visited in 1894. The Oxford opened in 1862; in 1868, D. L. & W. took over its operation (Murphy, "Transportation," 102). Peoples Coal operated the mine during a major 1909 cave-in ("Pillar Robbing," 1; see below).

15. "Competitive Agenda," 38–39; "County Business," 9, 68.

16. Healey, *Coal Industry,* 36 (quote); Lackawanna Heritage Valley Authority, *Anthracite Coal,* 54.

17. Healey, *Coal Industry,* 40 (quote); Lackawanna Heritage Valley Authority, *Anthracite Coal,* 54–55; Miller and Sharpless, *Kingdom of Coal,* 121.

18. Raught painted his first coal breaker in 1910, inaugurating a series of breaker paintings; one, the 1914 *Anthracite Coal Breaker in Winter,* may depict the Hyde Park breaker (da Costa Nunes, "Anthracite Mines," 17; Schruers, "Raught," 39).

19. "Public Cordially Invited."

20. For a photo of this coal breaker at the time of its construction, see Azzarelli, *Taylor,* 12. For the breaker in ruins, see 124–26.

21. Waschak v. Moffat, 379 Pa. 441, Supreme Court of Pennsylvania, 1954, available at http://academic.lexisnexis.com/ (accessed 5 September 2011). For a photo of a Taylor culm bank, see Azzarelli, *Taylor,* 23.

22. "Trifling inconveniences" and "one's bread": *Waschak v. Moffat*; "normal and customary": Freyfogle, *Land We Share,* 93 (see also 92).

23. Freyfogle, *Land We Share,* 93–94.

24. *Waschak v. Moffat.*

25. Leopold, *Sand County,* 137, 141.

26. Rathje and Murphy, *Rubbish!* 122. "Few people today have very much awareness that the local landfill is destined for an afterlife, or that many landscapes they take for granted conceal distinctly checkered pasts" (90).

27. See "Facility Information" on Alliance Landfill's website, at http://alliancelandfill .wm.com (accessed 5 September 2011).

28. See "Construction Standards" on Alliance Landfill's website.

29. *Alliance Sanitary Landfill,* 4.

30. See "Site History" and "Frequently Asked Questions" on Alliance Landfill's website.

31. See "Landfill Liner System" (quote) and "Projects" on Alliance Landfill's website.

32. See "Good Neighbor" on Alliance Landfill's website.

33. Rathje and Murphy, *Rubbish!* 4.

34. Sugarman, "Health," 140–41, 147–48, 152–53.

35. Rathje and Murphy, *Rubbish!* 103–4, 119; quotes on 112 and 8.

36. Ibid., 34–35, 90. For a map of the parts of the New York metropolitan area that have been extended in this way, see 91.

37. Ibid., 45.

38. Ammons, *Garbage,* 48.

39. The poem has been called "perhaps the most remarkable nineteenth-century contribution to the poetry of ecology in America" (Killingsworth, *Walt Whitman*). In the 1856 edition, the poem's title is "Poem of Wonder at the Resurrection of the Wheat."

40. U.S. Environmental Protection Agency, *Risk Assessment,* 7; Kilborn, "Hurricane."

41. Reynaud, "For Wanda," 237.

42. People around the world watched the lunar landings on TV. Aside from scattered short pieces in local papers, the filming of *Wanda* didn't make it into area media. The Scranton papers didn't know about the movie until its release. See Lew Marcus, "33 Area Residents Had Roles in 'Wanda,'" *Scrantonian,* 7 March 1971, Motion Pictures file, Lackawanna Historical Society.

43. See Melton, "Barbara Loden," 12–14 (quotes on 12 and 13); Marcus, "33 Area Residents"; Reynaud, "For Wanda," 231–32.

44. Reynaud, "For Wanda," 224–25, 236; DeLillo, "Woman" (quote).

45. "Pioneer female filmmaker": Reynaud, "For Wanda," 238; "make the antithesis": Melton, "Barbara Loden," 11.

46. See Melton, "Barbara Loden," 11–12 (quotes on 12); Marcus, "33 Area Residents"; Reynaud, "For Wanda," 232.

47. Reynaud, "For Wanda," 232. Bérénice Reynaud argues that "Wanda's historical importance lies precisely at this junction: Loden wanted to suggest, *from the vantage point of her own experience,* what it meant to be a damaged, alienated woman—not to fashion a 'new woman' or a 'positive heroine'" (231).

48. Melton, "Barbara Loden," 12.

49. The site is the Eddy Creek colliery in Olyphant, which had ceased operation by 1970. In bank mining, companies comb culm banks for usable coal.

50. "Knocked out": Melton, "Barbara Loden," 11; "hidden turmoil": Reynaud, "For Wanda," 227. Loden told an interviewer, "I had a compulsion to get the story of Wanda out of myself" (Melton, "Barbara Loden," 14).

51. Melton, "Barbara Loden," 12.
52. "Moviemakers Tap Forest."
53. Reynaud, "For Wanda," 240.
54. Melton, "Barbara Loden," 14, 13.
55. DeLillo, "Woman."
56. "Unprepossessing," "intimate knowledge," "without rancor," and "good and simple": Simon, "Championship," 616; "universal experiences": Henn, "Jason Miller."
57. Born in 1939, Jason Miller grew up in West Scranton, attended the University of Scranton as an English and philosophy major, and went on for a master's degree at Catholic University. In 1963, he left Scranton for New York; in the mid-1980s, he returned to his hometown, where he died in 2001. *That Championship Season* won a Pulitzer Prize in 1973. Revived on Broadway in 2011 by Miller's son Jason Patric, the play met poor reviews, which generally damned the drama as dated ("Jason Miller's Storied Career"; Henn, "Jason Miller"; Brantley, "Champs").
58. J. Miller, *Championship Season,* 40.
59. Ibid., 3. George remarks that Phil is "going out with this seventeen year old . . . up in Scranton" (8). People in the Lackawanna Valley generally use the words "up" and "down" to refer to one's geographical position relative to the ends of the valley. Scranton is "up" the valley from neighboring Taylor. In the movie based on the play, the house used as the set is located in Taylor. The high school in the play, Fillmore, shares the same name as the street where Miller grew up (Flannery, "Filmmakers"; "Jason Miller's Storied Career").
60. See Dublin, *Mines Closed,* 27–28, 36, 212; K. Munley, *West Side,* 120 (quotes).
61. Lauver, "Walk."
62. The heavily Catholic and Irish American Lackawanna Valley favored Kennedy; Roosevelt intervened in 1902 on the side of strikers to settle a major anthracite labor dispute; McCarthy appealed to people's patriotism during the Cold War.
63. "Lumber Demands Expected to Increase," *Scrantonian,* 19 November 1967, Charmin file, Lackawanna Historical Society. See also "Charmin Paper Products," 1.
64. Dublin and Licht, *Face of Decline,* 52. Strip mining made up 1.3 percent of all anthracite mined in Pennsylvania in 1915; by 1961, strip mining surpassed underground mining in total percentage of anthracite mined (Lackawanna Heritage Valley Authority, *Anthracite Coal,* 53–54).
65. "Sad End for One of Zoo's Prime Attractions," *Scranton Times,* 10 February 1966, Nay Aug Park file, Lackawanna Historical Society.
66. "Abandoned strip mine pit": "Tillie's Grave"; "extensive bloating": Kashuba, "Call." Tillie's burial site may have been in Taylor (Donna Adler, e-mail to Judi Keller and Mary Ann Moran-Savakinus, 24 June 2011). In the movie version of *That Championship Season,* Phil tries to bury the elephant Tillie in a mine shaft at the Moffat breaker in Taylor. The burial may have taken place where the Alliance Landfill now operates.
67. This is a culminating moment for Tom, a likely stand-in for the playwright. Although George and James believe that alcohol has affected Tom's memory, the drunker Tom becomes, the more strength he gathers to criticize the others' behavior (7, 15). For example, Tom tells George to "stop this . . . dishonesty" (32). He later tells Phil that he doesn't "care about the melodrama of [his] life" (40). Tom, a writer, tells the others, "We are a myth" (41).
68. John Simon notes that "another device Miller uses unobtrusively but compellingly is the parallel" (Simon, "Championship," 621).
69. Woods, Omernik, and Brown, *Level III and IV,* 28.
70. For photos of mine subsidence, see Percival and Kulesa, *Anthracite Era,* 54, 71.
71. Daily, "Legacy," A6.

72. See "Sunken Coal Mine"; Roberts, *Breaker Whistle,* 133–34 (quote on 141); Harper, "Marywood College"; Philbin, "Marywood University."

73. For photos of the Marvine colliery, see Percival and Kulesa, *Anthracite Era,* 59, 69.

74. See Mattes, *Tales,* 16; Mattes, "Mine-Cave," 369.

75. See "Pillar Robbing," 1 (quote); Petula and Morgan, *History,* 77; Fischel, *Regulatory Takings,* 27; Mattes, "Mine-Cave," 371. This subsidence happened three blocks from where poet W. S. Merwin spent part of his childhood.

76. "Big Mine Cave."

77. See Fischel, *Regulatory Takings,* 27, 32; Mattes, "Mine-Cave," 371; Friedman, "Search for Seizure," 3.

78. Carbonneau, "Coal Mines," 26, 29–30 (quote on 25); Kashuba, "Cave-Ins," D1.

79. Mattes, *Tales,* 18.

80. Fischel, *Regulatory Takings,* 17; Mattes, "Mine-Cave," 374 (quote).

81. See Mattes, *Tales,* 16; "Atty P. Mattes Is Dead at 92; Service Noted," 23 December 1979, Mattes file, Lackawanna Historical Society; Mattes, "Mine-Cave," 375 (quote); "Clark Vein."

82. Mattes, "Mine-Cave," 373. Four blocks from our house, the Pennsylvania Tunnel empties into the Lackawanna River. Burrowed beneath Fisk Street between 1903 and 1906 and about two miles long, the tunnel once drained mines beneath where present-day Keystone Landfill piles trash, including mine (Murley, "Underwood Mine"; "Clark Vein").

83. Fischel, *Regulatory Takings,* 32–33; Mattes, "Mine-Cave," 373–74.

84. Fischel, *Regulatory Takings,* 31.

85. Mattes, "Mine-Cave," 374.

86. Fischel, *Regulatory Takings,* 43; Wolensky, Wolensky, and Wolensky, *Knox Mine Disaster,* 154. By 1928, D. L. & W. owned or leased almost all of the coal under West Scranton (Murphy, "Transportation," 102).

87. Murphy, "Transportation," 103; Moore, "Anthracite Industry," 148.

88. W. H. Williams, *Mine Cave,* 14, 16, 19–20, 23; quotes on 15.

89. Ibid., 15.

90. "Surface Protective Association," Surface Protective Association file, Lackawanna Historical Society.

91. Fischel, *Regulatory Takings,* 33; Friedman, "Search for Seizure," 21.

92. See Fischel, *Regulatory Takings,* 18; B. Folsom, *Urban Capitalists,* 108; "Surface Association and City Hope to Intervene in Test of Kohler Law," *Scranton Times,* 7 September 1921, Surface Protective Association file, Lackawanna Historical Society; *Telephone Directory for Brooklyn, Carbondale* [etc.], Commonwealth Telephone, 1910, Lackawanna County Historical Society.

93. "Brought the suit" and "complicated": Fischel, *Regulatory Takings,* 18; "brusquely informed": Mattes, "Mine-Cave," 378. In his memoir, Mattes claims that the coal companies "started a test suit of their own to attack the constitutionality of the Kohler Act. They selected a plaintiff and a tribunal, Judge Fuller of Luzerne, whose sympathies were well known" (Mattes, *Tales,* 26).

94. Pennsylvania Coal Company v. Mahon, 260 US 393, Supreme Court of the United States, 1922, available at http://academic.lexisnexis.com/ (accessed 5 September 2011).

95. Freyfogle, *Land We Share,* 270, 84–85. See also Brandes, "Legal Theory," 1189; Friedman, "Search for Seizure," 85.

96. "Frustratingly vague": Freyfogle, *Land We Share,* 85; "trifling inconveniences": Pennsylvania Coal Company v. Sanderson, 113 Pa. 126, Supreme Court of Pennsylvania, 1886, available at http://academic.lexisnexis.com/ (accessed 5 September 2011). *Mahon* is the "original and most-cited Supreme Court decision on regulatory takings" (Fischel, *Regulatory*

Takings, 13). Oliver Wendell Holmes wrote the majority opinion; Louis Brandeis authored the lone dissent.

97. See M. Germaine O'Neill to W. A. May, 8 May 1914; W. A. May to M. Germaine O'Neill, 8 June 1916 (quote); Edward F. Blewitt to M. Germaine O'Neill, 13 December 1917 and 26 August 1919. All in Land Records file, Sisters, Servants of the Immaculate Heart of Mary, Scranton, Pa.

98. Fischel, *Regulatory Takings,* 13, 40, 42–43, 45.

99. Conner, "Mine-Caves," 259, 258.

100. "Knox Flooding Peril," 4. See also "Flushing Sketch," *Scranton Times,* 22 April 1965, Flushing file, Lackawanna Historical Society.

101. "Lower Hill Section Flushing Work Will Take 4–5 Months to Complete," *Scranton Tribune,* 25 December 1961, Flushing file, Lackawanna Historical Society; McIntosh, "Dark, Damp." Built in 1926/1927, the Von Storch colliery piled fifteen million tons of waste at four locations. A longtime worker there described the breaker as the "most nearly perfect breaker ever built in the anthracite field" (Edward Hopkins, "Story of the Von Storch Breaker," 1965, 1, 5, Lackawanna Historical Society).

102. Mrozinski, "Hole Opens."

103. "Most sensational": Krawczeniuk, "Guilty," A1 (see also A10); "shakedown scheme": McDonald, "Seeds"; "façade" and "so tirelessly": Kelly A9; "business as usual": "Verdicts Vital Accountability."

CODA

1. "Diminished thing": Frost, "Oven Bird," line 14; "grief and rage": Costello, "What to Make," 570.

2. "IORR"; "Wind Farms."

3. Scranton Sewer Authority and Lackawanna River Corridor Association. *Lackawanna River Clean,* 3.

4. "New Geothermal Project."

5. Singleton, "At Last," A1, A8.

6. Johanson, "Mary's Garden," 5–7. See also Johanson, "Transforming."

7. "Wild trout": Becker, "Police"; "raining so hard" and "frustrated": Mrozinski, "Officials."

8. U.S. Environmental Protection Agency, *NPL.* See also U.S. National Oceanic and Atmospheric Administration, *Keyser Avenue.*

9. U.S. Environmental Protection Agency, *Butler Mine.* See also Hughes, "Much Waste."

10. Pennsylvania Department of Environmental Protection, *Marcellus Active Operators.*

11. Pennsylvania Department of Environmental Protection, *Weekly Workload Report.*

12. Legere, "Boom Towns"; B. Walsh, "Gas Dilemma," 44; Ward and Kelsey, "Local Business"; Pennsylvania Department of Labor and Industry, *Fast Facts,* 4; Falchek, "Flurry" (quotes).

13. "Wells have blown out": B. Walsh, "Gas Dilemma," 48; "land, streams": Soeder and Kappel, "Water Resources," 4. See also Abdalla and Drohan, *Water Withdrawals,* 8; McConnell, "Activist."

14. "One of the top four": Devlin, letter; "most intact": Johnson, *Pennsylvania Energy,* 6. For leasing statistics, see "Natural Gas Development."

15. "More than 80 chemicals": Levy, "Chemical List"; "incapable of screening": B. Walsh, "Gas Dilemma," 48. See also Soeder and Kappel, "Water Resources," 5.

16. Osborn et al., "Methane Contamination," 2–4. The researchers point out that "dissolved methane in drinking water is not currently classified as a health hazard for ingestion" (2).

17. B. Walsh, "Gas Dilemma," 46; Legere, "Marcellus Shale."

18. Black, *Petrolia*, 32, 38, 54, 57, 81, 88, 90, 101. For photographs, see 112, 145, 151, 176, and the title page.

19. Engelder, "Marcellus 2008," 22.

20. "America's Champion": Chesapeake Energy, advertisement, *Forest City News*, 2 December 2009; "Let's Keep It": Endless Mountain Energy, advertisement; "Champion of Natural Beauty": Chesapeake Energy, advertisement, *Forest City News*, 2 September 2009.

21. "Water-efficient energy source": Chesapeake Energy, advertisement, *Sunday Times*; "I'm happy with Troy" and "work very closely": Chesapeake Energy, advertisement, *Forest City News*, 29 June 2011.

22. Gilliland, "State Tracks."

23. *Gasland* premiered on HBO on 21 June 2010.

24. See Engelder, "Marcellus Gas."

25. Delaware River Basin Commission, "DRBC Approves"; Delaware River Basin Commission, "Natural Gas."

26. Engelder, "Marcellus Gas."

27. David Messersmith, personal interview, 12 July 2011.

28. Engelder, "Marcellus Gas."

29. McConnell, "Keystone," A3; Legere, "Shale Drives," A1 (quote).

Bibliography

Abdalla, Charles W., and Joy R. Drohan. *Water Withdrawals for Development of Marcellus Shale Gas in Pennsylvania.* University Park, Pa.: Penn State Cooperative Extension, 2010.

Allen, Paula Gunn. *The Sacred Hoop: Recovering the Feminine in American Indian Traditions.* 1986. Reprint, Boston: Beacon Press, 1992.

Alliance Sanitary Landfill: History of Permitted Site Footprint and General Surroundings. Carbondale, Pa.: Kaufman Engineering, 2004.

Ammerman, Kristen. "Mount Pleasant Township." In *History of Wayne County, Pennsylvania, 1798–1998,* edited by Walter B. Barbe and Kurt A. Reed, 216–25. Honesdale, Pa.: Wayne County Historical Society, 1998.

Ammons, A. R. *Garbage.* New York: W. W. Norton, 1993.

Aristotle. *Rhetoric and Poetics.* Translated by W. Rhys Roberts and Ingram Bywater. New York: Modern Library, 1954.

Atlas of the City of Scranton. Philadelphia: G. M. Hopkins, 1877.

Austen, Ian. "Canada: New Mad Cow Case." *New York Times,* 19 December 2007. http://www.nytimes.com/2007/12/19/world/americas/19briefs-cow.html. Accessed 3 September 2011.

Austin, Mary. *The Land of Little Rain.* 1903. Reprinted with an introduction by Robert Hass. New York: Modern Library, 2003.

Azzarelli, Margo L. *Taylor.* Charleston, S.C.: Arcadia, 2010.

Ball, Eric L. "Literary Criticism for Places." *symploke* 14.1–2 (2006): 232–51.

Bartlett, Thomas. "Phoenix Risen." *Chronicle of Higher Education,* 10 July 2009, A1, A10–A13.

"Basin Hydrology." In *State of the Delaware River Basin Report,* by the Delaware River Basin Commission, 1–27. 2008. Accessed 30 August 2011.

Becker, Peter. "Police Seek Info on Oil Dumping." *Wayne Independent,* 14 April 2009. http://www.wayneindependent.com/article/20090414/NEWS/304149986. Accessed 30 August 2011.

Bedell, Rebecca. *The Anatomy of Nature: Geology and American Landscape Painting, 1825–1875.* Princeton: Princeton University Press, 2001.

"Berlin Township." In *History of Wayne County, Pennsylvania, 1798–1998,* edited by Walter B. Barbe and Kurt A. Reed, 258–60. Honesdale, Pa.: Wayne County Historical Society, 1998.

Berry, Wendell. "Is Life a Miracle?" In *Citizenship Papers,* 181–89. Washington, D.C.: Shoemaker and Hoard, 2003.

———. "The River Bridged and Forgot." In *Collected Poems, 1957–1982,* 255–57. San Francisco: North Point Press, 1984.

"Big Mine Cave in Back Yard." *Scranton Times,* 30 August 1909, 3.

Black, Brian. *Petrolia: The Landscape of America's First Oil Boom.* Baltimore: Johns Hopkins University Press, 2000.

Blomain, Karen. "Carbondale Cave-In." In *Coalseam: Poems from the Anthracite Region,* edited by Karen Blomain, 114–15. 2nd ed. Scranton, Pa.: University of Scranton Press, 1996.

Brandes, Evan B. "Legal Theory and Property Jurisprudence of Oliver Wendell Holmes, Jr., and Louis D. Brandeis: An Analysis of *Pennsylvania Coal Company v. Mahon.*" *Creighton Law Review* 38.5 (2005): 1179–202.

Brantley, Ben. "The Champs Reunite, Bearing the Nation's Scars." Review of *That Championship Season. New York Times,* 6 March 2011. http://theater.nytimes.com/2011/03/07/theater/reviews/07champ.html. Accessed 6 June 2011.

Braun, Duane D. "Surficial Geology of the Scranton 7.5-Minute Quadrangle, Lackawanna County, Pennsylvania." Pennsylvania Geological Survey, 4th ser., Open-File Report OFSM 06–07.0. 2006. http://www.dcnr.state.pa.us/cs/groups/public/documents/document/dcnr_015843.zip. Accessed 27 August 2011.

Broughton, Walter, and William Conlogue. "What Search Committees Want." In *Profession 2001,* 39–51. New York: Modern Language Association, 2001.

Brox, Jane. *Five Thousand Days Like This One.* Boston: Beacon Press, 1999.

Brunner, Edward J. *Poetry as Labor and Privilege: The Writings of W. S. Merwin.* Urbana: University of Illinois Press, 1991.

Bryson, J. Scott. *The West Side of Any Mountain: Place, Space, and Ecopoetry.* Iowa City: University of Iowa Press, 2005.

Buell, Lawrence. *Writing for an Endangered World: Literature, Culture, and Environment in the U.S. and Beyond.* Cambridge: Harvard University Press, 2001.

Bulfinch, Thomas. *The Golden Age of Myth and Legend.* Hertfordshire: Wordsworth Editions, 1993.

Burton, Gideon O. "Memory." Forest of Rhetoric, Brigham Young University, 26 February 2007. http://rhetoric.byu.edu/. Accessed 4 September 2011.

The Business of Building Men. Scranton, Pa.: International Correspondence Schools, 1930[?].

Carbonneau, Robert. "Coal Mines, St. Ann's Novena, and Passionist Spirituality in Scranton, Pennsylvania, 1902–2002." *American Catholic Studies* 115.2 (2004): 23–44.

Carlson, Ben. "BioArts International Ends Cloning Service; Blasts Black-Market Cloners." BioArts International, 10 September 2009. http://www.bioartsinternational.com/press_release/ba09_10_09.htm. Accessed 6 September 2011.

Casey, Robert. "Federal Government's Role in Energy Resource Development." Address delivered at "Marcellus Shale: Opportunities and Challenges," Marywood University, Scranton, Pa., 19 August 2010.

Cather, Willa. "Neighbour Rosicky." 1932. In *Norton Anthology of American Literature,* 2:1491–516. New York: W. W. Norton, 1979.

"Charmin Paper Products Co. Plant." *AAA Motorist of Northeastern Pennsylvania* 53.1 (1971): 1, 4.

Chesapeake Energy. Advertisement. *Forest City News,* 29 June 2011, 11.

———. Advertisement. *Forest City News,* 2 September 2009, 9.

———. Advertisement. *Forest City News,* 2 December 2009, 8.

———. Advertisement. *Sunday Times* (Scranton, Pa.), 5 September 2010, B3.

Christensen, Laird, and Hal Crimmel, eds. *Teaching About Place: Learning from the Land.* Reno: University of Nevada Press, 2008.

Cikovsky, Nicolai. "George Inness's *The Lackawanna Valley:* 'Type of the Modern.'" In *The Railroad in American Art: Representations of Technological Change,* edited by Susan Danly and Leo Marx, 71–91. Cambridge: MIT Press, 1988.

"City Prides Itself on Wonderful Water Supply." *Scranton Times,* 12 October 1926.

"City Pushes Report on Flushing Plan in Bid to Receive U.S. and State Aid." *Scranton Times,* 14 March 1960, 1, 8.

"Clark Vein." *No. 1 and 5 Colliery (Underwood), Pennsylvania Coal Company.* Map. Wilkes-Barre, Pa.: Office of Surface Mining, n.d.

Cohen, Michael. "Blues in the Green: Ecocriticism Under Critique." *Environmental History* 9.1 (2004): 9–36.

"Competitive Agenda for Renewing the Cities of Northeastern Pennsylvania." Joint Urban Studies Center, 2005. http://www.institutepa.org/PDF/Research/Brookings %20Follow%20Up.pdf. Accessed 5 September 2011.

Conforti, Joseph A. *Imagining New England: Explorations of Regional Identity from the Pilgrims to the Mid-twentieth Century.* Chapel Hill: University of North Carolina Press, 2001.

Conner, Eli T. "Mine-Caves Under the City of Scranton." In *Transactions of the American Institute of Mining Engineers,* 246–63. New York: American Institute of Mining Engineers, 1912.

Constitution of the Commonwealth of Pennsylvania. State of Pennsylvania. http://www .dced.state.pa.us/public/oor/constitution.pdf. Accessed 6 September 2011.

Conzen, Michael P. "The County Landownership Map in America: Its Commercial Development and Social Transformation, 1814–1939." *Imago Mundi* 36.1 (1984): 9–31.

Costello, Bonnie. "'What to Make of a Diminished Thing': Modern Nature and Poetic Response." *American Literary History* 10.4 (1998): 569–605.

"County Business Patterns: 1998–2007 Lackawanna and Luzerne Counties." Institute for Public Policy and Economic Development. February 2010. http://www.institutepa .org/PDF/Research/CBP2010.pdf. Accessed 5 September 2011.

"County-Level Results for 1870." Historical Census Browser, University of Virginia, 2007. http://mapserver.lib.virginia.edu/php/county.php. Accessed 4 August 2009.

Crimmel, Hal. *Teaching in the Field.* Salt Lake City: University of Utah Press, 2003.

Cronon, William. "The Trouble with Wilderness; or, Getting Back to the Wrong Nature." In *Uncommon Ground: Rethinking the Human Place in Nature,* edited by William Cronon, 69–90. New York: W. W. Norton, 1995.

da Costa Nunes, Jadviga M. "Pennsylvania's Anthracite Mines and Miners: A Portrait of the Industry in America Art, c. 1860–1940." *Journal of the Society for Industrial Archeology* 28.1 (2002): 11–32.

Daily, Stephen. "Coal Mining's Legacy: The Danger Resurfaces." *Sunday Times* (Scranton, Pa.), 16 February 2003, A1, A6.

Davis, Cheri. *W. S. Merwin.* Boston: Twayne, 1981.

De Blij, Harm. *The Power of Place: Geography, Destiny, and Globalization's Rough Landscape.* New York: Oxford University Press, 2009.

"DeLaval Announces World's First Automatic Milking Rotary." DeLaval, 14 September 2010. http://www.delaval.com/en/About-DeLaval/DeLaval-Newsroom/?nid=2718. Accessed 4 September 2011.

Delaware River Basin Commission. "DRBC Approves Stone Energy Water Withdrawal." DRBC, 15 July 2010. http://www.nj.gov/drbc/home/newsroom/news/approved/ 20100715_newsrel_naturalgas071510.html. Accessed 6 September 2011.

———. "Natural Gas Archives." DRBC, 4 October 2012. http://www.state.nj.us/drbc/ programs/natural/archives.html. Accessed 16 April 2013.

DeLillo, Don. *White Noise.* 1985. New York: Penguin, 1986.

———. "Woman in the Distance." *The Guardian,* 1 November 2008. http://www.guardian.co .uk/books/2008/nov/01/wanda-barbara-loden. Accessed 7 June 2011.

Derickson, Alan. *Black Lung: Anatomy of a Public Health Disaster.* Ithaca: Cornell University Press, 1998.

Devlin, Dan. Letter. *Times-Tribune* (Scranton, Pa.), 8 May 2008, A14.

Diamond State Data Services. *Pennsylvania from the U.S. Census, 1850.* Mount Pleasant Township, Wayne County, Pa., page 30. Diamond State Data Services, 10 December 2003. http://www.dsdata.com.au/cgi-bin/1850page.cgi?wayne030. Accessed 4 September 2011.

Digital Connections Council. *Harnessing Openness to Improve Research, Teaching, and Learning in Higher Education.* Committee for Economic Development, 2009. http://www.oerafrica.org/ResourceDownload.aspx?id=36722. Accessed 10 September 2011.

Dillon, Sam. "Troubles Grow for a University Built on Profits." *New York Times,* 11 February 2007. http://www.nytimes.com/2007/02/11/education/11phoenix.html. Accessed 14 August 2011.

Doerflinger, Thomas M. *A Vigorous Spirit of Enterprise: Merchants and Economic Development in Revolutionary Philadelphia.* Chapel Hill: University of North Carolina Press, 1986.

Donoghue, Frank. "Prestige." In *Profession 2006,* 155–62. New York: Modern Language Association, 2006.

Dublin, Thomas. *When the Mines Closed: Stories of Struggles in Hard Times.* Ithaca: Cornell University Press, 1998.

Dublin, Thomas, and Walter Licht. *The Face of Decline: The Pennsylvania Anthracite Region in the Twentieth Century.* Ithaca: Cornell University Press, 2005.

DuPuis, E. Melanie. *Nature's Perfect Food: How Milk Became America's Drink.* New York: New York University Press, 2002.

Dupuis, Roger. "Renovation Job Reveals Voids Under Courthouse." *Times-Tribune* (Scranton, Pa.), 6 January 2007, A1, A6.

"Early Development of Scranton's Water Supply." *Lackawanna Historical Society Bulletin* 4.1 (1969): 1.

Elliott, David L. "An Interview with W. S. Merwin." *Contemporary Literature* 29.1 (1988): 1–25.

Endless Mountain Energy. Advertisement. *Forest City News,* 2 September 2009, 8.

Engelder, Terry. "The Marcellus Gas Shale: Nature's Kitchen Under Wayne County." Presentation at the annual meeting of the Wayne County Cooperative Extension Service, Honesdale, Pa., 4 November 2009.

———. "Marcellus 2008: Report Card on the Breakout Year for Gas Production in the Appalachian Basin." *Fort Worth Basin Oil and Gas Magazine,* August 2009. http://www.marcellus.psu.edu/resources/PDFs/marcellusengelder.pdf. Accessed 28 August 2011.

Engelder, Terry, and Gary G. Lash. "Draft: Systematic Joints in Devonian Black Shale: A Target for Horizontal Drilling in the Appalachian Basin." Pittsburgh Association of Petroleum Geologists, n.d. http://www.shepstone.net/naturalgasnow/EngelderLash.pdf. Accessed 6 May 2008.

———. "Marcellus Shale Play's Vast Resource Potential Creating Stir in Appalachia." *American Oil and Gas Reporter,* May 2008. http://www.aogr.com/index.php/magazine/cover-story/marcellus-shale-plays-vast-resource-potential-creating-stir-in-appalachia. Accessed 28 August 2011.

Erikson, Kai T. *Everything in Its Path: Destruction of Community in the Buffalo Creek Flood.* New York: Simon and Schuster, 1976.

———. *A New Species of Trouble: The Human Experience of Modern Disasters.* New York: W. W. Norton, 1994.

Esch, Mary. "New York Senate OKs Moratorium on Natural Gas Drilling, Cites Dimock Contamination." *Republican Herald* (Pottsville, Pa.), 5 August 2010. http://republicanherald.com/news/new-york-senate-oks-moratorium-on-natural-gas-drilling-cites-dimock-contamination-1.923466. Accessed 30 August 2011.

"Evaluation of Faculty Members." In *Faculty Handbook*, 24–26. Marywood University, Scranton, Pa., 2008.

Fairchok, Sherry. "Culm Bank in Taylor, Pennsylvania." In *The Palace of Ashes*, 6–7. Fort Lee, N.J.: CavanKerry Press, 2002.

———. "Stoning the Breaker." In *The Palace of Ashes*, 14–16. Fort Lee, N.J.: CavanKerry Press, 2002.

———. "Three Towns." In *The Palace of Ashes*, 9. Fort Lee, N.J.: CavanKerry Press, 2002.

Falchek, David. "Flurry of Offers Greeting Marcellus Landowners." *Times-Tribune* (Scranton, Pa.), 17 September 2009, D1.

———. "State Loses Out in Drilling." *Sunday Times* (Scranton, Pa.), 6 July 2008, 1, 5.

Fifteenth Anniversary Exercises and Banquet. Scranton, Pa.: International Textbook Company, 1907.

"Fire Area 1500 Feet Nearer Midtown." *Carbondale Daily News*, 27 January 1954, 1.

"Fire Under the Streets." *Time*, 10 August 1959. http://www.time.com/time/magazine/article/0,9171,811233,00.html. Accessed 2 July 2009.

"First Wayne County Gas Well." *Forest City News*, 21 May 2008, 1.

Fischel, William A. *Regulatory Takings: Law, Economics, and Politics*. Cambridge: Harvard University Press, 1995.

Flannery, Joseph X. "Filmmakers Plan 20 Full Days of Shooting." *Scranton Times*, 6 July 1982, 8.

Folsom, Burton. *Urban Capitalists: Entrepreneurs and City Growth in Pennsylvania's Lackawanna and Lehigh Regions, 1800–1920*. 1981. 2nd ed. Scranton, Pa.: University of Scranton Press, 2001.

Folsom, Ed. "'I Have Been a Long Time in a Strange Country': W. S. Merwin and America." In *W. S. Merwin: Essays on the Poetry*, edited by Cary Nelson and Ed Folsom, 224–49. Urbana: University of Illinois Press, 1987.

Folsom, Ed, and Cary Nelson. Introduction to *W. S. Merwin: Essays on the Poetry*, edited by Cary Nelson and Ed Folsom, 1–18. Urbana: University of Illinois Press, 1987.

Francaviglia, Richard V. *Hard Places: Reading the Landscape of America's Historic Mining Districts*. Iowa City: University of Iowa Press, 1991.

Frazier, Charles. *Cold Mountain*. 1997. Reprint, New York: Vintage, 1998.

Frazier, Jane. *From Origin to Ecology: Nature and the Poetry of W. S. Merwin*. Madison, N.J.: Fairleigh Dickinson University Press, 1999.

Freyfogle, Eric T. "Introduction: A Durable Scale." In *The New Agrarianism: Land, Culture, and the Community of Life*, edited by Eric T. Freyfogle, xiii–xli. Washington, D.C.: Island Press, 2001.

———. *The Land We Share: Private Property and the Common Good*. Washington, D.C.: Island Press, 2003.

Friedman, Lawrence M. "A Search for Seizure: *Pennsylvania Coal Co. v. Mahon* in Context." *Law and History Review* 4.1 (1986): 1–22.

Frost, Robert. "A Brook in the City." In Lathem, *Poetry of Robert Frost*, 231.

———. "The Figure a Poem Makes." In *Robert Frost: Poetry and Prose*, edited by Edward Connery Lathem and Lawrance Thompson, 393–96. 1972. Reprint, New York: Henry Holt, 1984.

———. "The Gift Outright." In Lathem, *Poetry of Robert Frost*, 348.

———. "Mending Wall." In Lathem, *Poetry of Robert Frost*, 33–34.

———. "The Oven Bird." In Lathem, *Poetry of Robert Frost*, 119–20.

———. "The Pasture." In Lathem, *Poetry of Robert Frost*, 1.

———. "Pod of the Milkweed." In Lathem, *Poetry of Robert Frost*, 411–12.

———. "A Star in a Stoneboat." In Lathem, *Poetry of Robert Frost*, 172–74.

———. "The Wood-Pile." In Lathem, *Poetry of Robert Frost*, 101–2.

Galpin, Charles Josiah. *Rural Life*. New York: Century Company, 1920.

Gawande, Atul. "The Itch." *New Yorker*, 30 June 2008. Reprinted in *The Best American Science and Nature Writing 2009*, edited by Elizabeth Kolbert, 76–93. New York: Houghton Mifflin, 2009.

Gifford, Terry. *Reconnecting with John Muir: Essays in Post-pastoral Practice*. Athens: University of Georgia Press, 2006.

Gilliland, Donald. "State Tracks Anti-Marcellus Shale Drilling Groups, Notifies Law Enforcement." *Harrisburg Patriot-News*, 14 September 2010. http://www.pennlive.com/midstate/index.ssf/2010/09/post_122.html. Accessed 30 June 2011.

Glasgow, Ellen. *Barren Ground*. 1925. Reprint, New York: Harcourt, 1985.

Glassie, Henry. "The Variation of Concepts Within Tradition: Barn Building in Otsego County, New York." *Geoscience and Man*, 10 June 1974, 177–235.

"God Is Good in Blessing People with Good Water." *Scrantonian*, 3 April 1927.

Goin, Peter, and Elizabeth Raymond. "Living in Anthracite: Mining Landscape and Sense of Place in Wyoming Valley, Pennsylvania." *Public Historian* 23.2 (2001): 29–45.

Goodrich, Phineas G. *History of Wayne County*. Honesdale, Pa.: Haines and Beardsley, 1880.

Grun, Bernard. *The Timetables of History*. 3rd ed. New York: Simon and Schuster, 1991.

Haggerty, James. "Farmers Fleeing as Prices Plunge." *Times-Tribune* (Scranton, Pa.), 11 October 2009, A1, A7.

———. "Feds Probe Milk Pricing." *Times-Tribune* (Scranton, Pa.), 30 September 2009, A1, A7.

———. "Milk Pricing Imbalance Causing Many Local Dairy Farmers to Sell Off Herds." *Times-Tribune* (Scranton, Pa.), 3 May 2010. http://thetimes-tribune.com/news/milk-pricing-imbalance-causing-many-local-dairy-farmers-to-sell-off-herds-1.757309. Accessed 22 August 2011.

Hall, Sarah Hofius. "Plan Includes $44.7M Boost for Area Schools." *Times-Tribune* (Scranton, Pa.), 5 February 2009, A7.

Hamilton, Edith. *Mythology*. New York: New American Library, 1942.

Harper, Roland. "Marywood College Subsidence III." Complaint Investigation Report. Office of Surface Mining Reclamation and Enforcement, U.S. Department of Interior, 4 May 1994.

"A Haven from Prejudice: With Academia Elsewhere Closed to Teaching for Profit, the Company's Boss Turned to Arizona." *Financial Times*, 21 May 1996, 5.

Healey, Richard G. *The Pennsylvania Anthracite Coal Industry, 1860–1902*. Scranton, Pa.: University of Scranton Press, 2007.

Helleiner, Jane. *Irish Travellers: Racism and the Politics of Culture*. Toronto: University of Toronto Press, 2000.

Henn, Jennifer. "Jason Miller Dies." *Times-Tribune* (Scranton, Pa.), 14 May 2001. http://www.scrantontimestribune.com/zwire/jasonmiller/story1.htm. Accessed 2 June 2011.

Herbert, George. *The Country Parson*. 1652. In *The Works of George Herbert*, edited by F. E. Hutchinson, 223–90. Oxford: Clarendon Press, 1959.

"Here and there." In *Merriam Webster's Collegiate Dictionary*. 11th ed. 1998.

Hess, Scott. "Imagining Everyday Nature." *Interdisciplinary Studies in Literature and Environment* 17.1 (2010): 85–112.

Hitchcock, Frederick L. *History of Scranton and Its People.* Vol. 2. New York: Lewis Historical Publishing, 1914.

Hoffman, Jennifer. "Managing and Protecting Water Resources in the Susquehanna River
Basin." Presentation at "Marcellus Shale: Opportunities and Challenges," Marywood
University, Scranton, Pa., 19 August 2010.

Hole, Christina. *English Custom and Usage.* New York: Charles Scribner's Sons, 1946.

Hollister, Horace. *History of the Lackawanna Valley.* 1869. 5th ed. Philadelphia: J. B. Lippincott, 1885.

Hoskins, Donald M. "Celebrating a Century and a Half: The Geologic Survey." *Pennsylvania Heritage.* Pennsylvania Department of Environmental Protection, 5 April 2006.
http://www.portal.state.pa.us/portal/server.pt?open=514&objID=588479&mode=2.
Accessed 28 August 2011.

Howard, Jennifer. "The MLA Convention in Translation." *Chronicle of Higher Education,*
31 December 2009. http://chronicle.com/article/The-MLA-Convention-in/63379/.
Accessed 10 September 2011.

Hughes, Matt. "Much Waste Remains Under Pittston." *Times-Leader* (Wilkes-Barre, Pa.),
17 April 2011. http://www.scribd.com/doc/53179661/Times-Leader-04-17-2011.
Accessed 6 September 2011.

Hupkens, P., H. Boxma, and J. Dokter. "Tannic Acid as a Topical Agent in Burns: Historical
Considerations and Implications for New Developments." *Burns* 21.1 (1995): 57–61.

Insurance Maps of Scranton. Vol. 2. New York: Sanborn and Company, 1920. Includes a
September 1949 addendum.

"IORR: Iron Oxide Resource Recovery." Eastern Pennsylvania Coalition for Abandoned
Mine Reclamation, n.d. http://epcamr.org/home/current-initiatives/iorr-iron-oxide
-resource-recovery/. Accessed 5 July 2011.

"Jason Miller's Storied Career." *Times-Tribune* (Scranton, Pa.), 14 May 2001. http://www
.scrantontimestribune.com/zwire/jasonmiller/story5.htm. Accessed 5 September
2011.

Johanson, Patricia. "Mary's Garden, Marywood University: Narrative." In *Patricia Johan-
son at Marywood: The Mary's Garden Project in Context,* edited by Linda Dugan
Partridge and Pamela M. Parsons, 5–8. Exhibition catalog. Scranton, Pa.: Marywood
University, 2010.

———. "Transforming a Coal Mining Site with Nature: 'Mary's Garden' Reclamation." *Landscape Architect,* November 2010, 46–50, 52, 54, 56.

Johnson, Nels. *Pennsylvania Energy Impacts Assessment Report 1: Marcellus Shale Natural
Gas and Wind.* Nature Conservancy, 15 November 2010. http://www.nature.org/
media/pa/tnc_energy_analysis.pdf. Accessed 5 July 2011.

Kahrl, William L. "The Politics of California Water: Owens Valley and the Los Angeles
Aqueduct, 1900–1927." *California Historical Quarterly* 55.2 (1976): 98–120.

Kanjorksi, Paul. Address delivered at "Marcellus Shale: Opportunities and Challenges,"
Marywood University, Scranton, Pa., 19 August 2010.

Kashuba, Cheryl. *A Brief History of Scranton.* Charleston: History Press, 2009.

———. "Call of the Wild: Young, Old Campaigned to Bring Elephants to Scranton."
Times-Tribune (Scranton, Pa.), 27 June 2010, D1.

———. "Cave-Ins Threatened St. Ann's." *Sunday Times* (Scranton, Pa.), 18 July 2010, D1, D6.

Keary, Kathleen Marie. "The Foundation and Development of the International Correspondence Schools." Master's thesis, Marywood University, 1935.

Keenan, Michel. *The Sisters, Servants of the Immaculate Heart of Mary, Scranton, Pennsylvania, 1919–1974.* Pittsburgh: RoseDog Books, 2005.

Kelly, Chris. "Carefully Built Façade Crashes Around Pair." *Times-Tribune* (Scranton, Pa.), 22 June 2011, A1, A9.

Kelsey, Timothy. "Economic and Community Impacts." Presentation at "Marcellus Shale: Opportunities and Challenges," Marywood University, Scranton, Pa., 19 August 2010.

Kilborn, Peter T. "Hurricane Reveals Flaws in Farm Law as Animal Waste Threatens Carolina Water." *New York Times*, 17 October 1999. http://www.nytimes.com/1999/10/17/us/hurricane-reveals-flaws-in-farm-law-as-animal-waste-threatens-n-carolina-water.html. Accessed 22 August 2011.

Killingsworth, M. Jimmie. *Walt Whitman and the Earth: A Study in Ecopoetics.* Walt Whitman Archive, edited by Ed Folsom and Kenneth M. Price. http://www.whitmanarchive.org/. Accessed 5 September 2011. Originally published in 2004 by the University of Iowa Press.

Kim, Ann G., Thomas R. Justin, and John F. Miller. "Mine Fire Diagnostics Applied to the Carbondale, PA, Mine Fire Site." Bureau of Mines, U.S. Department of the Interior, 1992. http://www.cdc.gov/niosh/mining/works/coversheet1467.html. Accessed 28 September 2009.

Klaber, Kathryn. "Economics, Energy, and the Environment." Presentation at "Marcellus Shale: Opportunities and Challenges," Marywood University, Scranton, Pa., 19 August 2010.

Klein, Naomi. "Gulf Oil Spill: A Hole in the World." *The Guardian*, 19 June 2010. http://www.guardian.co.uk/theguardian/2010/jun/19/naomi-klein-gulf-oil-spill. Accessed 1 September 2011.

Knies, Michael. "International Correspondence Schools of Scranton, Pennsylvania, 1897–1996." Weinberg Memorial Library, University of Scranton, 27 March 2006. http://www.scranton.edu/academics/wml/bk-manuscripts/ics-aid.shtml. Accessed 7 September 2011.

"Knox Flooding Peril to County." *Scranton Times*, 12 March 1960, 1, 4.

Krawczeniuk, Borys. "Guilty." *Times-Tribune* (Scranton, Pa.), 22 June 2011, A1, A10.

Kumin, Maxine. "The Brown Mountain." In *Where I Live: New and Selected Poems, 1990–2010.* New York: W. W. Norton, 2010.

Kumpas, Charles. "Anthracite Mine Timbering." *Miner's Lamp* 13.4 (1996): 1, 4.

Kutz, Gregory D. "For-Profit Colleges: Undercover Testing Finds Colleges Encouraged Fraud and Engaged in Deceptive and Questionable Marketing Practices." Testimony before the Committee on Health, Education, Labor, and Pensions, U.S. Senate. Government Accountability Office, 4 August 2010. Reissued 30 November 2010. http://www.gao.gov/products/GAO-10-948T. Accessed 23 August 2011.

Lackawanna Heritage Valley Authority. *Anthracite Coal in Pennsylvania: An Industry and a Region.* Scranton, Pa.: Lackawanna Heritage Valley Authority, 1997.

Lackawanna River Corridor Association. *Lackawanna River Watershed Conservation Plan.* Lackawanna River Corridor Association, November 2001. http://www.dcnr.state.pa.us/cs/groups/public/documents/document/DCNR_001596.pdf. Accessed 23 August 2011.

Lamb, W. R. M. "General Introduction." In *Plato in Twelve Volumes*, vol. 2, edited by E. H. Warmington, translated by W. R. M. Lamb, ix–xix. Cambridge: Harvard University Press, 1967.

Lathem, Edward Connery, ed. *The Poetry of Robert Frost.* 1969. Reprint, New York: Henry Holt, 1979.

Lauver, Fred J. "A Walk Through the Rise and Fall of Anthracite Might." Pennsylvania Historical and Museum Commission, 2011. http://www.portal.state.pa.us/portal/server.pt/community/trails_of_history/4287/museum_of_anthracite_mining_%28ph

%29/472646. Accessed 9 July 2011. Originally published as "Visiting the Museum of Anthracite Mining: A Walk Through the Rise and Fall of Anthracite Might." *Pennsylvania Heritage Magazine* 27.1 (2001): 32–39.

Lee, Henry. "Town on a Hot Seat." *Pageant,* July 1957, 70–77.

Legere, Laura. "Boom Towns." *Times-Tribune* (Scranton, Pa.), 25 October 2009, A1, A8, A9.

———. "Dangers Surface." *Times-Tribune* (Scranton, Pa.), 21 June 2010, A1, A6.

———. "Do We Really Know What Effect Drilling Will Have?" *Times-Tribune* (Scranton, Pa.), 20 June 2010, A11.

———. "Marcellus Shale Drilling Site Rocked by Explosion." *Shamokin News-Item*, 4 January 2009. http://pqasb.pqarchiver.com/timesshamrock/access/2052695511.html?FMT=ABS&FMTS=ABS:FT&type=current&date=Jan+4%2C+2009&author=LAURA+LEGERE&pub=The+News+-+Item&edition=&startpage=A.7&desc=Marcellus+Shale+drill+site+rocked+by+explosion. Accessed 5 July 2011.

———. "Shale Drives Landfill Plan." *Times-Tribune* (Scranton, Pa.), 24 June 2011, A1, A9.

———. "State Shuts Down Cabot." *Times-Tribune* (Scranton, Pa.), 26 September 2009, A1, A8.

Lentricchia, Frank. *Robert Frost: Modern Poetics and the Landscapes of Self.* Durham: Duke University Press, 1975.

Leopold, Aldo. *A Sand County Almanac.* 1949. New York: Ballantine, 1991.

LeRoy, Edwin D. *The Delaware and Hudson Canal: A History.* Honesdale, Pa.: Wayne County Historical Society, 1950.

Lesley, J. P. "J. P. Lesley on High-Level Drift." *Geological Magazine* 9.7 (1882): 334–36.

———. "Letter of Transmittal." In *Second Geological Survey of Pennsylvania: Report of Progress/The Geology of Susquehanna County and Wayne County,* by I. C. White, v–vii. Harrisburg: Board of Commissioners for the Second Geological Survey, 1881.

Levy, Marc. "Chemical List Made Public." *Times-Tribune* (Scranton, Pa.), 29 June 2010, A10.

Lewin, Tamar. "Scrutiny Takes Toll on For-Profit College Company." *New York Times,* 9 November 2010. http://www.nytimes.com/2010/11/10/education/10kaplan.html. Accessed 14 August 2011.

Lewis, Corey Lee. "Beyond the Text: Literary Field Studies." *Academic Exchange Quarterly* 7.4 (2003): 88–92.

———. *Reading the Trail: Exploring the Literature and Natural History of the California Crest.* Reno: University of Nevada Press, 2005.

"Liberation from 'the White Whip.'" In *Reflections: A History of DeLaval,* 45–52. DeLaval, n.d. http://www.delaval.tm/NR/rdonlyres/F1D774B1-BEAE-4439-B7F1-A0596B6CDC82/0/ReflectionsAHistoryOfDeLaval_ch4.pdf. Accessed 9 September 2011.

"Looking Back." *Forest City News,* 14 December 2006.

Lowenthal, Larry. *From the Coalfields to the Hudson: A History of the Delaware and Hudson Canal.* Fleischmanns, N.Y.: Purple Mountain Press, 1997.

"Lubricant Spills at Gas Well." *Times-Tribune* (Scranton, Pa.), 18 September 2009, A3.

Lynen, John F. *The Pastoral Art of Robert Frost.* New Haven: Yale University Press, 1960.

Maclean, Annie Marion. "Life in the Pennsylvania Coal Fields with Particular Reference to Women." *American Journal of Sociology* 14.3 (1908): 329–51.

MacShane, Frank. "A Portrait of W. S. Merwin." *Shenandoah* 21.2 (1970): 3–14.

Major, William H. *Grounded Vision: New Agrarianism and the Academy.* Tuscaloosa: University of Alabama Press, 2011.

Marsh, Ben. "Continuity and Decline in the Anthracite Towns of Pennsylvania." *Annals of the Association of American Geographers* 77.3 (1987): 337–52.

Marshall, Ian. *Story Line: Exploring the Literature of the Appalachian Trail.* Charlottesville: University of Virginia Press, 1998.

Martin, Andrew. "Largest Recall of Ground Beef Is Ordered." *New York Times*, 18 February 2008. http://www.nytimes.com/2008/02/18/business/18recall.html. Accessed 3 September 2011.

Martin, George D. *Soil Survey of Wayne County Pennsylvania*. Washington, D.C.: USDA, 1985.

Marx, Leo. *The Machine in the Garden: Technology and the Pastoral Ideal in America*. 1964. Reprint, London: Oxford University Press, 1974.

———. "Pastoral Ideals and City Troubles." *Journal of General Education* 20.4 (1969): 251–71.

Mathews, Alfred. *History of Wayne, Pike, and Monroe Counties, Pennsylvania*. Philadelphia: R. T. Peck, 1886.

"Mattes, Philip." *Scranton Directory*. Scranton, Pa.: R. L. Polk, 1921. 474.

Mattes, Philip V. "The Mine-Cave Struggle." In *Jubilee History Commemorative of the Fiftieth Anniversary of the Creation of Lackawanna County, Pennsylvania*, edited by Thomas Murphy, 1:368–80. Topeka: Historical Publishing, 1928.

———. *Tales of Scranton*. Published by author, 1973.

Maxey, David W. "Of Castles in Stockport and Other Strictures: Samuel Preston's Contentious Agency for Henry Drinker." *Pennsylvania Magazine of History and Biography* 100 (1986): 413–46.

McConnell, Steve. "Activist Spurs Drilling Probe; Violations Found." *Times-Tribune* (Scranton, Pa.), 31 December 2009, A1, A6.

———. "Keystone No. 2 Landfill in State." *Sunday Times* (Scranton, Pa.), 20 March 2011, A3, A10.

———. "Philly Urges Gas Drilling in Watershed Be Denied." *Times-Tribune* (Scranton, Pa.), 30 March 2010, A4.

McDonald, Joe. "Seeds of Cordaro Corruption Case Fertilized in Pigeon Dung." *Times-Tribune* (Scranton, Pa.), 4 June 2011. http://thetimes-tribune.com/news/seeds -of-cordaro-corruption-case-fertilized-in-pigeon-dung-1.1157344. Accessed 4 September 2011.

McGurl, Bernard. *The Lackawanna River Guide*. 2nd ed. Scranton, Pa.: Lackawanna River Corridor Association, 2002.

McIntosh, Ronald E. "Dark, Damp, Silent Void: Relic of a Basic Industry." *Sunday Times* (Scranton, Pa.), 30 March 1969, B7.

McMurry, Sally. *Transforming Rural Life: Dairying Families and Agricultural Change, 1820–1885*. Baltimore: Johns Hopkins University Press, 1995.

McNarney, Michael. "Courthouse Makeover up in Air." *Sunday Times* (Scranton, Pa.), 14 November 2004, B1, B6.

———. "Decades of Dung Caves in Ceiling." *Times-Tribune* (Scranton, Pa.), 9 November 2004, A1, A5.

———. "Pigeon Droppings Threaten 2nd Judge." *Scranton Times*, 13 November 2004, A3.

McPhee, John. *Annals of the Former World*. 1998. Reprint, New York: Farrar, Straus and Giroux, 2000.

Melton, Ruby. "Barbara Loden on *Wanda*." *Film Journal* 1.2 (1971): 10–15.

Merrill, Christopher. "The Vibrancy of Life: An Interview with W. S. Merwin." *Orion* 13 (1994): 44–48.

Merritt, Jane T. *At the Crossroads: Indians and Empires on a Mid-Atlantic Frontier, 1700–1763*. Chapel Hill: University of North Carolina Press, 2003.

Merwin, W. S. "Burning Mountain." In *The Drunk in the Furnace*, 57–58. New York: Macmillan, 1960.

———. "The Drunk in the Furnace." In *The Drunk in the Furnace*, 64. New York: Macmillan, 1960.

———. "Empty Lot." In *The Shadow of Sirius*, 20. Port Townsend, Wash.: Copper Canyon Press, 2008.

———. "Flight Home." *Paris Review* 17 (Autumn/Winter 1957): 126–36.

———. Interview by Bill Moyers. *Bill Moyers Journal*. PBS. WVIA, Scranton. 26 June 2009.

———. "Lackawanna." In *The Carrier of Ladders*, 44–45. New York: Atheneum, 1970.

———. "Luzerne Street Looking West." *Hudson Review* 9 (Winter 1956–57): 509–10.

———. "The Miner." *Kenyon Review* 19.2 (1957): 195.

———. "No." In *The Shadow of Sirius*, 21. Port Townsend, Wash.: Copper Canyon Press, 2008.

———. *Summer Doorways*. Emeryville, Calif.: Shoemaker and Hoard, 2005.

"Middle British Colonies in North America." Map. In *A Topographical Description of the Dominions of the United States of America*, by Thomas Pownall, edited by Lois Mulkearn. Pittsburgh: University of Pittsburgh Press, 1949.

Miller, Donald L., and Richard E. Sharpless. *The Kingdom of Coal: Work, Enterprise, and Ethnic Communities in the Mine Fields*. Easton, Pa.: Canal History and Technology Press, 1998. Originally published in 1985 by the University of Pennsylvania Press.

Miller, Jason. *That Championship Season*. 1972. Reprint, New York: Dramatists Play Service, 2000.

Miner, Charles. *History of Wyoming, in a Series of Letters, from Charles Miner to His Son William Penn Miner, Esq.* Philadelphia: J. Crissy, 1845.

[Miner, Lewis H.]. *The Valley of Wyoming: The Romance of Its History and Its Poetry*. New York: Robt. H. Johnston, 1866.

Moore, P. H. "Anthracite Industry." In *Jubilee History Commemorative of the Fiftieth Anniversary of the Creation of Lackawanna County, Pennsylvania*, edited by Thomas Murphy, 1:131–52. Topeka: Historical Publishing, 1928.

"Mount Pleasant." Map. N.p., [1872].

"Moviemakers Tap Forest City for Film Scenes." *Forest City News*, 14 August 1969, 1.

Moyer, Paul B. *Wild Yankees: The Struggle for Independence Along Pennsylvania's Revolutionary Frontier*. Ithaca: Cornell University Press, 2007.

Mrozinski, Josh. "Hole Opens, Nearly Swallows Dump Truck." *Times-Tribune* (Scranton, Pa.), 16 June 2011, A3.

———. "Officials Seek Oil Dumpers." *Times-Tribune* (Scranton, Pa.), 9 April 2009, A4.

Munley, Anne. "Welcoming Remarks." Delivered at "Marcellus Shale: Opportunities and Challenges," Marywood University, Scranton, Pa., 19 August 2010.

Munley, Kathleen. "The Carbondale Mine Fire." Presentation delivered at Anthracite Heritage Museum, Scranton, Pa., 30 May 2009.

———. *The West Side Carbondale, Pennsylvania Mine Fire*. Scranton, Pa.: University of Scranton Press, 2011.

Murley, Chris. "Underwood Mine." Underground Miners, 2005. http://www.undergroundminers.com/underwood.html. Accessed 5 September 2011.

Murphy, Thomas. "Transportation Facilities." In *Jubilee History Commemorative of the Fiftieth Anniversary of the Creation of Lackawanna County, Pennsylvania*, edited by Thomas Murphy, 93–114. Topeka: Historical Publishing, 1928.

"Narrative Scholarship: Storytelling in Ecocriticism." Association for the Study of Literature and Environment, 1995. http://www.asle.org/site/resources/ecocritical-library/intro/narrative/. Accessed 19 January 2010.

Nash, Roderick Frazier. *Wilderness and the American Mind*. 1967. 4th ed. New Haven: Yale University Press, 2001.

"Natural Gas Development and State Forests: Shale Gas Leasing Statistics." Pennsylvania Department of Conservation and Natural Resources, December 2012. http://www.dcnr.state.pa.us/forestry/NaturalGas/DCNR_009675. Accessed 18 April 2013.

Nelson, Cary. "The Resources of Failure: W. S. Merwin's Deconstructive Career." In *W. S. Merwin: Essays on the Poetry,* edited by Cary Nelson and Ed Folsom, 78–121. Urbana: University of Illinois Press, 1987.

Nelson, Robert M. *Place and Vision: The Function of Landscape in Native American Fiction.* New York: Peter Lang, 1993.

"New Geothermal Project Achieves LEED Gold." Greenman-Pederson Inc., Scranton, Pa., 14 January 2011. http://www.gpinet.com/userfiles/file/GPI%20Scranton%20-%20New %20Geothermal%20Project%20Achieves%20LEED%20Gold.pdf. Accessed 6 September 2011.

Nissley, Erin, and David Singleton. "Reporters' Notebook." *Times-Tribune* (Scranton, Pa.), 7 June 2011, A7.

Noble, Allen G., and Richard K. Cleek. "Sorting Out the Nomenclature of English Barns." *Material Culture* 26.1 (1994): 49–63.

Norris, Frank. *The Octopus.* 1901. Reprint, New York: New American Library, 1981.

"Octagon School House." Wayne County Historical Society, 2010. http://waynehistorypa .org/plid/57. Accessed 6 September 2011.

O'Grady, Patricia. "Thales of Miletus." *The Internet Encyclopedia of Philosophy,* 17 September 2004. http://www.iep.utm.edu/thales/. Accessed 29 August 2011.

O'Hara, Paul L. *People and Places of Mount Pleasant Township, Wayne County, Pa.* Montrose: Montrose Publishing, 2009.

Osborn, Stephen G., Avner Vengosh, Nathaniel R. Warner, and Robert B. Jackson. "Methane Contamination of Drinking Water Accompanying Gas-Well Drilling and Hydraulic Fracturing." *PNAS (Proceedings of the National Academy of Sciences) Early Edition* 108.20 (2011): 1–5. http://www.nicholas.duke.edu/cgc/pnas2011.pdf. Accessed 10 May 2011.

"Overview." Information packet insert from "Marcellus Shale: Opportunities and Challenges," Marywood University, 19 August 2010.

Parini, Jay. "Anthracite Country." In *Anthracite Country,* 20. New York: Random House, 1982.

———. "The Lackawanna at Dusk." In *Anthracite Country,* 19. New York: Random House, 1982.

———. "A Lost Topography." In *Town Life,* 31. New York: Henry Holt, 1988.

———. "Why WS Merwin Deserves His Second Pulitzer Prize." *The Guardian,* 24 April 2009. http://www.guardian.co.uk/books/booksblog/2009/apr/24/pulitzerprize -poetry. Accessed 28 September 2009.

Pennsylvania Department of Environmental Protection. *Marcellus Active Operators.* Bureau of Oil and Gas Management, 24 August 2011. Web page no longer available. Accessed 6 September 2011.

———. *Weekly Workload Report: Week of 08/22/2011 to 08/26/2011.* Bureau of Oil and Gas Management, n.d. Web page no longer available. Accessed 6 September 2011.

Pennsylvania Department of Labor and Industry. *Marcellus Shale Fast Facts: September 2011 Edition.* Center for Workforce Information and Analysis, 2 September 2011. Web page no longer available. Accessed 6 September 2011.

Percival, Gwendoline E., and Chester J. Kulesa. *Illustrating an Anthracite Era: The Photographic Legacy of John Horgan, Jr.* Harrisburg: Pennsylvania Historical and Museum Commission, 1995.

Perry, Daniel K. *"A Fine Substantial Piece of Masonry": Scranton's Historic Furnaces.* Harrisburg: Pennsylvania Historical and Museum Commission, 1994.

Petula, Nicholas, and Thomas W. Morgan. *The History of Public Schools in Scranton, Pa.* Privately printed, 2008.

Philbin, David. "Marywood University Parking Lot Subsidence II." Complaint Investigation Report. Office of Surface Mining Reclamation and Enforcement, U.S. Department of Interior, 23 September 2004.

"Pillar Robbing Caused Big Cave-In; $100,000 Damage." *Scranton Times,* 30 August 1909, 1, 3.

Plato. *Protagoras.* Translated by W. R. M. Lamb. In *Plato in Twelve Volumes,* vol. 2, edited by E. H. Warmington, 85–257. Cambridge: Harvard University Press, 1967.

Poirier, Richard. *Robert Frost: The Work of Knowing.* New York: Oxford University Press, 1977.

Pollan, Michael. *The Omnivore's Dilemma.* 2006. Reprint, New York: Penguin, 2007.

Pownall, Thomas. *A Topographical Description of the Dominions of the United States of America.* Edited by Lois Mulkearn. Pittsburgh: University of Pittsburgh Press, 1949.

"Public Cordially Invited to See Beautiful Pictures Displayed in the Rooms of the Century Club." *Scranton Times,* 4 October 1915, 10.

Quigley, John. "Mineral Rights in Pennsylvania Parks and Forests." Presentation at "Marcellus Shale: Opportunities and Challenges," Marywood University, Scranton, Pa., 19 August 2010.

Rathje, William, and Cullen Murphy. *Rubbish! The Archaeology of Garbage.* New York: HarperCollins, 1992.

Raught, John Willard. "The Tragedy of Coal Mining." *Scranton Republican,* 6 February 1928, 8.

"Records of the Department of Education: Agency History." RG-22. Pennsylvania State Archives, Harrisburg, Pa., n.d. http://www.phmc.state.pa.us/bah/dam/rg/rg22ahr .htm. Accessed 6 September 2011.

"Reinhardt, John A." In *Scranton City Directory, 1907,* 713. Scranton, Pa.: R. L. Polk, 1907.

"Reinhart, John A." In *Scranton City Directory, 1908,* 625. Scranton, Pa.: R. L. Polk, 1908.

Reynaud, Bérénice. "For Wanda." In *The Last Great American Picture Show: New Hollywood Cinema in the 1970s,* edited by Thomas Elsaesser, Alexander Horwath, and Noel King, 223–47. Amsterdam: Amsterdam University Press, 2004.

Rhoads, Ann Fowler, and Timothy A. Block. *Trees of Pennsylvania: A Complete Reference Guide.* Philadelphia: University of Pennsylvania Press, 2005.

Ritchie, Mark. *The Loss of Our Family Farms: Inevitable Results or Conscious Policies?* Minneapolis: League of Rural Voters, 1979.

Roberts, Ellis W. *The Breaker Whistle Blows: Mining Disasters and Labor Leaders in the Anthracite Region.* Scranton, Pa.: Anthracite Museum Press, 1984.

Rodriguez, Richard. *Brown: The Last Discovery of America.* New York: Penguin, 2002.

Rogers, Henry Darwin. *The Geology of Pennsylvania: A Government Survey.* 2 vols. Philadelphia: J. B. Lippincott, 1858.

Rosin, Hanna. "Red, Blue, and Lots of Green: John Sperling Divides America into 'Metro' and 'Retro.'" *Washington Post,* 26 October 2004, C1.

Salaman, Redcliffe N. *The History and Social Influence of the Potato.* Cambridge: Cambridge University Press, 1949.

Sanderson, Dorothy Hurlbut. *The Delaware and Hudson Canalway: Carrying Coals to Rondout.* 2nd ed. Ellenville, N.Y.: Rondout Valley Publishing, 1974.

Sauthier, C. J. *Map of the Provinces of New York and New Jersey, with a Part of Pennsylvania and the Province of Quebec.* Map. 1777.

Schruers, Eric J. "John Willard Raught, Corwin Knapp Linson, and Stephen Crane: Picturing the Pennsylvania Coal Industry in Word and Image." *Journal of the Society for Industrial Archeology* 28.1 (2002): 33–42.

Scranton Sewer Authority and Lackawanna River Corridor Association. *Lackawanna River Clean: Downspout Disconnection.* Scranton, Pa.: Scranton Sewer Authority and Lackawanna River Corridor Association, 2010.

Seiden, Michael J. "For-Profit Colleges Deserve Some Respect." *Chronicle of Higher Education,* 10 July 2009, A80.

Shapiro, Elliot H. "Survival and Failure, Adaptation and Acceptance." *ADE Bulletin* 146 (2008): 18–27.

Shields, Alcuin F. *The Centennial History of St. Cecilia's Catholic Church, Hill Top, Wayne County, Pennsylvania, 1865–1965.* Montrose: Montrose Publishing, 1969.

Silko, Leslie Marmon. *Ceremony.* 1977. Reprint, New York: Penguin, 1986.

Simon, John. "That Championship Season." *Hudson Review* 25.4 (1972–73): 616–25.

Singleton, David. "At Last, a Balm for Area's Mine Scars." *Times-Tribune* (Scranton, Pa.), 11 August 2008, A1, A8.

Sloane, David Charles. *The Last Great Necessity: Cemeteries in American History.* Baltimore: Johns Hopkins University Press, 1991.

Smith, Sidonie. "The Presidential Theme for the 2011 MLA Convention: Narrating Lives." Modern Language Association, 2010. http://www.mla.org/pdf/pres_theme_letter_rev .pdf. Accessed 19 January 2010.

Snyder, Gary. *The Practice of the Wild.* Emeryville, Calif.: Shoemaker and Hoard, 1990.

Soeder, Daniel J., and William M. Kappel. "Water Resources and Natural Gas Production from the Marcellus Shale." Fact Sheet 2009-3032. U.S. Geological Service, May 2009. http://pubs.usgs.gov/fs/2009/3032/pdf/FS2009-3032.pdf. Accessed 6 September 2011.

Soraghan, Mike. "Groundtruthing Academy Award Nominee 'Gasland.'" *New York Times,* 24 February 2011. http://www.nytimes.com/gwire/2011/02/24/24greenwire -groundtruthing-academy-award-nominee-gasland-33228.html. Accessed 30 June 2011.

"Statement and Implementation of Undergraduate Core Curricular Purpose: Living Responsibly in an Interdependent World." In *Undergraduate Catalog, 2011–2013.* Marywood University, Scranton, Pa.

Stefon, Frederick J. "The Wyoming Valley." In *Beyond Philadelphia: The American Revolution in the Pennsylvania Hinterland,* edited by John B. Frantz and William Pencak, 133–52. 1998. Reprint, University Park: Pennsylvania State University Press, 2000.

Stevens, Wallace. "Anecdote of the Jar." 1919. In *Norton Anthology of American Literature,* 2:1154–55. New York: W. W. Norton, 1979.

St. John, David. "The Last Troubadour." *Kenyon Review* 19.3–4 (1997): 197–202.

Sugarman, Jeffery. "Environmental and Community Health: A Reciprocal Relationship." In *Restorative Commons: Creating Health and Well-Being Through Urban Landscapes,* edited by Lindsay Campbell and Anne Wiesen, 138–53. Gen. Tech Rep. NRS-P-39. Forest Service, Northern Research Station, U.S. Department of Agriculture, 2009. http://www.nrs.fs.fed.us/pubs/gtr/gtr_nrs-p-39r.pdf. Accessed 5 September 2011.

"Sunken Coal Mine." *New York Times,* 20 December 1869. New York Times Archive. http:// www.nytimes.com/ref/membercenter/nytarchive.html. Accessed 5 September 2011.

That Championship Season. Directed by Jason Miller. Beverly Hills, Calif.: Metro-Goldwyn-Mayer, 1982. DVD.

"Then and Now." *Sunday Times* (Scranton, Pa.), 1 August 2010, D2.

Thoreau, Henry David. *Walden.* 1854. In *Thoreau: Walden and Other Writings,* edited by Joseph Wood Krutch, 107–351. 1962. Reprint, New York: Bantam, 1971.

Throop, B. H. *Historical Notes: The Settlement of Providence Township and Reminiscences of Early Scranton.* Scranton, Pa.: Lackawanna Institute of Science and History, 1887.

"Tillie's Grave Secret but City Files Sketch." *Scranton Times,* 11 February 1966, 3.

Torrey, David. *Memoir of Major Jason Torrey of Bethany, Wayne County, PA.* Scranton, Pa.: James S. Horton, 1885.

"University of Phoenix." MTV. Comcast Cable channel 40. Scranton, Pa. 6 January 2010.

U.S. Census Bureau. *Census of Population and Housing, 1850 Census.* 1852. U.S. Census Bureau, n.d. 26 August 2008. http://www.census.gov/prod/www/decennial.html #y1850. Accessed 8 August 2009.

———. *Census of Population and Housing, 1870 Census.* Vol. 1. 1872. U.S. Census Bureau, n.d. 26 August 2008. http://www.census.gov/prod/www/decennial.html#y1870. Accessed 8 August 2009.

———. *Census of Population and Housing, 2000 Census.* U.S. Census Bureau, 2002. 26 August 2008. http://www.census.gov/prod/www/decennial.html#y2000. Accessed 8 August 2009.

———. *Community Facts: Population.* Forest City Borough, Pa. U.S. Census Bureau, 2010. http://factfinder2.census.gov/faces/nav/jsf/pages/community_facts.xhtml. Accessed 24 August 2011.

———. *1970 Census of Population: Advance Report, Final Population Counts.* Pennsylvania. U.S. Census Bureau, n.d. http://www.census.gov/prod/www/decennial.html #y1970. Accessed 26 August 2011.

———. *1980 Census of Population and Housing: Summary Characteristics for Governmental Units and Standard Metropolitan Statistical Areas.* Washington, D.C.: GPO, 1982.

U.S. Environmental Protection Agency. *Butler Mine Tunnel.* Mid-Atlantic Superfund, 16 June 2011. http://www.epa.gov/reg3hscd/super/sites/PAD980508451/. Accessed 27 June 2011.

———. *NPL Site Narrative for Keyser Avenue Borehole.* Environmental Protection Agency, 21 February 1990. http://www.epa.gov/superfund/sites/npl/nar1033.htm. Accessed 6 September 2011.

———. *Risk Assessment Evaluation for Concentrated Animal Feeding Operations.* Office of Research and Development National Risk Management Research Laboratory, 2004. http://cfpub.epa.gov/si/si_public_record_report.cfm?dirEntryId=85107. Accessed 5 September 2011.

U.S. National Oceanic and Atmospheric Administration. *Keyser Avenue Borehole.* Office of Response and Restoration, 1989. http://archive.orr.noaa.gov/book_shelf/442_Keyser .pdf. Accessed 28 June 2011.

U.S. Office of the Press Secretary. Remarks by President Clinton and President Kim of South Korea at Dedication of Korean War Veterans Memorial. White House, 27 July 1995. http://clinton6.nara.gov/1995/07/1995-07-27-pres-clinton-and-kim-at-korean -memorial-dedication.html. Accessed 5 December 2009.

VanBriesen, Jeanne. "Water Quantity and Quality Issues in Unconventional Shale Gas Development." Presentation at "Marcellus Shale: Opportunities and Challenges," Marywood University, Scranton, Pa., 19 August 2010.

"Verdicts Vital Accountability." Editorial. *Times-Tribune* (Scranton, Pa.), 22 June 2011, A14.

Vobejda, Barbara. "Agriculture No Longer Counts." *Washington Post,* 9 October 1993, A1, A13.

Wallace, Paul A. W. *Indians in Pennsylvania.* 1961. Reprint, Harrisburg: Pennsylvania Historical and Museum Commission, 1970.

Walsh, Bryan. "The Gas Dilemma." *Time,* 11 April 2011, 40–48.

Walsh, William S. *Curiosities of Popular Customs.* 1897. Reprint, Philadelphia: J. B. Lippincott, 1914.

Ward, Melissa M., and Timothy W. Kelsey. "Local Business Impacts of Marcellus Shale Development: The Experience in Bradford and Washington Counties, 2010." Pennsylvania State University, 2011. http://extension.psu.edu/pubs/ee0005. Accessed 5 July 2011.

Watkinson, James D. "'Education for Success': The International Correspondence Schools of Scranton, Pennsylvania." *Pennsylvania Magazine of History and Biography* 120.4 (1996): 343–69.

Welling, Bart H. "Ecoporn: On the Limits of Visualizing the Nonhuman." In *Ecosee: Image, Rhetoric, Nature,* edited by Sidney I. Dobrin and Sean Morey, 53–77. Albany: State University of New York Press, 2009.

Whaley, Samuel. *History of the Township of Mount Pleasant, Wayne County, Pennsylvania.* New York: M. W. Dodd, 1856.

White, I. C. *Second Geological Survey of Pennsylvania: Report of Progress/The Geology of Susquehanna County and Wayne County.* Harrisburg: Board of Commissioners for the Second Geological Survey, 1881.

Whitman, Walt. "Song of Myself." In *Leaves of Grass,* 1881–82 ed. Walt Whitman Archive, edited by Ed Folsom and Kenneth M. Price. http://www.whitmanarchive.org/. Accessed 3 September 2011.

———. "This Compost." In *Leaves of Grass,* 1867 ed. Walt Whitman Archive, edited by Ed Folsom and Kenneth M. Price. http://www.whitmanarchive.org/. Accessed 5 September 2011.

Wilkinson, Norman B. "The 'Philadelphia Fever' in Northern Pennsylvania." *Pennsylvania History* 20.1 (1953): 41–56.

Williams, Jeffrey. "The New Belletrism." *Style* 33.3 (1999): 414–42.

Williams, W. H. *Mine Cave Problems.* Scranton, Pa.: Hudson Coal Company, 1920.

Williamson, James R., and Linda A. Fossler. *The Susquehanna Frontier: Northeastern Pennsylvania During the Revolutionary Years.* Wilkes-Barre: Wilkes University Press, 1997.

Wills, Garry. *Lincoln at Gettysburg.* New York: Simon and Schuster, 1992.

Wilson, Charles Reagan. Introduction to *The New Regionalism,* edited by Charles Reagan Wilson, ix–xxiii. Jackson: University Press of Mississippi, 1998.

"Wind Farms in Pennsylvania." Pennsylvania Wind Working Group, n.d. http://www .pawindenergynow.org/pa/farms.html. Accessed 27 June 2011.

Wolensky, Robert P., Kenneth C. Wolensky, and Nicole H. Wolensky. *The Knox Mine Disaster, January 22, 1959: The Final Years of the Northern Anthracite Industry and the Effort to Rebuild a Regional Economy.* Harrisburg: Pennsylvania Historical and Museum Commission, 1999.

Woods, Alan J., James M. Omernik, and Douglas D. Brown. *Level III and IV Ecoregions of Delaware, Maryland, Pennsylvania, Virginia, and West Virginia.* "EPA Region 3 Descriptions." Western Ecology Division, Environmental Protection Agency, 1999. http://www.epa.gov/wed/pages/ecoregions/reg3_eco.htm. Accessed 9 July 2008.

Wordsworth, William. *Tintern Abbey.* In *English Romantic Poetry,* edited by Stanley Appelbaum, 25–29. Mineola, N.Y.: Dover, 1996.

———. "The Two-Part Prelude of 1799." In *The Prelude: 1799, 1805, 1850,* edited by Jonathan Wordsworth, M. H. Abrams, and Stephen Gill, 1–27. New York: Norton, 1979.

"Wreath-Laying Ceremony Marks Knox Disaster First Anniversary." *Scranton Times,* 22 January 1960, 3, 25.

Yarina, Margaret. *Marywood, the First Seventy-Five Years: A Retrospective.* Scranton, Pa.: Marywood College, 1990.

Index